PASSIONS WITHIN REASON

THE STRATEGIC ROLE OF THE EMOTIONS

PASSIONS WITHIN REASON

THE STRATEGIC ROLE OF THE EMOTIONS

ROBERT H. FRANK

CORNELL UNIVERSITY

W. W. NORTON & COMPANY

NEW YORK · LONDON

Drawing by Modell; © 1971 The New Yorker Magazine, Inc.

Drawing by Ed Arno; © 1974 The New Yorker Magazine, Inc.

Photograph of Woody Allen courtesy of Philippe Halsman

Photograph of J. Bunny with startled face courtesy of The Bettmann
Archive, Inc.

Photograph of baseball player courtesy of Leo de Wys, Inc.

Aztec Two Step lyric from "Faster Gun" © 1975 by Mannequin
Music, Inc./Harry's Tune Music, Inc.

Appendix reprinted by permission of The American Economic
Review

Illustrations from Darwin, 1872, reproduced courtesy of The New
York Public Library, Astor, Lenox, and Tilden Foundations.

The text of this book is composed in Adroit Light, with display type
set in Adroit Medium. Composition by The Maple-
Vail Book Manufacturing Group.
Book design by Charlotte Staub.

Library of Congress Cataloging-in-Publication Data

Frank, Robert H.
   Passions within reason.

   Bibliography: p.
   Includes index.
   1. Emotions.   2. Altruism.   3. Ethics.
4. Motivation (Psychology)   5. Rationalism—
Psychological aspects.   I. Title.
BF531.F73   1988   152.4   88–1224

ISBN 0-393-96022-6

W.W. Norton & Company, Inc.
500 Fifth Avenue, New York, N.Y. 10110
W.W. Norton & Company, Ltd.
10 Coptic Street, London WC1A 1PU

6 7 8 9 0

One can lie with the mouth, but with the accompanying grimace one nevertheless tells the truth.
—Nietzsche

Immoderate self-love does very ill consult its own interest; and how much soever a paradox it may appear, it is certainly true that even from self-love we should endeavor to get over all inordinate . . . consideration of our own happiness.
—Joseph Butler

CONTENTS

PREFACE

In recent years, the message from behavioral scientists has been that people are fundamentally selfish. Biologists tell us that behavior is shaped ultimately by material rewards, that the relentless pressures of natural selection will cull out any organism that forgoes opportunities for personal gain. Psychologists affirm this view, noting the pervasive role of material rewards in the learning process. Economists, for their part, point with pride to the power of self-interest to explain and predict behavior, not only in the world of commerce but in networks of personal relationships as well.

And yet the plain fact is that many people do not fit the me-first caricature. They give anonymously to public television stations and private charities. They donate bone marrow to strangers with leukemia. They endure great trouble and expense to see justice done, even when it will not undo the original injury. At great risk to themselves, they pull people from burning buildings, and jump into icy rivers to rescue people who are about to drown. Soldiers throw their bodies atop live grenades to save their comrades. Seen through the lens of modern self-interest theory, such behavior is the human equivalent of planets traveling in square orbits.

In this book, I make use of an idea from economics to suggest how noble human tendencies might not only have survived the ruthless pressures of the material world, but actually have been nurtured by them. The idea rests on a simple paradox, namely, that in many situations the conscious pursuit of self-interest is incompatible with its attainment. We are all comfortable with the notion that someone who strives to be spontaneous can never succeed. So too, on brief reflection, will it become apparent that someone who always pursues self-interest is doomed to fail.

The essence of the difficulty can be seen clearly in this simple example: Jones has a $200 leather briefcase that Smith covets. If Smith steals it, Jones must decide whether to press charges. If Jones does, he will have to go to court. He will get his briefcase back and Smith will spend 60 days in jail, but the day in court will cost Jones $300 in lost earnings. Since this is more than the briefcase is worth, it would clearly not be in his material interest to press charges. (To eliminate an obvious complication, suppose Jones is about to move to a distant city, so there is no point in his adopting a tough stance in order to deter future theft.) Thus, if Smith knows Jones is a purely rational, self-interested person, he is free to steal the briefcase with impunity. Jones may threaten to press charges, but his threat would be empty.

But now suppose that Jones is *not* a pure rationalist; that if Smith steals his briefcase, he will become outraged, and think nothing of losing a day's earnings, or even a week's, in order to see justice done. If Smith knows Jones will be driven by emotion, not reason, he will let the briefcase be. If people *expect* us to respond irrationally to the theft of our property, we will seldom *need* to, because it will not be in their interests to steal it. Being predisposed to respond irrationally serves much better here than being guided only by material self-interest.

The difficulty confronting self-interested people is not confined to situations where aggression must be deterred. It also includes ventures that require trust, from which we make every effort to exclude these people in favor of others we believe to be honest. It extends as well to situations that involve bargaining, where purely selfish people tend to perform less effectively than others who have strong emotional commitments to norms of fairness. And it spills over into the realm of personal relationships, where egoists often fare poorly, even in purely material terms, by comparison with those who are motivated primarily by love and affection.

Views about human nature are not merely a subject of debate among behavioral scientists. They also have important practical consequences. They affect a corporation's strategy for getting workers to perform tasks that are difficult to monitor, how it bargains with its unions, even how it sets its prices. They also have important implications for government policy—for the conduct of foreign affairs, the design and scope of economic regulation, and the structure of taxation. In our personal lives, they affect how we choose mates and jobs, how we spend our incomes, and the extent to which we rely on formal contracts.

More important, our beliefs about human nature help shape human nature itself. What we think about ourselves and our possibilities determines what we aspire to become; and it shapes what we teach our children, both at home and in the schools. Here the pernicious effects of the self-interest theory have been most disturbing. It tells us that to behave morally is to invite others to take advantage of us. By encouraging us to expect the worst in others, it brings out the worst in us: dreading the role of the chump, we are often loath to heed our nobler instincts.

We will see that the modern presumption of a severe penalty for behaving morally is utterly without foundation. My claim is not that self-interest is an unimportant human motive, but that material forces allow room, apparently a great deal of room, for more noble motives as well. We have always known that society as a whole is better off when people respect the legitimate interests of others. What has not been clear, least of all to modern behavioral scientists, is that moral behavior often confers material benefits on the very individuals who practice it.

That such benefits exist is an extraordinarily encouraging piece of news. Largely as a result of the self-interest model's influence, our bonds of trust have taken a heavy beating in recent years. My deepest hope in writing this book is that it may encourage people to feel greater concern for the interests of others. If it succeeds for even a single person, it will have been well worth the effort.

ACKNOWLEDGMENTS

I first sketched a crude version of the idea that an emotional predisposition can be advantageous in a paper I wrote in the winter of 1981. But it was not until 1984 that I began to appreciate its full scope. At that time I believed, with characteristically naive optimism, that I had stumbled onto something original and profoundly important. I still believe the idea is important, but have long since abandoned any illusion that I was the first to see it. That it builds on one from Thomas Schelling's 1960 book, *The Strategy of Conflict,* was clear to me from the beginning. What I did not know at first, however, was that he had even suggested my particular refinement of it in a one-page paper published in 1978. George Akerlof, in 1983, published a clearer and more complete statement of the idea. A year later, Jack Hirshleifer wrote a paper that went still further. Amartya Sen discussed the benefits of narrowly irrational behavior in a 1985 paper. And, also in 1985, David Gauthier published a very thoughtful book on a closely related set of issues. If the idea that irrational predispositions can be advantageous turns out to be one that matters, these authors deserve a full measure of credit for it.

In order for such predispositions to be advantageous, others must be able to discern that we have them. Although the question of whether, and if so, how, this can happen is of central importance, none of these other authors pursued it. When I began work on it in earnest in 1985, it was still unclear whether the parts would fit together into a coherent whole. If this book constitutes an original contribution of any sort, it is in showing that the parts do indeed seem to fit.

In writing it, I have incurred more than my usual share of debts. I especially thank Larry Seidman for his insightful comments and enthusiastic encouragement through several earlier drafts. I also benefited from the suggestions and support of more friends, colleagues, and correspondents than I can hope to recall. With sincere apologies to those I neglect to mention, I thank George Akerlof, Robert Axelrod, Philip Cook, Jon Elster, Stephen Emlen, Tom Gilovich, Henry Hansmann, Robert Heilbroner, Richard Herrnstein, Jack Hirshleifer, Laurence Iannacone, Martin Kilduff, Hartmut Kliemt, Simon Levin, George Loewenstein, Andy McLennan, Douglas Mook, Christopher Morris, Dennis Regan, Elizabeth Adkins Regan, John Robertson, Thomas Schelling, Nicholas Sturgeon, Richard Thaler, Robert Trivers, Gordon Winston, and Richard Zeckhauser. I also gratefully acknowledge the National Science Foundation, which supported various parts of my research under grant numbers SES-8707492 and SES-8605829.

Finally, I thank Drake McFeely, Donald Lamm, Avery Hudson, and the many others at Norton who have done so much to improve this book.

PASSIONS WITHIN REASON

THE STRATEGIC ROLE OF THE EMOTIONS

ONE

BEYOND
SELF-INTEREST

The bloody feud between the Hatfields and McCoys began more than a century ago. It took place along the remote, mountainous border between Kentucky and West Virginia, and lasted more than 35 years. To this day, no one is sure how it actually started. But once under way, its pattern was one of alternating attacks, each a retaliation for the one preceding, and thus also the provocation for the one to follow.

On New Year's night of 1888, the Hatfields attempted to end the feud once and for all by killing the remaining members of the main branch of the McCoy family. Led by James Vance, they set fire to the McCoy farmhouse, planning to shoot the McCoys as they tried to escape. As she emerged from the kitchen door, young Alifair McCoy was the first cut down.

Upon hearing that Alifair had been shot, Sarah McCoy, her mother, rushed to the back door . . . and continued toward her dying daughter. Vance bounded toward her and struck her with the butt of his rifle. For a moment she lay on the cold ground, stunned, groaning, and crying. Finally, she raised herself on her hands and knees and tried to crawl to Alifair. . . . she pleaded with the attackers, "For God's sake let me go to my girl." Then, realizing the situation, she cried, "Oh, she's dead. For the love of God, let me go to her." Sarah put out her hand until she could almost touch the feet of Alifair. Running down the doorsill, where Alifair had fallen, was blood from the girl's wounds. Johnse [Hatfield], who was standing against the outside wall of the kitchen, took his revolver and crushed Sarah's skull with it. She dropped to the ground and lay motionless.[1]

Although Alifair and her brother Calvin were killed, and their mother and several others in the family seriously injured, the Hatfield attack fell short. Randolph McCoy, Alifair's father, was among those who escaped.

In nineteenth-century Appalachia, few citizens had faith in the power of law to resolve their disputes. So we are not surprised that the main project of Randolph and the other McCoys in the ensuing years was to kill as many of the remaining Hatfields as they could. Before hostilities finally ended, several more members of both families lost their lives.

Where the force of law is weak, cycles of attack and revenge are familiar. They pervade life in the Middle East today and have been recorded throughout human history. Probably very few of us have never experienced the impulse to seek revenge. And yet the costs of acting on it are often ruinous. The McCoys, or the Hatfields, could have ended the violence at any moment by not retaliating for the most recent attack. At each juncture, it was clear that to retaliate would produce still another round of bloodshed. Yet for almost four decades they persisted.

What prompts such behavior? Surely not a clear-headed assessment of self-interest. If a rational action is one that promotes the actor's interests,* it is manifestly irrational to retaliate in the face of such devastating costs.

The self-destructive pursuit of vengeance is not the only way we ignore our narrow, selfish interests. We trudge through snowstorms to cast our ballots, even when we are certain they

---

*There are almost as many definitions of rationality as there are people who have written on the subject. Many authors (for example, Harsanyi, 1977) define it as the use of efficient means in the pursuit of a given end (no matter how self-destructive that end might be). By this standard, it might be possible to call even the bloodiest family feud rational (if the participants' overwhelming motive was merely to avenge the latest provocation). In this book, by contrast, I will use the terms "rational behavior" and "self-interested behavior" to mean the same thing. Needless to say, nothing of importance turns on this choice of definitions.

will make no difference. We leave tips in restaurants in distant cities we will never visit again. We make anonymous contributions to private charities. We often refrain from cheating even when we are sure cheating would not be detected. We sometimes walk away from profitable transactions because we believe the terms to be "unfair." We battle endless red tape merely to get a $10 refund on a defective product. And so on.

Behavior of this sort poses a fundamental challenge to those who believe that people generally pursue self-interest. Philosophers, biologists, economists, and others have invested much effort trying to account for it. Their explanations generally call attention to some ancillary gain implicit in the seemingly irrational action. Biologists, for example, tell us that someone may give up her life to save several of her immediate relatives, thereby increasing the survival rate of genes like the ones she carries. Or, economists will explain that it makes sense for the Internal Revenue Service to spend $10,000 to prosecute someone who owes $100 in taxes, because it thereby encourages broader compliance with the tax laws.

Much of the time, however, there appear to be no such ancillary gains. The war between the British and the Argentines over the Falklands is a clear case in point. The Argentine writer Jorge Luis Borges likened it to two bald men fighting over a comb. Both sides knew perfectly well that the windswept, desolate islands were of virtually no economic or strategic significance. At one point in history, it might have made sense for Britain to defend them anyway, as a means of deterring aggression against other, more valuable parts of its far-flung empire. But today, of course, there is no such empire left to protect. For much less than the British spent in the conflict, they could have given each Falklander a Scottish castle and a generous pension for life. And yet very few British citizens seem to regret having stood up to the Argentines.

Many actions, purposely taken with full knowledge of their consequences *are* irrational. If people did not perform them, they would be better off and they know it. Much has been written about the tendency of passions and other nonrational sources of motivation to interfere with the reasoned pursuit of self-interest.[2] The message of this literature is that passions are always something we do better to control.

My claim, on the contrary, is that passions often serve our interests very well indeed. The apparent contradiction arises not because of any hidden gains from the impassioned actions themselves, but because we face important problems that simply cannot be solved by rational action. The common feature of these problems is that to solve them we must commit ourselves to behave in ways that may later prove contrary to our interests.

THE COMMITMENT PROBLEM

Thomas Schelling[3] provides a vivid illustration of this class of problems. He describes a kidnapper who suddenly gets cold feet. He wants to set his victim free, but is afraid he will go to the police. In return for his freedom, the victim gladly promises not to do so. The problem, however, is that both realize it will no longer be in the victim's interest to keep this promise once he is free. And so the kidnapper reluctantly concludes that he must kill him.

Schelling suggests the following way out of the dilemma: "If the victim has committed an act whose disclosure could lead to blackmail, he may confess it; if not, he might commit one in the presence of his captor, to create a bond that will ensure his silence."[4] (Perhaps the victim could allow the kidnapper to photograph him in the process of some unspeakably degrading act.) The blackmailable act serves here as a *commitment device,* something that provides the victim with an incentive to keep his promise. Keeping it will still be unpleasant for him once he is freed; but clearly less so than not being able to make a credible promise in the first place.

In everyday economic and social interaction, we repeatedly encounter commitment problems like the one confronting Schelling's kidnapper and victim. My claim is that specific emotions act as commitment devices that help resolve these dilemmas.

Consider a person who threatens to retaliate against anyone who harms him. For his threat to deter, others must believe he will carry it out. But if others know that the costs of retaliation are prohibitive, they will realize the threat is empty. Unless, of course, they believe they are dealing with someone who simply *likes* to retaliate. Such a person may strike back even when it is not in his material interests to do so. But if he is known in advance to have that preference, he is not likely to be tested by aggression in the first place.

Similarly, a person who is known to "dislike" an unfair bargain can credibly threaten to walk away from one, even when it is in her narrow interest to accept it. By virtue of being known to have this preference she becomes a more effective negotiator.

Consider, too, the person who "feels bad" when he cheats. These feelings can accomplish for him what a rational assessment of self-interest cannot—namely, they can cause him to behave honestly even when he *knows* he could get away with cheating. And if others realize he feels this way, they will seek him as a partner in ventures that require trust.

Being known to experience certain emotions enables us to make commitments that would otherwise not be credible. The clear irony here is that this ability, which springs from a *failure* to pursue self-interest, confers genuine advantages. Granted, following through on these commitments will always involve avoidable losses—not cheating when there is a chance to, retaliating at great cost even after the damage is done, and so on. The problem, however, is that being unable to make credible commitments will often be even more costly. Confronted with the commitment problem, an opportunistic person fares poorly.

EMOTIONS AS COMMITMENTS

It is no longer controversial to say that we come into the world equipped with nervous systems that predispose us to behave in particular ways. Brain circuits that exist before birth cause a person with low levels of sugar in his bloodstream to feel hungry, and it is that feeling, not any rational meditation about goals, that prompts him to eat. Conscious thoughts may intervene, of course, as when the dieter restrains himself from eating. But even these "conscious" interventions are themselves merely expressions of the basic motivational pattern: the dieter envisions the social and medical consequences of being overweight, and the anxiety summoned by these images battles the competing feelings of hunger.

In addition to inborn tastes, habits, too, are an important component of motivation. So far as we know, people are not born with a taste for drinking coffee in the morning. But people who regularly do so will develop a powerful taste for it. And if they attempt to abandon their habit, the difficulty they will feel is real, not imagined.

Innate behavior patterns and the capacity to form habits are adaptive in a broad sense. Yet the behaviors they motivate should not be viewed as having sprung from a rational, case-by-case assessment of self-interest. Rational analysis can, as noted, trigger feelings that affect behavior. It may even guide our choice of which habits to adopt. In this picture, however, the rational assessment is only one of many forces that can arouse the feelings that govern behavior directly.

A person's feelings "commit" him to act in certain ways. A person who has not eaten for several days is "committed" to eat; someone who has not slept for several days is "committed" to sleep. Such commitments are often advantageous even though we might be able to show in a particular case that it is not in a hungry person's interest to eat.

Within broad limits, commitments of this sort are neither strictly binding nor irrevocable. They are merely incentives to behave in a particular way. The person who feels hungry and doesn't eat must endure continued hunger. The unjustly injured party who doesn't seek revenge must go on feeling outraged. A behavioral predisposition, in economic terms, is thus much like a tax on not behaving in a particular way.

Our concern here will be with the role of such emotions as guilt, anger, envy, and even love. These emotions often predispose us to behave in ways that are contrary to our narrow interests, and being thus predisposed can be an advantage. For it to be, others must have some way of discovering we have these emotional commitments. But how do people know that a person's feelings commit him to behave honestly in the face of a golden opportunity to cheat? Or that he will seek revenge, even when it is too late to undo the injury he has suffered? Or that he really will walk away from an unfair bargain, even when he would do better by accepting it? Much of the evidence I will later discuss concerns the subtle clues by which we infer such behavioral predispositions in others.

CLUES TO BEHAVIORAL PREDISPOSITIONS

One fall day, almost twenty years ago, black activist Ron Dellums was speaking at a large rally on the University of California campus in Berkeley. Polls suggested he would soon become the Berkeley–North Oakland district's first radical congressman. Crowds were easily galvanized in those days, and this one was in especially high spirits. But at least one young man was not moved by Dellums's speech. He sat still as a stone on the steps of Sproul Plaza, lost to some drug, his face and eyes empty of expression.

Presently a large Irish setter appeared, sniffing his way through the crowd. He moved directly to the young man sitting on the steps and circled him once. He paused, lifted his leg, and, with no apparent malice, soaked the young man's back. He then set off again into the crowd. The boy barely stirred.

Now, the Irish setter is not a particularly intelligent breed. Yet this one had no difficulty locating the one person in that crowd who would not retaliate for being sprayed. Facial expressions and other aspects of demeanor apparently provide clues to behavior that even dogs can interpret. And although none of us had ever witnessed such a scene before, no one was really surprised when the boy did nothing. Before anything even happened, it was somehow *obvious* that he was just going to go right on sitting there.

Without doubt, however, the boy's behavior was unusual. Most of us would have responded angrily, some even violently. Yet we already know that no real advantage inheres in this "normal" response. After all, once the boy's shirt was soaked, it was already too late to undo the damage. And since he was unlikely ever to encounter that particular dog again, there was little point in trying to teach the dog a lesson. On the contrary, any attempt to do so would have courted the risk of being bitten.

Our young man's problem was not that he failed to respond angrily, but that he failed to communicate to the dog that he was so *predisposed*. The vacant expression on his face was somehow all the dog needed to know he was a safe target. Merely by wearing "normal" expressions, the rest of us were spared.

There are numerous behavioral clues to people's feelings. Posture, the rate of respiration, the pitch and timbre of the voice, perspiration, facial muscle tone and expression, and movement of the eyes, are among the signals we can read. We quickly surmise, for example, that someone with clenched jaws and a purple face is enraged, even when we do not know what, exactly, may have triggered his anger. And we apparently know, even if we cannot articulate, how a forced smile differs from one that is heartfelt.

At least partly on the basis of such clues, we form judgments about the emotional makeup of the people with whom we deal. Some people we sense we can trust, but of others we remain ever wary. Some we sense can be taken advantage of, others we know instinctively not to provoke.

Being able to make such judgments accurately has always been an obvious advantage. But it may be no less an advantage that others be able to make similar assessments about our own propensities. A blush may reveal a lie and cause great embarrassment at the moment, but in circumstances that require trust there can be great advantage in being known to be a blusher.

THE PROBLEM OF MIMICRY

If there are genuine advantages in being vengeful or trustworthy and being perceived as such, there are even greater advantages in appearing to have, but not actually having, these qualities. A liar who appears trustworthy will have better opportunities than one who glances about furtively, sweats profusely, speaks in a quavering voice, and has difficulty making eye contact.

Adolf Hitler was apparently someone who could lie convincingly. In a September 1938 meeting, Hitler promised British Prime Minister Neville Chamberlain that he would not go to war if the borders of Czechoslovakia were redrawn to meet his demands. Following that meeting, Chamberlain wrote in a letter to his sister: ". . . in spite of the hardness and ruthlessness I thought I saw in his face, I got the impression that here was a man who could be relied upon when he gave his word."[5]

Clues to behavioral predispositions are obviously not perfect. Even with the aid of all of their sophisticated machinery, experienced professional polygraph experts cannot be sure when someone is lying. Some emotions are more difficult to simulate than others. Someone who feigns outrage, for example, is apparently easier to catch than someone who pretends to feel joyful. But no matter what the emotion, we can almost never be certain that what we see is genuine.

Indeed, the forces at work are such that it will always be possible for at least *some* people to succeed at deception. In a world in which no one cheated, no one would be on the lookout. A climate thus lacking in vigilance would create profitable opportunities for cheaters, so there would inevitably be a niche for at least some of them.

Useful lessons about the nature of this problem are contained in the similar instances of mimicry that abound in nature. There are butterflies, such as the monarch, whose foul taste defends them against predators. This taste would be useless unless predators had some way of telling which butterflies to avoid. Predators have learned to interpret the monarch's distinctive wing markings for this purpose.

The monarch has created a profitable opportunity for other butterflies, such as the viceroy, who bear similar wing markings but lack the bad taste. Merely by looking like the unpalatable monarchs, viceroys have escaped predation without having had to expend the bodily resources needed to produce the objectionable taste itself.

In such instances, it is clear that if mimics could *perfectly* simulate the wing markings with neither cost nor delay, the entire edifice would crumble: the comparatively efficient mimics would eventually overwhelm the others, and the predators' original reason for avoiding that particular marking would thereby vanish. So in cases where mimics coexist alongside the genuine article for extended periods, we may infer that perfect mimicry either takes time or entails substantial costs. The fact that the bearer of the genuine trait has the first move in this game will often prove a decisive advantage.

Similar considerations apply in the case of those who mimic emotional traits. If the signals we use for detecting these traits had no value, we would have long since ceased to rely on them. And yet, by their very nature, they cannot be perfect. Symptoms of character, after all, cannot be scrutinized without effort. If no one ever cheated, it would never pay anyone to expend this effort. The irony, of course, is that this would create irresistible opportunities to cheat.

The inevitable result is an uneasy balance between people who really possess the underlying emotions and others who merely seem to. Those who are adept at reading the relevant signals will be more successful than others. There is also a payoff to those who are able to send effective signals about their own behavioral predispositions. And, sad to say, there will also be a niche for those who are skillful at pretending to have feelings they really lack.

Indeed, at first glance the largest payoff of all appears to go to shameless liars. Yet most of us reserve special contempt for such persons, and will go to great trouble to inform others when we stumble upon them. Even if such persons are caught only very rarely, it is on this account far from clear that they command any special advantage.

The ecological balance between more and less opportunistic strategies is at once in harmony with the view that self-interest underlies all action and with the opposing view that people often transcend their selfish tendencies. The key to resolving the tension between these views is to understand that the ruthless pursuit of self-interest is often self-defeating. As Zen masters have known all along, the best outcome is sometimes possible only when people abandon the chase. Here, we will see that self-interest often requires commitments to behave in ways that will, if triggered, prove deeply contrary to our interests.

Much of the time, the practical means for accomplishing these commitments will be emotions that have observable symptoms. I will later survey persuasive evidence that at least some of these emotions are inborn. But even if they were transmitted only by cultural indoctrination, they would serve equally well. What is necessary in either case is that people who have them be observably different, on the average, from those who do not.

For convenience, I will use the term *commitment model* as shorthand for the notion that seemingly irrational behavior is sometimes explained by emotional predispositions that help solve commitment problems. The competing view, that people always act efficiently in the pursuit of self-interest, I will call the *self-interest model.*

On purely theoretical grounds, the commitment model suggests that the moving force behind moral behavior lies not in rational analysis but in the emotions. This view is consistent with an extensive body of empirical evidence reviewed by developmental psychologist Jerome Kagan. As he summarizes his interpretation of that evidence:

> Construction of a persuasive rational basis for behaving morally has been the problem on which most moral philosophers have stubbed their toes. I believe they will continue to do so until they recognize what Chinese philosophers have known for a long time: namely, feeling, not logic, sustains the superego.[6]

The emotions may indeed sustain the superego. But as the commitment model will make clear, it may well be the logic of self-interest that ultimately sustains these emotions.

A SIMPLE THOUGHT EXPERIMENT

The critical assumption behind the commitment model, again, is that people can make reasonable inferences about character traits in others. By "reasonable inference" I do not mean that it is necessary to be able to predict other people's emotional predispositions with certainty. Just as a weather forecast of a 20 percent chance of rain can be invaluable to someone who must plan outdoor activities, so can probabilistic assessments of character traits be of use to people who must choose someone to trust. It would obviously help to be accurate in every instance. But it will often suffice to be right only a fraction of the time.

Is it reasonable to assume we can infer emotional predispositions in others? Imagine you have just gotten home from a crowded concert and discover you have lost $1000 in cash. The cash had been in your coat pocket in a plain envelope with your name written on it. Do you know anyone, not related to you by blood or marriage, who you feel certain would return it to you if he or she found it?

For the sake of discussion, I will assume that you are not in the unenviable position of having to answer no. Think for a moment about the person you are sure would return your cash; call her "Virtue." Try to explain *why* you feel so confident about her. Note that the situation was one where, if she had kept the cash, you could not have known it. On the basis of your other experiences with her, the most you could possibly know is that she did not cheat you in *every* such instance in the past. Even if, for example, she returned some lost money of yours in the past, that would not prove she didn't cheat you on some other occasion. (After all, if she *had* cheated you in a similar situation, you wouldn't know it.) In any event, you almost certainly have no logical basis in experience for inferring that Virtue would not cheat you now. If you are like most people, you simply believe you can fathom her inner motives: you are sure she would return your cash because you are sure she would feel terrible if she did not.

The thought experiment also calls attention to the fact that such emotional predispositions may depend on circumstance. Think, for example, about your relationship with Virtue. Typically, she is a close friend. This is natural, for at least two reasons. First, you have had much more opportunity to observe the behavior of close friends; if situations that shed light on a person's character occur only rarely, it is much more likely you will have witnessed one. But second, and perhaps more important, you are much more inclined to trust a friend because you believe she feels a special loyalty to you. Indeed, your belief that Virtue will return your cash does not necessarily imply a belief that she would have returned an envelope bearing the name of a perfect stranger. Her predisposition to return your money may be contingent on her relationship to you.

Your intuitions may also tell you that the amount of cash in the envelope could matter. Most people believe they know many more people who would return $100 than $1000. By the same token, a person who would unhesitatingly return $1000 might instead hang onto an envelope with $50,000.

People's feelings of right and wrong are clearly not the only forces that govern their behavior. As Walter Mischel[7] and other social psychologists have long emphasized, behavior of almost every sort is strongly influenced by the details and nuances of context. But despite the obvious importance of situational factors, they do not tell the whole story. On the contrary, most participants in this thought experiment respond that they know someone they feel sure would return the cash of a perfect stranger, or indeed even that of someone deeply disliked, no matter how large the amount. I do not mean to deny the obvious importance of context, now or in later chapters, when I speak of traits of character that differ between persons. It would be a mistake to pretend that character traits account for all important differences in behavior. But it is perhaps a more serious error to suppose that behavior is guided *only* by context.

Of course, the fact that you may feel sure that a particular person would return a stranger's cash does not necessarily make it so. Plenty of apparently trustworthy people have let even close friends down in situations like the one in the thought experiment. What the experiment does establish (on the assumption that you responded affirmatively) is that you accept the crucial premise of the commitment model. The evidence we will see in later chapters, though far from decisive, can only strengthen your belief that we can, in fact, identify emotional predispositions in others.

THE IMPORTANCE OF TASTES

The self-interest model assumes certain tastes and constraints, and then calculates what actions will best serve those tastes. Widely used by military strategists, social scientists, game theorists, philosophers, and others, it influences decisions that affect all of us. In its standard form, it assumes purely self-interested tastes; namely, for present and future consumption goods of various sorts, leisure, and so on. Envy, guilt, rage, pride, love, and the like typically play no role.*

* In fairness I must note that among economists and other behavioral scientists, there are many who recognize the limitations of the strict self-interest model. See, in particular,

The commitment model, by contrast, emphasizes the role of these emotions in behavior. The rationalists speak of tastes, not emotions, but for analytical purposes, the two play exactly parallel roles. Thus, for example, a person who is motivated to avoid the emotion of guilt may be equivalently described as someone with a "taste" for honest behavior.

Tastes have important consequences for action. The inclusion of tastes that help solve commitment problems substantially alters the predictions of self-interest models. We will see that it may pay people to feel envious, because feeling that way makes them better bargainers. But people who feel envious will accept different jobs, earn different salaries, spend them in different ways, save different amounts, and vote for different laws than predicted by self-interest models.*

Feelings of envy are also closely linked to feelings about fairness. Without taking the latter into account, we cannot hope to predict what prices stores will charge, what wages workers will demand, how long business executives will resist a strike, what taxes governments will levy, how fast military budgets will grow, or whether a union leader will be re-elected.

The presence of conscience alters the predictions of self-interest models. These models predict clearly that when interactions between people are not repeated, people will cheat if they know they can get away with it. Yet evidence consistently shows that most people do not cheat under these circumstances. Self-interest models also suggest that the owner of a small business will not contribute to the lobbying efforts of trade associations. Like one man's vote, her own contribution will seem too small a part of the total to make any difference. Yet many small businesses do pay dues to trade associations, and many people do vote. Charitable institutions also exist on a far grander scale than would ever be predicted by self-interest models.

Schelling, 1978; Akerlof, 1983; Hirshleifer, 1984; Sen, 1977, 1985; and Arrow, 1975. See also Leibenstein, 1976; Scitovsky, 1976; Harsanyi, 1980; Phelps, 1975; Collard, 1978; Margolis, 1982; and Rubin and Paul, 1979.

*I develop these particular claims at length in my 1985 book.

There is nothing mystical about the emotions that drive these behaviors. On the contrary, they are an obvious part of most people's psychological makeup. What I hope to show here is that their presence is in perfect harmony with the underlying requirements of a coherent theory of rational behavior.

The self-interest model has proven its usefulness for understanding and predicting human behavior. But it remains seriously incomplete. Most analysts regard "irrational" behavior motivated by the emotions as lying beyond the scope of the model. As we will see, however, it is neither necessary nor productive to adopt this view. With careful attention to the things people care about, and to *why* they care about them, we can gain a much clearer understanding of why we behave as we do.

MOTIVES FOR HONESTY

When an opportunistic person is exhorted to behave morally, his immediate, if unspoken, question is "What's in it for me?" The traditional rationale for the maxim, "Honesty is the best policy," responds that penalties for cheating are often severe and you can never be sure you will not be caught. The rationale further asserts that living up to your promises on one occasion creates the impression you will do so in the future. This, in turn, makes people more inclined to trust you, which is often a decisive advantage.

In some cases it is easy to see why honesty might indeed be the best policy for the reasons traditionally given. Consider, for example, a practice clearly built on trust: that of tipping in restaurants. Because, by custom, tips are left at the end of the meal, the waiter or waitress must rely on the diner's implicit promise to reward prompt and courteous service.* Having

---

*A recent *New Yorker* cartoon suggested a way of curtailing the waiter's risk. It portrayed a solitary diner in the midst of his meal. On the table was a plate with a few coins on it and a small placard reading, "Your tip so far."

already received good service, the diner is in a position to stiff the waiter. But while this occasionally does happen, it would not be a sensible strategy for most people, who eat repeatedly in the same restaurants. A person who leaves a generous tip each time he visits his favorite restaurant may thus be viewed as making a rational investment in obtaining good service in the future. Living up to his implicit promise is clearly consistent with—indeed, required by—the vigorous pursuit of self-interest.

The difficulty is that the tipper's behavior here does not really capture what we understand by the term "honesty." It is perhaps more fittingly described as "prudence." He has lived up to his implicit promise, to be sure; but since failure to do so would have led to bad service on future occasions, we cannot conclude that fidelity to the promise was an important motivating factor.

Whether people honor their agreements when they expect to interact repeatedly with us is obviously important. But in much of life, we are concerned instead with how they behave either in fleeting encounters or in ones where their behavior simply cannot be observed. These cases, after all, are the ones that seriously test a person's character. In them, an honest action will be one that, by definition, requires personal sacrifice. The tip left in a restaurant in a distant city is a clear example. When a traveler breaks the implicit promise to tip he will save some money, and his disgruntled waiter will have no opportunity to retaliate.

With situations like these in mind, many people react cynically to the notion that honesty is the best policy. They realize that guaranteed success is *not* a prerequisite for cheating to be profitable. Of course there is always *some* possibility that an angry waiter will make a scene that will be witnessed by someone you know. But celebrities apart, this risk is negligible, or at any rate far too small to be seriously considered a self-interested reason for tipping. The difficulty with traditional self-interest appeals to morality is that they suggest no reason not to cheat in situations where detection is all but impossible.

The commitment model suggests an altogether different rationale for honesty, one that is both self-interested and at the same time relevant for situations where cheating cannot be detected: If character traits like honesty are observable in a person, an honest person will benefit by being able to solve important commitment problems. He will be trustworthy in situations where the purely self-interested person would not, and will therefore be much sought after as a partner in situations that require trust.

The decision to tip in the distant city is in part a decision about the kinds of character traits one wishes to cultivate. For while modern biologists have established that the capacity to develop various character traits is inherited, no one has successfully challenged the nineteenth-century view that indoctrination and practice are required for them to emerge. The direction of causality between character and behavior thus runs both ways. Character influences behavior, of course. But behavior also influences character. Despite our obvious capacities for self-deception and rationalization, few people can maintain a predisposition to behave honestly while at the same time frequently engaging in transparently opportunistic behavior.

The opportunist's goal is to appear honest while availing himself of every prudent opportunity for personal gain. He wants to seem like a good guy to the people who count, but at the same time to refrain from tipping in distant cities. If character traits are discernible, however, this may not be possible. In order to *appear* honest, it may be necessary, or at least very helpful, to *be* honest.

In these observations lie the seeds of a very different reason for leaving a tip in the distant restaurant. The motive is not to avoid the possibility of being caught, but to maintain and strengthen the predisposition to behave honestly. My failure to tip in the distant city will make it difficult to sustain the emotions that motivate me to behave honestly on other occasions.

It is this change in my emotional makeup, not my failure to tip itself, that other people may apprehend.

Moral philosophers and others have long stressed the adverse social consequences of the unbridled pursuit of self-interest. The utilitarians, for example, urge us to practice restraint because the world would be a better place if everyone did so. For opportunistic persons, however, such appeals have not proved compelling. They reason, with seemingly impeccable logic, that their own behavior will not much affect what others do. Because the state of the world is thus largely independent of how they themselves behave, they conclude that it is best to take what they can and assume others will do likewise. As more and more people adopt this perspective, it becomes increasingly difficult for even basically honest persons not to do so.

Many of my friends, and I too in years past, have complained of feeling like chumps for paying all of our income taxes when so many people evade theirs so brazenly. More recently, however, my work on the commitment model has sharply altered my feelings on this issue. I am still annoyed if a plumber asks me to pay in cash; but now my resentment is tempered by thinking of tax compliance as an investment in maintaining an honest predisposition. Virtue is not only its own reward here; it may also lead to material rewards in other contexts. Whether this outside payoff is larger than what I could safely steal from the government, I cannot be sure. But the evidence, we will see, suggests that it might be.

Even the mere possibility of such rewards transforms a person's choice about whether to cultivate an honest predisposition. On traditional views of morality, opportunists have every reason to break the rules (and to teach their children to do likewise) whenever they can profitably do so. The commitment model challenges this view at its core. That, for me, is by far its most exciting message. Because the model suggests an intelligible answer to the pressing question of "What's in it for me?," I hope it will encourage even the most hardened cynic to feel greater regard for others.

TWO

THE ALTRUISM PARADOX

I n *Growing Up,* Russell Baker tells of his mother's relatives sitting around the kitchen table late at night during the Depression talking about the long-lost family fortune. Its existence had been discovered many years earlier by his grandfather—"Papa"—when he journeyed to England to investigate the family history. There, he learned they were descended from a "fabulously rich old Bishop of London back in the time of Marlborough and Queen Anne."

The bishop, it seems, had willed his fortune to his Virginia kin—that is, to Baker's forebears—but the inheritance somehow never made it across the Atlantic. Papa was told it had all "reverted to the Crown," and was now the property of the Empire. The family felt sure, however, that their rightful fortune had been embezzled by "British connivers."

By their account, the loss was substantial. "Probably a million dollars in today's money," as Russell's Uncle Allen put it. "'More like fifty or sixty million," according to his Uncle Hal.

Young Russell, age eleven, was intoxicated by the erstwhile family riches. But his sister Doris, two years younger, was more tough-minded. As Baker tells it:

> My excitement about the great lost fortune was dampened by Doris when, grousing one evening about having to sell magazines, I said, "If Mama's father had got the family fortune, I wouldn't have to work."
> "You don't believe any of that baloney, do you?" she replied.

I quit believing it then and there. No nine-year-old girl was going to beat me at skepticism.

Like young Baker, most behavioral scientists deeply fear being thought naive by their peers. They feel uneasy, for example, when called upon to explain why a dentist serves without pay on the board of directors of a local charity. Perhaps he volunteers out of pure generosity of spirit, but worldly behavioral scientists are reluctant to speak of such motives. They feel on much firmer ground when they imagine that the dentist hopes to win favorable attention, thereby to lure, in time, more teeth to extract. And sure enough, when we examine membership lists of Rotary Clubs and other "service" organizations, we find a surfeit of lawyers, insurance agents, and others with something to sell, but not many postal employees or airline pilots.

The flint-eyed researcher fears no greater humiliation than to have called some action altruistic, only to have a more sophisticated colleague later demonstrate that it was self-serving. This fear surely helps account for the extraordinary volume of ink behavioral scientists have spent trying to unearth selfish motives for seemingly self-sacrificing acts. In this chapter, I will examine the most important of these efforts, and suggest that they account for some, but by no means all, of our failure to pursue self-interest.

THE INVISIBLE HAND

The modern behavioral scientist's focus on self-interest traces directly to Adam Smith. The Scottish philosopher's penetrating insight, distilled into two brief sentences, was that

It is not from the benevolence of the butcher, the brewer, or the baker that we expect our dinner, but from their regard of their own interest. We address ourselves not to their humanity, but to their self-love, and never talk to them of our necessities, but of their advantage.

In Smith's scheme, the quest for personal gain often benefits others. The merchant in pursuit of his own profits acts as if guided by an invisible hand to supply the products we most desire. Yet Smith held no illusions that the consequences were always benign. "People of the same trade," he wrote, "seldom meet together but the conversation ends in a conspiracy against the public, or in some diversion to raise prices."

Many people, behavioral scientists conspicuously few among them, are offended by the notion that behavior is so strongly governed by self-interest. Even Adam Smith himself, in his earlier book, *The Theory of Moral Sentiments,* wrote movingly of man's compassion for his fellows:

> How selfish soever man may be supposed, there are evidently some principles in his nature, which interest him in the fortune of others, and render their happiness necessary to him, though he derives nothing from it, except the pleasure of seeing it. Of this kind is pity or compassion, the emotion which we feel for the misery of others, when we either see it, or are made to conceive it in a very lively manner. That we often derive sorrow from the sorrow of others, is a matter of fact too obvious to require any instances to prove it; for this sentiment, like all the other original passions of human nature, is by no means confined to the virtuous and humane, though they perhaps may feel it with the most exquisite sensibility. The greatest ruffian, the most hardened violator of the laws of society, is not altogether without it.[1]

Yet who would deny that most people look out first for themselves and their families? Or that this view has obvious power to explain behavior? When a detective investigates a murder, his first question is "Who stood to benefit from the victim's death?" When an economist studies a government regulation, she wants to know whose incomes it enhances. When a senator proposes a new spending project, the political scientist tries to discover which of the senator's constituents will be its primary beneficiaries. That it is so useful to ask such questions obviously does not prove that selfish motives are the *only* ones that matter. Even so, their importance is scarcely open to doubt.

SELFISHNESS AND THE DARWINIAN MODEL

The strongest intellectual foundation for the self-interest model came not from Smith's *Wealth of Nations* but from the 1859 publication of Charles Darwin's *The Origin of Species*. Darwin explained that the only way an inherited characteristic can become more widespread is for it to enhance the reproductive fitness of the *individuals* who bear it. The effect of a characteristic on the well-being of populations as a whole is of little significance in the Darwinian scheme.

Some of the most conspicuous evidence for this proposition comes in the form of characteristics favored by sexual selection. The peahen, for example, is for some reason attracted to peacocks with large, colorful displays of tail feathers—the larger the better. This preference may have originated because large displays are a useful signal of overall robustness, a good trait for her to pass along to her offspring. But whatever its source, once the preference exists, it will tend to be self-perpetuating. A peahen concerned about the reproductive success of her own male offspring needs no better reason to favor large tail displays than that most other peahens favor them. Any peahen who mated with a peacock with a small tail feathers would be more likely to have sons with small tail feathers, who in turn would find it difficult to attract mates of their own.

If the peacocks with the largest displays sire the most offspring, there will inevitably be a "tail feathers arms race" among the males. In each round, sexual selection favors the males with the largest tail displays. The result is that surviving males will eventually have such large displays that they become more vulnerable to predators. Peacocks *taken as a group* would clearly do better if all had smaller tail feathers. And yet a mutant male with a significantly smaller display would do worse than the others, because he would be less attractive to peahens.

The peacock example drives home the critical point that the unit of selection in the Darwinian model is the individual, not the group or species. Given the level at which selection takes place, the behavior and physical characteristics of any species must evolve in ways that favor the reproductive interests not of the species as a whole but of its individual members. Faced with a choice between an action that will benefit others and one that will serve its own narrow interests, each animal is said to have been programmed by evolutionary forces to follow the second path.

This principle is fundamental. It applies not only to the size of tail feathers but also to the question of whether to cheat. British biologist Richard Dawkins illustrates the idea with the following description of the behavior of hatchling birds:

> Many birds are fed in the nest by parents. They all gape and scream, and the parent drops a worm or other morsel in the open mouth of one of them. The loudness with which each baby screams is, ideally, proportional to how hungry he is. Therefore, if the parent always gives the food to the loudest screamer, they should all tend to get their fair share, since when one has had enough he will not scream so loudly. At least this is what would happen in the best of all possible worlds, if individuals do not cheat. But in the light of our selfish gene concept we must expect that individuals *will* cheat, *will* tell lies about how hungry they are. This will escalate, apparently rather pointlessly because it might seem that if they are all lying by screaming too loudly, this level of loudness becomes the norm and ceases, in effect, to be a lie. However, it cannot de-escalate, because any individual who takes the first step in decreasing the loudness of his scream will be penalized by being fed less and is more likely to starve.[2]

If human nature, too, was shaped by the forces of natural selection, the apparently inescapable conclusion is that people's behavior must be fundamentally selfish in the manner Dawkins ascribes to the baby birds. This extension of the Darwinian model to human behavior remains deeply controversial, however, in large measure because of the reluctance many feel to deny the existence of genuinely charitable impulses in people.

KIN-SELECTION

Biologists have made numerous attempts to explain behavior that, on its face, appears self-sacrificing. Many of these make use of William Hamilton's notion of kin selection.[3] According to Hamilton, an individual will often be able to promote its own genetic future by making sacrifices on behalf of others who carry copies of its genes. Indeed, for some individuals in some species (such as the worker ant, who cannot reproduce), helping relatives is the *only* way of promoting the survival of copies of their genes. The kin-selection model predicts that parents will make "altruistic" sacrifices on behalf of their offspring, brothers on behalf of sisters, and so on. (Anticipating Hamilton's argument by several decades, J. B. S. Haldane once remarked that it would make sense for him to lay down his own life to save the lives of eight of his cousins—since first cousins, on the average, have one-eighth of their genetic material in common.)

The kin-selection model fits comfortably within the Darwinian framework, and has clearly established predictive power. E. O. Wilson, for example, has shown that the extent to which ants assist one another is very accurately predicted by their degree of relatedness.[4] Robert Trivers has even shown that the kinship model predicts specific *conflicts* between relatives. He predicted mother-offspring conflicts over weaning, for example, by showing that the suckling period that best serves the mother's reproductive interests is significantly shorter than the one that best serves her offspring's.[5]

Sacrifices made on behalf of kin are an example of what E. O. Wilson calls " 'hard-core' altruism, a set of responses relatively unaffected by social reward or punishment beyond childhood."[6] Viewed from one perspective, the behavior accounted for by the kin-selection model is not really self-sacrificing behavior at all. When an individual helps a relative, it is merely helping that part of itself that is embodied in the relative's genes.

As philosopher Philip Kitcher observes, however, this perspective gives short shrift to the incredible personal costs sometimes borne by those who sacrifice on behalf of kin.

> When we recall cases of altruistic actions toward kin, we do not primarily think of the instinctive responses of parents who pluck their children from danger almost before they appreciate the threat to themselves. We focus instead on the political prisoners who submit to torture in order to shield their kin, on Cordelia accompanying her father to prison, on Antigone's resolve to bury her brother. These are not cases that we are inclined to dismiss as involving responses "relatively unmodified beyond childhood." Instead, they seem to reveal courageous self-sacrifice after deep reflection.[7]

But the ultimate difficulty of the kin-selection model, for present purposes, is not that it fails to account for at least *some* of the noble behaviors that come under the rubric of hard-core altruism. The problem is rather that, by definition, it does not account for the many clear cases of genuinely unselfish behavior toward nonrelatives.

Some observers have suggested that hard-core altruism may be an evolutionary vestige, a pattern shaped by kin selection during a time when humans existed only among groups of close relatives. On this view, it was never particularly advantageous to discriminate between kin and nonkin because *everyone* was kin.

To be sure, our ancestors did exist in small kin groups during most of the course of human evolution, and it makes perfectly good sense to say that traits favored during this period may have survived into the modern era. But even in the early hunter-gatherer groups, the kin-selection model would not have predicted indiscriminately altruistic behavior.

That is simply because genetic relatedness declines extremely rapidly once we leave the confines of the nuclear family. Siblings share half of their genes in common, on the average, first cousins only one-eighth, and second cousins only one thirty-second. Thus, in genetic terms, second cousins are little different from perfect strangers, and the kin-selection model predicts a small payoff indeed from helping them. Insects have been shown to discriminate in their helping behavior on the basis of much smaller variations in relatedness than that.[8] Because there was always very substantial variation in genetic relatedness among the members of even the smallest hunter-gatherer groups, the forces of kin-selection are not likely to have produced indiscriminately altruistic behavior.

RECIPROCAL ALTRUISM

Trivers and others have attempted to explain altruism toward nonkin with a theory of "reciprocal altruism," in which people act benevolently toward others in the expectation of being recognized and rewarded by some reciprocal act of kindness in the future.[9] Mutual grooming among unrelated animals is a frequently cited example. Animals have difficulty picking parasites off their own heads, but can easily pick them off the heads of others. Each animal can thus benefit by joining another in a figurative contract to provide mutual grooming services.

For such contracts to succeed, it is necessary for animals to have the ability to recognize specific individuals and withhold grooming services from those who refuse to reciprocate. Otherwise, populations would eventually become dominated by cheaters, those who accept grooming but expend none of their valuable time grooming others.

A wide variety of symbiotic relationships prosper in nature. Approximately fifty species of fish, for example, are known to make their living by cleaning parasites from the surfaces of larger fish. To perform these tasks, it is sometimes necessary for the smaller fish to swim into the mouths of the larger ones. It is difficult to imagine an action more demanding of trust than that.

The cleaner needs some form of assurance that he will not be gobbled up. The cleanee, likewise, needs some reason to believe that the cleaner will not bite a chunk out of him. Both the cleaner and the cleanee have evolved highly specialized body markers and behavior patterns that identify them to one another. And although some mimicry and cheating apparently does take place in these relationships, they are for the most part remarkably stable.

Man, of course, has the greatest capacity of any animal to recognize and remember the past behavior of other members of his species. Indeed, we now know that a specific area of the brain houses the ability to identify individual faces. (Stroke victims who suffer damage to this area in both hemispheres function normally for the most part, but cannot recognize the faces even of close relatives.) So there is surely merit in Trivers's account of reciprocal altruism among humans.

And yet many of the predictions of his model do not correspond very well to what we observe in the world. Consider, for example, its prediction about a bystander's decision about whether to rescue someone who is drowning. According to the formal logic of the model, if the probability of the rescuer drowning during the rescue attempt is, say, 1 in 20, then the attempt should be made only if there is a greater than 1 in 20 chance that the victim will someday return the favor. By such reckoning, we ought to see precious few rescue attempts.

Yet rescue attempts have always been common, even when they involve great peril to the rescuer. On a bitter cold evening in mid-January of 1982, for example, Lenny Skutnik dove into the icy Potomac River to rescue one of the survivors of Air Florida's Flight 90, which minutes earlier had collided with the 14th Street bridge. There was no assurance he would reach the struggling woman in time and, even if he did, it was far from certain he would be able to make it back to shore. In the end, he did manage to bring her in, one of only five survivors of the disaster.

We celebrate Skutnik's courage, to be sure. But his and countless other similar displays of valor are surely not the result of any expectation of reciprocal benefits. Indeed, if they *were*, what reason would we have to celebrate them?

Skutnik's action was a clear instance of hard-core altruism. Reciprocal altruism, by contrast, is an example of what Wilson calls "soft-core altruism," actions undertaken with the expectation that society will reciprocate.[10] Our task here, once again, is to try to understand hard-core altruism.

TIT-FOR-TAT AND THE PRISONER'S DILEMMA

As we saw in Chapter 1, the pursuit of self-interest often leads people astray. In many circumstances, we can achieve what we seek only if we each set aside personal interest. During heat waves in New York, the Consolidated Edison Company tells people they will have plenty of electricity for essential needs if no residential customers turn on their air conditioners before 10 PM. Rather than endure the disruption of a power outage, most customers would gladly wait that long. But the fear that others will not hold up their end of the bargain foils many such attempts at cooperation. Once someone hears a neighbor's air conditioner humming at 7 PM, the agreement quickly unravels.

Dilemmas of this sort have long been a favorite topic of behavioral scientists and game theorists. The most frequently discussed example is the "prisoner's dilemma." The mathematician A. W. Tucker is credited with having discovered this simple game, which derives its name from the anecdote originally used to illustrate it. Two prisoners are held in separate cells for a serious crime that they did, in fact, commit. The prosecutor, however, has only enough hard evidence to convict them of a minor offense, for which the penalty is, say, a year in jail. Each prisoner is told that if one confesses while the other remains silent, the confessor will go scot-free while the other spends 20 years in prison. If both confess, they will get an intermediate sentence, say 5 years. (These payoffs are summarized in Table 2.1.) The two prisoners are not allowed to communicate with one another.

The dominant strategy in the prisoner's dilemma is to confess. No matter what Y does, X gets a lighter sentence by speaking out: if Y too confesses, X gets 5 years instead of 20; and if Y remains silent, X goes free instead of spending a year in jail. The payoffs are perfectly symmetric, so Y also does better to confess, no matter what X does. The difficulty, here again, is that when each behaves in a self-interested way, both do worse than if each had shown restraint. Thus, when both confess, they get 5 years, instead of the 1 year they could have gotten by remaining silent.

Although the prisoners are not allowed to communicate with one another, it would be a mistake to assume that this is the real source of difficulty. Their problem is rather a lack of *trust*. A simple promise not to confess does not change the material payoffs of the game. (If each could promise not to confess, each would *still* do better if he broke his promise.)

In one early study, psychologists Anatol Rapoport and Albert Chammah investigated how people actually behave when con-

TABLE 2.1. The Prisoner's Dilemma

		PRISONER Y	
		CONFESS	REMAIN SILENT
PRISONER X	CONFESS	5 years for each	0 yr for X 20 yr for Y
	REMAIN SILENT	20 yr for X 0 yr for Y	1 year for each

fronted with repeated instances of the prisoner's dilemma.[11] Their experiments, like hundreds of others that have followed, gave pairs of players two choices: "cooperate" or "defect." The payoffs were small sums of money rather than years in jail, but the structure of their game was otherwise identical to the prisoner's dilemma. A typical game is shown in Table 2.2.

As before, the dominant strategy for a single play of the game is to defect. A higher payoff is achieved by defecting, no matter what the other player does. As in the original prisoner's dilemma, however, the players each do better when both cooperate than when both defect.

The central discovery by Rapoport and Chammah was that people show a strong tendency to cooperate *when they play repeatedly with the same partner*. The reason is simple. If the game is to be played many times, a cooperator has the opportunity to retaliate if his partner defects. Once it becomes apparent that defection invites retaliation, both parties usually settle into a pattern of mutual cooperation. Rapoport and Chammah dubbed the strategy of rewarding cooperation and retaliating against defection "tit-for-tat."

In his recent book, Robert Axelrod investigated how the tit-for-tat strategy performed against a broad range of ingenious counterstrategies.[12] Tit-for-tat is defined formally as "cooperate on the first move, then on each successive move do whatever the other player did on the previous move." It is a "nice"

TABLE 2.2. The Prisoner's Dilemma with Monetary Payoffs

		PLAYER Y	
		DEFECT	COOPERATE
PLAYER X	DEFECT	2¢ for each	6¢ for X 0 for Y
	COOPERATE	0 for X 6¢ for Y	4¢ for each

strategy, in the sense that it shows an initial inclination to cooperate. But it is a tough-minded strategy as well, in that it promptly punishes defections from the other side. If each of two players plays tit-for-tat, the result is perfect cooperation in every play of the game. A pair of tit-for-tat players thus receives the largest possible aggregate payoff.

Axelrod examined hypothetical populations of players in which not only tit-for-tat but also numerous other strategies were represented. He performed computer simulations to discover the conditions that favor the emergence of cooperation. He discovered that tit-for-tat performed extremely well against a host of cynical strategies that had been designed for the specific purpose of defeating it.

In Axelrod's scheme, the emergence of cooperation requires a reasonably stable set of players, each of whom can remember what other players have done in previous interactions. It also requires that players have a significant stake in what happens in the future, for it is only the fear of retaliation that keeps people from defecting. When these conditions are met, cooperators can identify one another and discriminate against defectors.* The higher payoffs inherent in successful cooperation then cause cooperators to comprise a growing share of the population.

The conditions called for by the tit-for-tat model are often met in human populations. Many people do interact repeatedly and most keep track of how others treat them. Axelrod has assembled persuasive evidence that these forces help explain how people actually behave. Perhaps the most impressive of

---

*Strictly speaking, the emergence of cooperation in Axelrod's scheme also requires that the players not know exactly how many times they will interact with one another. If, for example, they knew they would interact exactly 100 times, each player would know that on the 100th, or last, interaction the self-interested strategy would be to defect, because there will be no way for anyone to retaliate. But that means that there can be no effective threat of retaliation on the 99th interaction either, which in turn means that it will be best to defect then too. Because the same argument applies step by step to every interaction, the tit-for-tat solution unravels. Kreps, Milgrom, Roberts, and Wilson (1982) argue that cooperative play may nonetheless be rational in these circumstances if there is some probability that others will irrationally follow the tit-for-tat strategy.

all this evidence comes from accounts of the "live-and-let-live" system that developed in the trench warfare in Europe during World War I. In many areas of the war, the same units lay encamped opposite one another in the trenches over a period of several years. Units were often closely matched, with the result that neither side had much hope of quickly eliminating the other. Their choices were to fight intensively, with both sides sustaining heavy casualties, or to exercise restraint.

The conditions of interaction described in historian Tony Ashworth's account of the trench fighting closely resemble those required for the success of tit-for-tat.[13] The identities of the players were more or less stable. Interactions between them were repeated, often several times daily, for extended periods. Each side could easily tell when the other side defected. And each side had a clear stake in keeping its future losses to a minimum.

There is little doubt that tit-for-tat often did emerge as the strategy of choice for both Allied and German fighting units. Although strongly discouraged as a matter of official policy, restraint was sometimes conspicuously apparent. Referring to night patrol squads operating out of the trenches. Ashworth writes:

> both British and Germans on quiet sectors assumed that should a chance face-to-face encounter occur, neither patrol would initiate aggression, but each would move to avoid the other. Each patrol gave peace to the other where aggression was not only possible, but prescribed, provided, of course, the gesture was reciprocated, for if one patrol fired so would the other.[14]

In the words of one of the participants in the conflict:

> we suddenly confronted, round some mound or excavation, a German patrol . . . we were perhaps twenty yards from one another, fully visible. I waved a weary hand, as if to say, what is the use of killing each other? The German officer seemed to understand, and both parties turned and made their way back to their own trenches.[15]

Often, bombardments would occur only at specified times of day and would be directed away from the most vulnerable times and positions. Mealtimes and hospital tents, for example, were usually tacitly off limits.

The conditions discussed by Axelrod help to explain not only when people will cooperate, but also when they are most likely to *refrain* from cooperation. Thus, he notes that mutual restraint in trench warfare began to break down once the end of the war was clearly in sight.

As in warfare, so, too, in the world of business. Companies pay their bills on time, Axelrod suggests, not because it is the right thing to do but because they require future shipments from the same suppliers. When future interactions appear unlikely, this tendency to cooperate often breaks down: "[An] example is the case where a business is on the edge of bankruptcy and sells its accounts receivable to an outsider called a 'factor.' " This sale is made at a very substantial discount because

> once a manufacturer begins to go under, even his best customers begin refusing payment for merchandise, claiming defects in quality, failure to meet specifications, tardy delivery, or what-have-you. The great enforcer of morality in commerce is the continuing relationship, the belief that one will have to do business again with this customer, or this supplier, and when a failing company loses this automatic enforcer, not even a strong-arm factor is likely to find a substitute.[16]

Not even academe is exempt: "a visiting professor is likely to receive poor treatment by other faculty members compared to the way these people treat their regular colleagues."[17]

It is impossible to quarrel with the notion that trust and cooperation often emerge for the reasons suggested by these authors. The material world is a difficult environment, and the penalty for uncritically charitable behavior will often be failure to survive.

But again, the difficulty, for our purposes, is that tit-for-tat is simply not genuinely *altruistic* behavior. Rather, it is, like reciprocal altruism, a straightforward illustration of *prudent* behavior—enlightened prudence, to be sure, but self-interested behavior all the same. The person whose cooperation is summoned only by the conditions specified by these theories can hardly lay claim to the moral high ground. Those who would search for deeper, more noble impulses in people must look elsewhere.

MEDIATING EMOTIONS

Trivers clearly has such impulses in mind when he writes, "Selection may favor distrusting those who perform altruistic acts without the emotional basis of generosity or guilt because the altruistic tendencies of such individuals may be less reliable in the future."[18] He mentions parallel roles for other mediating emotions such as "moralistic aggression," friendship, and sympathy.

The presence of such emotions can help account for many of the observations that pure calculations about reciprocity cannot. As noted in Chapter 1, for example, the expectation of reciprocal benefits is no reason to tip in a restaurant in a distant city. But generosity or sympathy may provide ample motive to do so.

What Trivers does not explain clearly is how these emotions would benefit the individual in material terms. To see the difficulty, recall that the basic problem both theories attempt to solve is the repeated prisoner's dilemma.* As both Trivers and Axelrod emphasize, each individual has a purely selfish motive for cooperating in this context, namely, that failure to do so will provoke retaliation. But Axelrod also stresses that this motive, *by itself,* is sufficient to assure maximum benefits.

Persons with some *additional* motive will tend to fare worse because they will sometimes cooperate when it is not in their

---

*Axelrod poses the problem explicitly in these terms; Trivers implies it by his emphasis on repeated interactions and the need to be able to remember how specific individuals behaved in the past.

material interests to do so. A person who wants to avoid guilt, for example, will sometimes cooperate even in a one-shot prisoner's dilemma—he may pay his bills even when it looks like his creditor is about to go out of business. Tit-for-tat, by contrast, does not even apply in this case, where the optimal strategy is simply to defect.

A person who experiences sympathy may be excessively reluctant to retaliate. In Axelrod's terms, the latter tendency is characteristic of people who play "tit-for-two-tats"—the strategy of retaliating only against partners who defect twice in succession. In all of the environments Axelrod studied, tit-for-tat performed considerably better than tit-for-two-tats.

Trivers argues that moralistic aggression may be useful because it motivates us to punish people who refuse to return a favor. But again, tit-for-tat does this as well and, as Axelrod emphasizes, in precisely the desired contexts and to precisely the desired degree. Someone motivated by moralistic aggression may waste energy trying to punish others with whom he knows he will never interact again. This is often a good thing from society's point of view, of course, but any individual would do better by leaving costly aggression to others. Another difficulty with moralistic aggression is that people motivated by it may retaliate excessively against ongoing trading partners. ("Friends are even killed over apparently trivial disputes."[19]) In Axelrod's terms, moralistic aggression is thus akin to "two-tits-for-a-tat," another of the many strategies defeated by tit-for-tat.

If tit-for-tat required people to make complex computations, then mediating emotions might prove useful as rules-of-thumb. If they motivated maximizing behavior sufficiently often, and if they saved a lot of computational time and energy, they might perform better, on the average, than tit-for-tat. But in view of tit-for-tat's exceedingly simple nature, such a role hardly appears plausible. Even the most slow-witted persons can easily meet the computational demands imposed by this strategy.

To summarize, the advantage of Trivers's account is that his mediating emotions help explain why people might act altruistically even in situations in which it does not pay them to do so. In Axelrod's story, which makes no mention of the emotions, such behavior remains a mystery. The disadvantage in Trivers's account is that he doesn't offer a clear explanation of how the mediating emotions confer material advantages on individuals. Where the behaviors favored by these emotions differ from those dictated by tit-for-tat, the latter seem to serve better. And where the two mechanisms lead to the same behaviors, the mediating emotions appear unnecessary. Although the two accounts of cooperation are very similar, Trivers's appears more in harmony with our observations on altruistic behavior, whereas Axelrod's seems more in harmony with Darwin's individual selection model.*

I do not mean to say, however, that the mediating emotions described by Trivers serve no purpose. On the contrary, I will argue in the next two chapters that they are very useful indeed. My point here is that much more needs to be said about *how,* exactly, they are helpful.

GROUP SELECTION

Group-selection models are the favored turf of biologists and others who feel that people are genuinely altruistic. Many biologists are skeptical of these models, which reject the central Darwinian assumption that selection occurs at the individual level.** In his recent text, for example, Trivers includes a chapter entitled "The Group Selection Fallacy."[20] With thinly veiled contempt, he defines group selection as "the differential reproduction of groups, often imagined to favor traits that are individually disadvantageous but evolve because they benefit the

---

*Of course, Trivers originally proposed his model of reciprocal altruism more than a decade before the appearance of Axelrod's book. Even in his most recent writings (1985), however, he continues to stress the importance of mediating emotions.

**For an excellent survey of the technical difficulties confronting group selection models, see Wilson, 1975, Chapter 5.

larger group." Group selectionists have attempted to show that genuine altruism, as conventionally defined, is just such a trait. A propensity not to cheat even when there is no possibility of being detected is a convenient example. In cases where cheating cannot be detected, tit-for-tat and other forms of reciprocal altruism have no apparent path to success, since it is impossible for cooperators to retaliate against defectors.

Could altruism have evolved via group selection? For this to have happened, altruistic groups would have had to prosper at the expense of less altruistic groups in the competition for scarce resources. This requirement, by itself, is not problematic. After all, altruism *is* efficient at the group level (recall that pairs of cooperators in the prisoner's dilemma do better than pairs of defectors), and we can imagine ways that altruistic groups might avoid being taken advantage of by less altruistic groups. For example, an altruistic group might be totally isolated from other groups. Such isolation, while rare, can happen.[21]

But even if we suppose that the superior performance of the altruistic group enables it to triumph over all other groups, the group selection story still faces a formidable hurdle. The conventional definition, again, is that nonaltruistic behavior is advantageous *to the individual.* Even in an altruistic group, not every individual will be equally altruistic. When individuals differ, there will be selection pressure in favor of the least altruistic members. And as long as these individuals get higher payoffs, they will comprise an ever-larger share of the altruistic group.

So even in the event that a purely altruistic group triumphs over all other groups, the logic of selection at the individual level appears to spell ultimate doom for genuinely altruistic behavior. It can triumph only when the extinction rate of groups is comparable to the mortality rate for individuals within them. As Wilson stresses, this condition is rarely if ever met in practice.[22]

Although the book is far from closed on the group selection debate, most biologists now reject the notion that genuinely altruistic behavior could have emerged via group selection.

Indeed, many seem to regard group selectionists much as Doris Baker once regarded her brother Russell.

CULTURAL PRESSURES

Perhaps altruism and other forms of self-sacrificing behavior are not biologically rooted at all, but instead the result of cultural conditioning. This appears to be William Hamilton's view when he writes,

> ... the animal part of our nature is expected to be more concerned with "getting more than the average" than with "getting the maximum possible." ... [This] implies ... a complete disregard for any values, either of individuals or of groups, which do not serve competitive breeding. This being so, the animal in our nature cannot be regarded as a fit custodian for the values of civilized man.[23]

Virtually every human culture we know of has invested great effort in both the teaching and enforcement of moral codes of conduct. Most of these codes oppose the "animal in our nature," calling on people to forego personal advantage out of consideration for others. Perhaps these codes are the real explanation for self-sacrificing behavior.

We know, however, that there are at least *some* forms of self-sacrificing behavior that culture clearly cannot explain. The pursuit of vengeance, discussed briefly in Chapter 1, is one example. Most cultures not only do not encourage the pursuit of vengeance, they take positive steps to curtail it. Contrary to impressions, the biblical reference, "an eye for an eye, a tooth for a tooth," is not an exhortation to *seek* vengeance, but a plea to *restrain* it to the scale of the original provocation. We may safely presume that, where a cultural norm attempts to restrain a given behavior, people left to their own devices would tend to do even more of it. Thus, it hardly makes sense to offer cultural conditioning as the explanation for why we see such behavior in the first place.

The same objection, however, clearly does not apply in the case of culturally *encouraged* behaviors, such as honesty or charity. Many have argued that these behaviors would not exist at all were it not for the pressure of cultural forces. After all, the very definition of honesty differs widely from culture to culture, and across groups within cultures. The Mafia soldier follows a code of conduct vastly different from the Presbyterian deacon's. This tells us that there is nothing so simple as a biological urge to "be honest." If there is any sort of inherited instinct at work here, it must be extremely flexible—something like "pay attention to what the people around you teach, and try to follow that."

Is such an instinct necessary, or are cultural norms, in and of themselves, sufficient to account for the presence of altruistic behavior? It is easy to credit that cultural norms might be a *prerequisite* for the emergence of altruistic behavior. We know, after all, that precious little altruism is found in cultures that do not actively encourage it.

It is also easy to see why even an inherently selfish person would be pleased to live in a culture that promulgated altruistic norms, for if these norms are effective, they will result in his being treated more favorably by others.

From the skeptical behavioral scientist's perspective, however, the real mystery is why a self-interested individual would *follow* such a code. In other words, we must explain why there would not be a decisive advantage to breaking the moral norms whenever one could profitably do so. Some people, of course, do precisely that. But most people are considerably less opportunistic. In a world in which there is apparently a high payoff to opportunistic behavior, how does anything less than complete opportunism survive?

I should stress here that by "complete opportunism" I do not mean conspicuously antisocial behavior. The true opportunist cooperates when it is in his interests to do so and will often refrain from cheating when there is even only a small likelihood of being caught. Indeed, he may appear to be a model citizen. But there are any number of ways a seemingly model citizen can defect with virtually no chance of penalty. He can, among other things,

- keep the cash in a wallet he finds;
- fail to report that cash to the IRS;
- pad expense accounts and insurance claims;
- refrain from tipping when he is on the road;
- leave litter on a lonely beach;
- disconnect his car's smog control device.

Perhaps some people do all of these things. Many more do some of them. It is in the nature of these acts that, while we may know *someone* is doing them, we cannot know *who.* Yet we do know that not everyone does all of these things. If all smog control devices were unhooked, the air would be even browner than it is; if everyone littered, the beaches would be even dirtier.

Do the people who refrain from defecting in these situations necessarily do worse than others? Many religions teach that virtuous people may look forward to great rewards in the next life. But the conventional wisdom is that, in this life, virtue must be its own reward. In material terms, the defectors in each of the above-mentioned situations surely will do better. This is the fundamental paradox of the Darwinian model and other materialist theories of human existence. They leave no apparent room for virtuous behavior, yet hard evidence of such behavior abounds.

While cultural norms may be necessary, they do not seem sufficient to account for this behavior. There is first of all the question of why opportunistic parents would cooperate in the effort to teach their children to behave unopportunistically. Why don't they just say "Be a cheerful member of the group, deliver on your commitments where failure to do so can be observed, but otherwise avail yourself of every opportunity for gain."?

Laws could be passed, presumably, to make it more difficult for opportunistic parents to transmit such messages. We have compulsory education, for example, and try to impart benign cultural values in our schools. Yet we know there are at least some people—sociopaths, for example—who are insensitive to even the most intense forms of cultural conditioning. And if opportunists consistently outperform all others, the inexorable logic of the evolutionary model is that we should end up with only such people.

Yet this has not happened. In Chapter 1, I suggested that one reason it may not have is that unopportunistic persons may be observably different from others, and that in this difference may lie the clue to their survival. Let us now turn to the details of this explanation.

THREE

A THEORY OF MORAL SENTIMENTS

I n the early hours of March 13, 1964, Winston Moseley stalked a young woman as she walked from her car near a train station in Queens, New York. He caught up with her on the sidewalk in front of a bookstore near her apartment, then wrestled her to the pavement and stabbed her in the chest. As she screamed for help, lights went on and several windows opened in the surrounding apartments. From his seventh-floor vantage, one neighbor yelled, "Let that girl alone!"

Moseley retreated. But he later said, "I had a feeling this man would close his window and go back to sleep and then I would return." Return he did. He stalked his screaming victim to a stairwell in her apartment house, where he stabbed her eight more times and sexually assaulted her. New York police did not receive their first call about the incident until 3:50 AM, some thirty minutes after the cries of distress first awakened neighbors. By the time they arrived, Kitty Genovese was beyond help.

Among the neighbors later interviewed by police, 38 admitted to having heard her screams. Any one of them might have saved her life with a single phone call, yet all held back. Investigators heard explanations like "I was tired"; "We thought it was a lovers' quarrel"; and "Frankly, we were afraid." One couple had doused their lights and watched the assault from behind their curtains.

In the ensuing years, the case has become a celebrated symbol of human indifference to a victim in distress. Almost everyone familiar with the story expresses moral outrage at Kitty Genovese's neighbors. Yet, in the face of so many people having failed to act, it may be a mistake for critics to feel certain they would have behaved otherwise.

The Genovese case, and others like it, are often cited in support of the purely self-serving portrait of human nature. And yet there are equally vivid episodes that support a much less dismal portrait. A surviving witness tells, for example, of how three CBS technicians came upon Margaret Barbera being dragged by a man through an isolated parking garage along the Hudson River in Manhattan. Even though the assailant was brandishing a long-barreled pistol, the three men rushed to Barbera's aid. It was hardly selfish motives that led Leo Kuranski, Robert Schulze, and Edward Benford to their deaths that evening in the spring of 1982. Most certainly, they were not engaged in a prudent act of reciprocal altruism.

In his 1759 book with nearly the same title as this chapter's, Adam Smith wrote about sympathy and other moral sentiments that motivate people to put others' interests ahead of their own. Smith believed nature endowed us with these sentiments for the good of mankind.[1] In modern terms, we recognize his view as the familiar group-selectionist account—noble instincts impose costs on those who hold them, but persist because they promote the survival of people as a species. As noted in the previous chapter, however, most biologists vehemently reject this view. And yet the individual-selectionist explanations they offer in its place are at best incomplete, at worst transparently inadequate.

The evolutionary view of human nature insists that behaviors and other traits exist for a single purpose—to promote the survival of the genes carried by the individuals that bear them. Sugar tastes sweet, for example, because apes who had a taste for ripened fruit were more likely than others to survive and leave offspring. By the same token, purely self-interested individuals should do better than altruists, and should therefore eventually make up the entire population. Material forces seem to assure that we end up only with people like Kitty Genovese's neighbors, none like Kuranski, Schulze, and Benford. The individual-selectionist framework, once again, leaves no obvious pathway for the emergence of unopportunistic behavior.

For precisely this reason, many insist the evolutionary model does not apply to human behavior. Rather than deny noble tendencies exist, when we have compelling evidence they do, these people find it easier to say Darwinism stops with apes. By this view, culture and other nonbiological forces are so important for humans that we do better simply to ignore evolutionary influences.

My task in this chapter is to make use of a simple idea from economics to sketch an alternative individual-selectionist avenue along which altruism and other forms of apparently non-self-serving behavior might have emerged. The mechanism I will describe differs from those we saw in Chapter 2 in that the behaviors it tries to explain are non-self-serving in the strictest sense: if individuals could *selectively* refrain from performing them, they and their relatives would be better off in material terms. In later chapters, I will survey a variety of evidence that is consistent with the account I offer here. But it is well beyond the scope of this work to suggest that this mechanism is *the* explanation, or even the most important one, for non-self-serving behavior. My hope is to establish merely that it is a plausible candidate and thus, perhaps, to stimulate others to investigate it further.

Before proceeding with the details of the argument, it will be helpful to clarify what I am *not* trying to accomplish. In presenting earlier versions of this work, I have always encountered a few people in every audience who become hostile at the mere mention of biological forces playing a role in human choices. To such people I emphasize that it is not my purpose to try to persuade anyone that biological forces play such a role. Rather, it is to establish that even if biological forces were the *only* ones that influenced behavior, it would *still* be possible for unopportunistic behavior to emerge. My main point is simply that standard sociobiological models have not dealt adequately with an important class of problems that people confront in social environments; and that the behaviors required to solve these problems are very different from the ones that emerge in standard models.

To engage in this discussion, it is not necessary to accept the view that biological forces are important. Neither, of course, is it necessary to reject it.

MORAL SENTIMENTS AS PROBLEM-SOLVING DEVICES

For a trait to emerge in evolutionary models, it must be not only beneficial to the individual, but also *more* beneficial than other traits that could have been supported by the same bodily resources. Consider the evolution of eyesight. Human beings and other animals see only a fraction of the potentially visible spectrum. A person who could see well into the infrared spectrum would have certain obvious advantages over the rest of us; in particular, she would have better night vision. And yet human vision stops with the color red. The reason, in evolutionary terms, is that the neurological capacity needed to support infrared vision has more important uses. What a person would gain by being able to see the infrared spectrum is apparently not as valuable as having, for example, generally keener vision through a more limited spectrum.

For a moral sentiment to evolve, then, it must somehow confer not just an advantage, but an important one. The theory of moral sentiments I will sketch here suggests that these sentiments do precisely that. They help us solve an important and recurring problem of social interaction—namely, the *commitment problem* introduced in Chapter 1.

•   •   •

EXAMPLES OF THE COMMITMENT PROBLEM

The commitment problem, recall, arises when it is in a person's interest to make a binding commitment to behave in a way that will later seem contrary to self-interest.* Some examples:

Cheating. Two persons, Smith and Jones, can engage in a potentially profitable venture, say, a restaurant. Their potential for gain arises from the natural advantages inherent in the division and specialization of labor. Smith is a talented cook, but is shy and an incompetent manager. Jones, by contrast, cannot boil an egg, but is charming and has shrewd business judgment. Together, they have the necessary skills to launch a successful venture. Working alone, however, their potential is much more limited.

Their problem is this: Each will have opportunities to cheat without possibility of detection. Jones can skim from the cash drawer without Smith's knowledge. Smith, for his part, can take kickbacks from food suppliers.

If only one of them cheats, he does very well. The non-cheater does poorly, but isn't sure why. His low return is not a reliable sign of having been cheated, since there are many benign explanations why a business might do poorly. If the victim also cheats, he, too, can escape detection, and will do better than by not cheating; but still not nearly so well as if both had been honest.

Once the venture is under way, self-interest unambigu-

---

*What I am calling "commitment problems" here will be familiar to some readers as "precommitment problems," the name used by most economists to describe them (Strotz, 1956; Williamson, 1977; Dixit, 1980; Eaton and Lipsey, 1981; Schmalensee, 1978). I have indeed referred to them by that name myself (Frank, 1985). The economists' term is probably chosen to emphasize that the solutions to these problems require people to commit themselves *in advance.* But how else can one commit oneself to anything, if not in advance? The term "precommitment" is a redundancy. It is less salient than the remark by a sports announcer that the home team had "won eight consecutive games in a row without a loss," but it is a poorly chosen term nonetheless.

ously dictates cheating. Yet if both could make a binding commitment not to cheat, they would profit by doing so. The difficulty they confront is much the same as in Schelling's kidnap example from Chapter 1 and the prisoner's dilemma from Chapter 2.

· **Deterrence.** Suppose Smith grows wheat and Jones raises cattle on adjacent plots of land. Jones is liable for whatever damage his steers do to Smith's wheat. He can prevent damage altogether by fencing his land, which would cost him $200. If he leaves his land unfenced, his steers will eat $1000 worth of wheat. Jones knows, however, that if his steers do eat Smith's wheat, it will cost Smith $2000 to take him to court.

These court costs notwithstanding, Smith threatens to sue Jones for damages if he does not fence his land. But if Jones believed Smith to be a rational, self-interested person, this threat is not credible. Once the wheat has been eaten, there is no longer any use for Smith to go to court. He would lose more than he recovered.

If Smith could make a binding commitment to go to court in the event of damage, however, his problem would be solved. Knowing a damage suit was inevitable, Jones would then have nothing to gain by not fencing his land, and there would thus be no need for Smith to incur the costs of suing.*

· **Bargaining.** In this example, Smith and Jones again face the opportunity of a profitable joint venture. There is some task that they alone can do, which will net them $1000 total. Jones has no pressing need for extra money, but Smith has impor-

---

*Note that in this instance the problem is solved with a "contingent" commitment, one that will trigger action only if a particular condition occurs. In the cheating problem, the solution required that each party actually follow through on its commitment to forfeit advantage, by not cheating. (Granted, each party benefited even more by the other's not cheating). Here, by contrast, Smith must forsake personal advantage only on the condition that Jones does not fence his land. And if Jones knows Smith has made a contingent commitment to sue, that contingency will not arise. In the end, it will not prove necessary for Smith to forego self-interest.

tant bills to pay. It is a fundamental principle of bargaining theory that the party who needs the transaction least is in the strongest position. The difference in their circumstances thus gives Jones the advantage. Needing the gain less, he can threaten, credibly, to walk away from the transaction unless he gets the lion's share of the take, say $800. Rather than see the transaction fall through, it will then be in Smith's interest to capitulate.

Smith could have protected his position, however, had he been able to make a binding commitment not to accept less than, say, half of the earnings. One possible way of accomplishing this would be to sign a contract that requires him to contribute $500 to the Republican party in the event he accepts less than $500 from his joint venture with Jones. (Smith is a lifelong Democrat and finds the prospect of such a gift distasteful.) With this contract in place, it would no longer be in his interest to give in to Jones's threat. (If Smith accepted $200, for example, he would have to make the $500 contribution, which would leave him $300 worse off than if he hadn't done the job with Jones at all.) Jones's threat is suddenly stripped of all its power.

Marriage. As a final example of the commitment problem, consider the difficulty confronting a couple who want to marry and raise a family. Each considers the other a suitable mate. But marriage requires substantial investment, which each person fears could be undercut if the other were to leave for an even more attractive opportunity in the future. Without reasonable assurance that this will not happen, neither is willing to make the investments required to make the most of their marriage.

They could solve their problem if they could write a detailed marriage contract that would levy substantial penalties on whichever of them attempted to leave. They are, after all, willing to forego potentially attractive opportunities in the future in order to make it in their interests to invest in the present effort of raising a family. It would serve their purposes to take steps now that would alter the incentives they face in the future.

Two features stand out in these examples. First, the problems themselves, if not the proposed solutions, are by no means contrived or unimportant. In joint ventures, practical difficulties almost always stand in the way of being able to monitor other people's performance. Again and again, cheating on all sides leads to a worse outcome for everyone. In these situations, having the means to make binding commitments not to cheat would benefit every party. In competitive environments, similarly, opportunities for predation are widespread. And where such opportunities exist, there is a ready supply of cynical people to exploit them. To be able to solve the deterrence problem would be an asset of the first magnitude. Bargaining problems are no less important. To live is to haggle. People must repeatedly dicker with one another about how to divide the fruits of their collective efforts. Those who can deal successfully with these problems would have an obvious advantage. Finally, almost everyone confronts some version of the marriage problem. That there would be significant value in being able to solve this problem can hardly be questioned.

The second obvious feature of the four examples is that the proposed solutions are either hopelessly vague or decidedly impractical. Indeed, no suggestion was even offered about how a commitment not to cheat could be made where the detection of cheating is impossible; or of how a commitment to retaliate might be implemented when an aggressor realizes that retaliation would not be rational. Contracts like the one suggested as a solution to the bargaining problem are probably not legally binding, and there are a variety of reasons for wanting them not to be. Finally, various penalties already do exist for the termination of formal marriage contracts, and yet few people regard them as sufficient to bind partners together who believe their interests lie elsewhere.

EMOTIONS AS INCENTIVES

The irony of the commitment problem is that it arises because material incentives at a given moment prompt people to behave in ways contrary to their ultimate material interests. The solutions suggested in the examples all try to alter the relevant material incentives. In Chapter 1, for example, recall that Schelling's kidnap victim solved the cheating problem by giving the kidnapper self-incriminating evidence to ensure his silence. The contracts proposed for the bargaining and marriage problems, similarly, work by changing people's material payoffs.

As noted, however, it will often be impractical to alter material incentives in the desired ways. Fortunately, there is a potentially fruitful alternative approach. Material incentives are by no means the only force that governs behavior. Even in biological models, where these incentives are the ultimate concern, they play no *direct* role in motivation. Rather, behavior is directly guided by a complex psychological reward mechanism.

The system that governs food intake provides a clear illustration of this mechanism. Man or beast, an individual does not eat in response to a rational calculation about caloric needs. Instead, a complex of biological forces causes it to "feel hungry" when its stomach contents, blood sugar level, and other nutritional indexes fall below various threshold values. To feel hungry is to experience a subjective sensation of displeasure in the central nervous system. Experience, and perhaps even inborn neural circuits, tell us that food intake will relieve this sensation.

In a proximate sense, this is *why* we eat. There is a material payoff to eating, to be sure. Any organism that did not eat obviously would not be favored by natural selection. But the relevant material payoffs are more likely to be realized if eating is motivated directly through the reward mechanism. When food is scarce, finding something to eat requires great effort, no mean feat for someone who is already weakened by lack of nourishment. For such a person, feelings of intense hunger can mobilize reserves of energy in a way that mere rational calculations cannot.

The fit between the behaviors favored by the reward mechanism and those favored by rational calculation is at best imperfect. The reward mechanism provides rules of thumb that work well much of the time, but not in all cases. Indeed, when environmental conditions differ substantially from the ones under which the reward mechanism evolved, important conflicts often arise.

The reward system governing food intake again provides a convenient illustration. It is now believed that food shortages were a common occurrence during most of evolutionary history. Under such conditions, it paid to have a reward mechanism that favored heavy food intake whenever abundant food was available. People thus motivated would be more likely to fatten up as a hedge against periods of famine. In modern industrial societies, however, people are much more likely to die of heart attacks than of starvation. A rational calculation of self-interest currently dictates that we stay slim. This calculation, needless to say, is at war, often on the losing side, with the reward mechanism.

To say that the reward mechanism often defeats intentions motivated by rational assessment of material payoffs is not to say that rational assessment is unimportant for survival. On the contrary, our ability to make purposeful, rational calculations has surely played a major role in our ability to persist in competition with animal species that are far stronger, faster, and more prolific than we are.

The critical point, for present purposes, is that rational calculations play only an indirect role. Suppose, for example, a hungry person calculates that being fat is not in his interests, and for this reason refrains from eating. His rational calculation has clearly played a role, but it is an indirect one. It is still the reward mechanism that directly governs his behavior. The rational calculation informs the reward mechanism that eating will have adverse consequences. This prospect then triggers unpleasant feelings. And it is these feelings that compete directly with the impulse to eat. Rational calculations, understood in this way, are an *input* into the reward mechanism.

Feelings and emotions, apparently, are the proximate causes of most behaviors. The biochemical workings of some of them— hunger, anger, fear, and mating urges, for example—are sufficiently well understood that they can be induced by electrical stimulation of specific brain sites. Others are less well mapped. Yet they are so consistently recognized across cultures that they, too, likely have some neuroanatomical basis.

Certain of the emotions—anger, contempt, disgust, envy, greed, shame, and guilt—were described by Adam Smith as moral sentiments. The reward theory of behavior tells us that these sentiments, like feelings of hunger, can and do compete with the feelings that spring from rational calculations about material payoffs. For exactly this reason, they can help people solve the commitment problem.

It is clear, at any rate, that these sentiments can alter people's incentives in the desired ways. Consider, for example, a person capable of strong guilt feelings. This person will not cheat even when it is in her material interests to do so. The reason is not that she fears getting caught but that she simply does not *want* to cheat. Her aversion to feelings of guilt effectively alters the payoffs she faces.* That it is not necessary to monitor such a person to prevent her from cheating precludes the difficulty that there is often no practical way to do so.

By the same token, someone who becomes enraged when dealt with unjustly does not need a formal contract to commit him to seek revenge. He will seek revenge because he *wants* to, even when, in purely material terms, it does not pay. His feelings of anger will offset his material incentives.

---

*In purely material terms, of course, her payoffs remain the same. And since, in biological theories of behavior, these are the only payoffs that matter, her aversion to cheating does not make her dilemma any less real.

This same sense of justice can serve as the commitment device needed to solve the bargaining problem. Smith was in a weak bargaining position, recall, because he needed money more than Jones did. But if Smith is concerned not only about how much money he gets, in absolute terms, but also about how the total is divided, he will be much more inclined to reject an unfair division. Being concerned about justice is like signing a contract that prevents him from accepting the short end of a one-sided transaction.

And it is no surprise, finally, that the marriage problem is likewise better solved by moral sentiments than by awkward formal contracts. The best insurance against a change in future material incentives is a strong bond of love. If ten years from now one partner falls victim to a lasting illness, the other's material incentives will be to find a new partner. But a deep bond of affection will render this change in incentives irrelevant, which opens the door for current investments in the relationship that might otherwise be too risky.

By themselves, however, the described changes in incentives are not sufficient to solve the commitment problem. Granted, strong feelings of guilt *are* enough to prevent a person from cheating. And the satisfying feeling someone gets from having done the right thing is, in a very real sense, its own reward. But our task here, once again, is to explain how such sentiments might have evolved in the material world. We can't eat moral sentiments. For them to be viable in competitive environments, they must have a material payoff.

The potential gain from being honest, recall, is to cooperate with others who are also honest. In order for the noncheater to benefit in material terms, others must thus be able to recognize her as such, and she, in turn, must be able to recognize other noncheaters. The impulse to seek revenge is likewise counterproductive unless others have some way of anticipating that one has it. The person in whom this sentiment resides unrecognized will fail to deter potential predators. And if one is going to be victimized anyway, it is better *not* to desire revenge. It is the worst of both worlds, after all, to end up spending $2000 to recover $1000 worth of damaged wheat. For similar reasons, a sense of justice and the capacity to love will not yield material payoffs unless they can be somehow communicated clearly to others.

But how to communicate something so subjective as a person's innermost feelings? Surely it is insufficient merely to *declare* them. ("I am honest. Trust me.") The essential ingredients of the commitment mechanism I have in mind are nicely captured in the Frank Modell drawing reproduced in Figure 3.1. The wary couple must decide whether to buy a pencil from the gentleman with the whip. If they believe him to be a fully rational, self-interested person, the presence of the whip should make no difference. The man would realize that no amount of added pencil sales could possibly compensate him for the jail term he would get if he actually used it. But if they believe he

FIGURE 3.1 The Extortionist
Drawing by Modell: © 1971 The New Yorker Magazine, Inc.

is *not* in full control, the whip will matter. It will then be in their interests to buy a pencil whether they want one or not. And in that event, the man gets the extra sale without so much as lifting the whip from his side.

Note that the sign around the man's neck is not the only, or even a very good, signal that he is not fully rational. On the contrary, that he seems to have realized the sign might serve his purposes can only detract from its ability to do so. It is the expression on his face that really makes his point. People who are fully in control of themselves just don't often *look* like that.

ILLUSTRATION: THE CHEATING PROBLEM

If moral sentiments are so useful, why are there so many dishonest people in the world? What forces have kept moral sentiments from driving out the less noble sentiments that are also such an obvious component of human nature? To help focus on these questions, let us examine a specific illustration of the cheating problem.

Consider again the restaurant example. Smith and Jones both have the options of cheating or not, which gives rise to four possible combinations of behavior. For the sake of concreteness, suppose the payoffs to these combinations are as summarized in Table 3.1. The terms "defect" and "cooperate" are used to represent "cheat" and "not cheat," respectively.

The payoffs in Table 3.1 are the same as the ones we saw in the monetary prisoner's dilemma in Chapter 2. As before, it is thus a dominant strategy to defect on one's partner. Jones gets a higher payoff by defecting, no matter what Smith does, and the same is true for Smith. If Jones believes Smith will behave in a self-interested way, he will predict that Smith will defect. And if only to protect himself, he will likely feel compelled to defect as well. When both defect, each gets only a 2-unit payoff. The frustration, as in all dilemmas of this sort, is that both could have easily done much better. Had they cooperated, each would have gotten a 4-unit payoff.

TABLE 3.1. Monetary Payoffs in a Joint Venture

		SMITH	
		DEFECT	COOPERATE
JONES	DEFECT	2 for each	6 for Jones 0 for Smith
	COOPERATE	0 for Jones 6 for Smith	4 for each

Now suppose we have not just Smith and Jones but a large population. Pairs of people again form joint ventures and the relationship between behavior and payoffs for the members of each pair is again as given in Table 3.1. Suppose further that everyone in the population is of one of two types—cooperator or defector. A cooperator is someone who, possibly through intensive cultural conditioning, has enhanced a genetically endowed capacity to experience a moral sentiment that predisposes him to cooperate. A defector is someone who either lacks this capacity or has failed to develop it.

In this scheme, cooperators are hard-core altruists in the sense described in Chapter 2. They refrain from cheating even when there is no possibility of being detected, and this behavior is clearly contrary to their material interests. Defectors, by contrast, are pure opportunists. They always make whatever choice will maximize their personal payoff. Our task is to determine what will happen when people from these two groups are thrown into a survival struggle against one another. How well each type fares will depend on whether (and if so, how easily) the two groups can be distinguished. I will consider several cases in turn.

When Cooperators and Defectors Look Alike

First, suppose that cooperators and defectors look exactly alike. In such a population, the two types will pair at random. Naturally, cooperators (and defectors, for that matter) would like nothing better than to pair with cooperators, but they have no choice in the matter. Because everyone looks the same, they must take their chances. The expected payoffs to both defectors and cooperators therefore depend on the likelihood of pairing with a cooperator, which in turn depends on the proportion of cooperators in the population.

Suppose, for example, the population consists almost entirely of cooperators. A cooperator is then virtually certain to have a cooperator for a partner, and so expects a payoff of nearly 4 units. The rare defector in this population is similarly almost certain to get a cooperator for a partner, and can expect a payoff of nearly 6 units. (The defector's unlucky partner, of course, gets a payoff of zero, but his singular misfortune does not significantly affect the average payoff for cooperators as a group.)

Alternatively, suppose the population consists of half cooperators, half defectors. Each person is then just as likely to pair with a defector as with a cooperator. Cooperators thus have equal chances of receiving either zero or 4 units, which gives them an average payoff of 2 units. Defectors, in turn, have equal chances of receiving 2 or 6 units, so their average payoff will be 4 units. In general, the average payoffs for each type will rise with the proportion of cooperators in the population—the cooperator's because he is less likely to be exploited by a defector, the defector's because he is more likely to find a cooperator he can exploit. The exact relationships for the particular payoffs assumed in this illustration are shown in Figure 3.2.

When cooperators and defectors look exactly the same, how will the population evolve over time? In evolutionary models, each individual reproduces in proportion to its average payoff: those with larger material payoffs have the resources necessary to raise larger numbers of offspring.* Since defectors always

* In very recent times, of course, there has been a *negative* relationship between income and family size. But if sentiments were forged by natural selection, the relationship that matters is the one that existed during most of evolutionary history. And that relationship was undisputedly positive: periods of famine were frequent and individuals with greater material resources saw many more of their children reach adulthood. Moreover, most early societies were polygynous—their most wealthy members usually claimed several wives, leaving many of the poor with none.

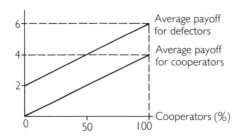

**FIGURE 3.2   Average Payoffs When Cooperators and
Defectors Look Alike**

receive a higher average payoff here, their share of the population will grow over time. Cooperators, even if they make up almost the entire population to begin with, are thus destined for extinction. When cooperators and defectors look alike, genuine cooperation cannot emerge. In a crude way, this case epitomizes the traditional sociobiological characterization of behavior.

When Cooperators Are Easily Identified

Now suppose everything is just as before except that cooperators and defectors are perfectly distinguishable from each other. Imagine that cooperators are born with a red "C" on their foreheads, defectors with a red "D." Suddenly the tables are completely turned. Cooperators can now interact selectively with one another and be assured of a payoff of 4 units. No cooperator need ever interact with a defector. Defectors are left to interact with one another, for which they get a payoff of only 2 units.

Since all element of chance has been removed from the interaction process, payoffs no longer depend on the proportion of cooperators in the population. (See Figure 3.3.) Cooperators always get 4, defectors always get 2.

This time the cooperators' larger payoffs enable *them* to raise larger families, which means they will make up an ever-grow-

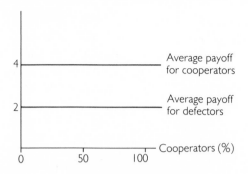

**FIGURE 3.3   Average Payoffs When Cooperators and
Defectors Are Perfectly Distinguishable**

ing share of the population. When cooperators can be easily
identified, it is the defectors who face extinction.

Mimicry without Cost or Delay

The defectors need not go gentle into the night, however.
Suppose there arises a mutant strain of defectors, one that
behaves exactly like other defectors, but in which each individual has not a red "D" on his forehead but a red "'C." Since this
particular strain of defectors looks exactly the same as cooperators, it is impossible for cooperators to discriminate against
them. Each imposter is therefore just as likely to interact with
a cooperator as a genuine cooperator is. This, in turn, means
that the mutant defectors will have a higher expected payoff
than the cooperators.

The nonmutant defectors—those who continue to bear the
red "D"—will have a lower payoff than both of these groups
and, as before, are destined for extinction. But unless the cooperators adapt in some way, they too face the same fate. When
defectors can perfectly mimic the distinguishing feature of
cooperators with neither cost nor delay, the feature loses all
power to distinguish. Cooperators and the surviving defectors
again look exactly alike, which again spells doom for the cooperators.

Costs of Scrutiny

Defectors, of course, have no monopoly on the power to adapt. If random mutations alter the cooperators' distinguishing characteristic, the defectors will be faced with a moving target. Imagine that the red "C" by which cooperators originally managed to distinguish themselves has evolved over time into a generally ruddy complexion—a blush of sorts—and that some defectors have a ruddy complexion as well. But because cooperators actually experience the emotions that motivate cooperator, they have a more intense blush, on the average.

In general, we might expect a continuum of intensity of blushes for both groups.* For the sake of simplicity, however, suppose that complexions take one of only two discrete types: (1) heavy blush and (2) light blush. Those with heavy blushes are cooperators, those with light blushes, defectors. If the two types could be distinguished at a glance, defectors would again be doomed. But suppose it requires effort to inspect the intensity of a person's blush. For concreteness, suppose inspection costs 1 unit. For people who pay this cost, the veil is lifted: cooperators and defectors can be distinguished with 100 percent accuracy. For those who don't pay the 1-unit cost of scrutiny, the two types are perfectly indistinguishable.

To see what happens this time, suppose the payoffs are again as given in Table 3.1 and consider the decision facing a cooperator who is trying to decide whether to pay the cost of scrutiny. If he pays it, he can be assured of interacting with another cooperator, and will thus get a payoff of $4-1=3$ units. If he does not, his payoff is uncertain. Cooperators and defectors will look exactly alike to him and he must take his chances. If he happens to interact with another cooperator, he will get 4 units. But if he interacts with a defector, he will get zero. Whether it makes sense to pay the 1-unit cost of scrutiny thus depends on the likelihood of these two outcomes.

Suppose the population share of cooperators is 90 percent.

---

*I describe the details of a model that allows this feature in the Appendix.

By not paying the cost of scrutiny, a cooperator will interact with another cooperator 90 percent of the time, with a defector only 10 percent. His payoff will thus have an average value of $(.9 \times 4) + (.1 \times 0) = 3.6$. Since this is higher than the 3-unit net payoff he would get if he paid the cost of scrutiny, it is clearly better not to pay it.

Now suppose the population share of cooperators is not 90 percent but 50 percent. If our cooperator does not pay the cost of scrutiny, he will now have only a 50–50 chance of interacting with a defector. His average payoff will thus be only 2 units, or 1 unit less than if he had paid the cost. On these odds, it would clearly be better to pay it.

The numbers in this example imply a "break-even point" when the population share of cooperators is 75 percent. At that share, a cooperator who does not pay the cost has a 75 percent chance at a payoff of 4 units, and a 25 percent chance of getting zero. His average payoff is thus 3 units, the same as if he had paid the cost. When the population share of cooperators is below 75 percent, it will always be better for him to pay the cost of scrutiny; and when the share of cooperators is above 75 percent, it will never be better to pay the cost.

With this rule in mind, we can now say something about how the population will evolve over time. When the population share of cooperators is below 75 percent, cooperators will all pay the cost of scrutiny and get a payoff of 3 units by cooperating with one another. It will not be in the interests of defectors to bear this cost, because the keen-eyed cooperators would not interact with them anyway. The defectors are left to interact with one another, and get a payoff of only 2 units. Thus, if we start with a population share of cooperators less than 75 percent, the cooperators will get a higher average payoff, which means that their share of the population will grow.

In populations that consist of more than 75 percent cooperators, the tables are turned. Now it no longer makes sense to pay the cost of scrutiny. Cooperators and defectors will thus interact at random, which means that defectors will have a higher average payoff. This difference in payoffs, in turn, will cause the population share of cooperators to shrink.

For the values assumed in this example, the average payoff schedules for the two groups are plotted in Figure 3.4. As noted, the cooperators' schedule lies above the defectors' for shares smaller than 75 percent, but below it for larger shares. The sharp discontinuity in the defectors' schedule reflects the fact that, to the left of 75 percent, all cooperators pay to scrutinize while, to the right of 75 percent, none of them does. Once the population share of cooperators passes 75 percent, defectors suddenly gain access to their victims. The evolutionary rule, once again, is that higher relative payoffs result in a growing population share. This rule makes it clear that the population in this example will stabilize at 75 percent cooperators.

Now, there is obviously nothing magic about this 75 percent figure. Had the cost of scrutiny been higher than 1 unit, for example, the population share of cooperators would have been smaller. A reduction in the payoff when cooperators pair with one another would have a similar effect on the equilibrium population shares. The point of the example is that when there are costs of scrutiny, there will be pressures that pull the population toward some stable mix of cooperators and defectors. Once the population settles at this mix, members of both groups have the same average payoff and are therefore equally likely to survive. There is an ecological niche, in other words, for both groups. This result stands in stark contrast to the traditional sociobiological result that only opportunism can survive.

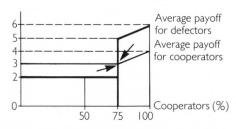

FIGURE 3.4   Average Payoffs with Costs of Scrutiny

ARE INHERITED CAPACITIES NECESSARY?

According to the commitment model, the survival of trust-worthiness derives in part from a tendency to be receptive to cultural training. In this respect, it is no different from the story told by critics of the biological model, who insist that culture is the sole explanation for human altruism. As we saw in Chapter 2, however, the critics' story runs into difficulty in the case of people who are unreceptive to cultural conditioning. Specifically, it does not explain why these people would not eventually dominate. And since we know there are many such people, this is a substantive difficulty.

If we are to account for altruism within a purely materialist framework, receptiveness to cultural training is not sufficient. In order for a behavioral predisposition to help solve the commitment problem, recall, it is essential that others be able to discern that we have it. It is easy to imagine that cultural training could instill a moral sentiment. But it is far from clear that it could, *by itself*, also account for a blush or some other observable symptom of the sentiment.

To the traditional story about the role of culture, we must thus add some mechanism whereby a person who has internalized a cultural message becomes observably different in a way that is at least partly insulated from purposeful control. In the case of physical symptoms like a blush, it is hard to see how this mechanism could be completely nonbiological. Critics of the biological approach may continue to insist that it is purely by accident that an honest person blushes when he tells a lie. Indeed, in Chapter 6 we will see that many symptoms of emotional arousal probably did originate for reasons quite independent of their role as signals of intention. But if altruistic behavior is to have a material payoff in the manner set forth by the commitment model, at least some sort of biological symptom of emotion, accidental or not, appears necessary.

Moral sentiments predispose us to behave in certain ways, much as a spinning gyroscope is predisposed to maintain its initial orientation. In thinking about the separate roles of nature and culture, I find it a helpful metaphor to imagine that nature's role is to have endowed us with a capacity that is much like a gyroscope at rest; and that culture's role is to spin it and establish its orientation. Each of these roles is indispensable.

THE IMPORTANCE OF SYMPATHY

If the prospect of unpleasant guilt feelings were the sole deterrent of cheating, we would have to wonder how the capacity to feel guilt could ever be recognized in a person. The logical difficulty is that if having this capacity is what prevents people from cheating in the first place, people who have it will never have an opportunity to display its symptoms. In order to sustain the commitment model's account of how honest persons survive, some emotional precursor to guilt therefore appears necessary.

Sympathy is a natural candidate. In order for an act that harms another person to summon guilt, it is necessary that we feel at least some sympthy for the victim. The French villager who lied when a Nazi storm trooper asked if there were Jews hidden in his basement, for example, felt no guilt because he felt no sympathy for persons harmed by his lie.

If the presence of sympathy is a good predictor of the capacity to feel guilt, it may then be possible to identify trustworthy persons using symptoms not of guilt but of sympathy. Indeed, many people report just such a basis for their predictions in the thought experiment discussed in Chapter 1 (where the task, recall, was to think of someone who would return a lost envelope with $1000 in it).

THE ROLE OF STRENGTH IN NUMBERS

An important force behind the emergence of unopportunistic behavior in the commitment model is strength in numbers—"economies of scale" in the economist's parlance. If two could not produce more efficiently than one, there would be no reason to expose ourselves to the possibility of being cheated by interacting with another person. Nor would there be any reason to spend effort haggling over how to divide the fruits of collective efforts. It would be much easier simply to work alone.

The marriage problem is perhaps the most conspicuous example of the gains from specialization. One person acting in isolation will never get far trying to raise a family.

Of the specific commitment problems discussed, the deterrence problem depends least on the existence of scale economies. But even it is affected by them. Deterrence would never be required if it were practical to isolate ourselves completely from interaction with other persons. Economies of scale, however, are a powerful reason to avoid isolation. To take advantage of them, we must engage in social interaction. The more closely we interact, the more opportunities for predation arise and the greater becomes our need for an effective deterrence strategy.

This is not to say that vengeance-seekers will always benefit in the presence of economies of scale. It would be an obvious mistake, for example, to claim that the Hatfields and the McCoys did better because of a moral sentiment that compelled them to seek revenge. But that is not my claim. Rather, it is that persons endowed with such a sentiment may do better, *on the average,* than persons who lack it. The potential usefulness of the sentiment lies in its capacity to deter aggression. When it works, persons with the sentiment obviously do better. When it fails, as with the Hatfields and McCoys, they do worse. As things turned out, either family would have done much better to leave the area once the first shot was fired. But that does not imply that in general a person would do better to be born without the tendency to seek revenge.

Sociologist Jack Weller notes that crime rates in Appalachian communities are very low, which he attributes to the "unwillingness of mountaineers to do anything that neighbors might construe as interference with them or that otherwise might stir ill will."[2] With the vivid history of the Hatfields and McCoys in mind, it is easy to imagine the source of this unwillingness. The important point, for our purposes, is that it is advantageous not to be victimized by our neighbors. Provided the violent tempers that deter such aggression are not tested too frequently, they can be very useful indeed.

The issues are similar in the case of perilous rescue attempts. It would be absurd to maintain that Kuranski, Schulze, and Benford did better because of their impulse to assist the woman in the Manhattan parking garage. But, again, that is not my claim. The payoff, if there is one, lies in such people being observably different—and more attractive—to others, which puts them in a better position to reap the material benefits of social cooperation. Thus, as in the deterrence example, it is a gamble to be a strongly empathic person. If the conditions that trigger a rescue attempt happen to arise, you probably lose. Otherwise, you win. We *like* empathic people and are more likely to favor them with our trust. If rescue attempts motivated by strong feelings of empathy are sufficiently infrequent, such feelings can obviously be useful.

Moral sentiments could not emerge under the commitment model, however, if there were not substantial economies of scale in social interaction.

A NOTE ON RATIONAL BEHAVIOR

The notion that moral sentiments might solve the commitment problem helps clarify some of the ambiguity about what it means to behave in a rational way. The philosophical literature distinguishes at least two main accounts of rational behavior.[3] In the so-called "present aim theory," rationality is taken to be the efficient pursuit of whatever aims one has at the moment of deliberation and action. A person who, for example, refrains from cheating because of guilt feelings would thus be considered rational by this standard, even if there were no possibility that cheating could have been detected.

By the same token, however, a person who drank cyanide because he felt a compelling desire to do so would also be considered rational under the present aim standard. The obvious difficulty of this standard is that it permits virtually any behavior to be considered rational merely by asserting that a person prefers it.

The second account of rationality, the "self-interest theory," tries to get around this problem. It says an act is rational if it efficiently promotes the interests of the person who performs it. A person—even one who is motivated by moral sentiments—who does not cheat when he could get away with cheating is thus judged, by the self-interest standard, to have acted irrationally.

Ironically, however, the self-interest version allows us to say that a self-interested person might very well *want* to be motivated by precisely such moral sentiments (provided, again, that their presence is recognizable by others). He may even take purposeful steps to enhance the likelihood that he will develop these sentiments. (He may join a church, for example, or look for opportunities to practice being honest.) Once he acquires the sentiments, of course, the behavior they provoke will still be officially categorized as irrational by the self-interest standard. But the commitment model may at least help us understand why such behavior, rational or not, might be widespread.

The commitment model is like the conventional evolutionary account in that it predicts the inevitability of opportunistic behavior. In at least one critical respect, however, it differs: opportunistic behavior here is not the *only* viable strategy. There is also room, possibly even a wide berth, for behavior that is unopportunistic in the truest sense.

I must stress again that the commitment model does not view cooperators as automatons, genetically programmed to eschew self-interest. On the contrary, it allows—indeed, in some cases almost certainly requires—a central role for cultural conditioning in the acquisition of moral sentiments. People may even make rational choices about the sorts of conditioning they expose themselves to. Thus, according to the model, a tendency to cooperate may or may not be a trait that some people inherit. The model can function even if its biological component is confined to an inherited complex of symptoms that manifests itself in people who have assimilated a cooperative predisposition. Surely not even the fiercest critic of biological theories will find this requirement unacceptable.

The honest individual in the commitment model is someone who values trustworthiness for its own sake. That he might receive a material payoff for such behavior is completely beyond his concern. And it is precisely because he has this attitude that he can be trusted in situations where his behavior cannot be monitored.

Trustworthiness, provided it is recognizable, creates valuable opportunities that would not otherwise be available.* The fact that trustworthy persons *do* receive a material payoff is of course what sustains the trait within the individual selectionist framework. But even if the world were to end at midnight, thus eliminating all possibility of penalty for defection, the genuinely trustworthy person would not be motivated to cheat.

Tit-for-tat, reciprocal altruism, kin selection, and other conventional evolutionary accounts of unopportunistic behavior paint a very different picture of human nature. Indeed, for all their obvious value, these accounts do not explain genuinely unopportunistic behavior at all.

Of course, a brief example involving people with "Cs" and "Ds" on their foreheads is hardly much better. If the claim that we can benefit from a predisposition to cooperate is to be made plausible, much more must be said about how, exactly, this

---

*George Akerlof (1983) makes a similar point.

predisposition arises and can be identified by others. This issue is of crucial importance* and will occupy our attention for the next three chapters.

*David Gauthier (1985) also notes that predispositions to behave in non-self-interested ways can be advantageous, but he does not focus on how they are achieved or how others discern them.

FOUR

REPUTATION

H. L. Mencken once called conscience the inner voice that tells you somebody may be looking. The distinguished sociobiologist Robert Trivers seems to have had much the same notion in mind when he wrote, ". . . it is possible that the common psychological assumption that one feels guilt even when one behaves badly in private is based on the fact that many transgressions are *likely* to become public knowledge."[1]

The examples we saw in Chapter 3 were ones in which a selfish person would have no use for a conscience as warning device. In those examples, recall, cheating was impossible to detect. Perhaps there occasionally are such cases in real life. But whether a person could ever feel *certain* he would not be caught is a different matter. Our history is filled with examples of "perfect" crimes gone awry. Even the person who finds a wallet full of cash in a deserted park may wonder whether it was deliberately placed there as part of a "Candid Camera" episode.

Someone who is caught cheating on one occasion creates the presumption he may do so again, which can obviously limit his future opportunities. From observations like these springs the maxim, "Honesty is the best policy." On this commonly held view, even a merely prudent person—one with no "real" concern about doing the right thing—does best simply to pass up all opportunities for cheating, no matter how seemingly attractive. By so doing, he will develop a reputation for being honest, which will serve him in the same way a heavy-blush complexion served honest persons in the last chapter—namely, as a credible signal of trustworthiness.

Trivers suggests that the emotion of guilt might have been favored by natural selection for its capacity to protect people against getting caught cheating, thereby helping them to establish favorable reputations. Guilt may indeed have been favored for this purpose, but not for the reasons that are commonly given.

THE "BAD-OUTCOME-IMPLIES-BAD-DECISION" FALLACY

The reputation argument sounds good but, on a closer look, seems to have a critical logical flaw. Stated in brief, the argument says that, by never cheating, a person will acquire a good reputation, the benefits of which will outweigh whatever gains he could expect from cheating. It is thus equivalent to saying that just because there is always *some* possibility of being caught, it is *never* rational to cheat. Taken literally, this is surely false. It is a clear example of the "bad-outcome-implies-bad-decision" fallacy.

To illustrate the fallacy, suppose someone offers you the following gamble: You are to draw a single ball from an urn containing 999 white balls and 1 red ball. If you draw a white ball, as you most probably will, you win $1000. If you draw the lone red ball, however, you lose $1. Suppose you accept the gamble and then draw the red ball. You lose $1. Do you now say you made a bad decision? If you do, you commit the fallacy. The decision, when you made it, was obviously a good one. Almost every rational person would have decided in the same way. The fact that you lost is too bad, but tells you nothing about the quality of your decision.

My colleague Richard Thaler illustrates the same fallacy with this episode from the 1980 American League Championship Series: There are two outs in the eighth inning of game two and the Yankees are down 3 to 2. Willie Randolph is on first when Yankee first baseman Bob Watson drills a double into the left-field corner. The Royals' left fielder chases it down, then throws over the shortstop, who is the cutoff man. Seeing the high throw, third-base coach Mike Ferraro waves Randolph home. But George Brett, the Royals' third baseman, is backing up the throw and makes a perfect relay to the plate. Randolph is called out on an extremely close play. Yankee owner George Steinbrenner becomes enraged; eventually, he fires Ferraro. In doing so, Steinbrenner commits the bad-outcome-implies-bad-decision fallacy (and, as Yankee watchers know, not for the first or last time). Ferraro's call, when he made it, was clearly the right one.*

Adam Smith seems to have had the hapless Ferraros of the world in mind more than two centuries ago when he wrote, "That the world judges by the event, and not by the design, has been in all ages the complaint, and is the great discouragement of virtue."[2] The bad-outcome-implies-bad-decision fallacy discourages not only virtuous conduct but also any other conduct, such as cheating, where a clear risk of a bad outcome exists.

Yet it is not irrational to cheat no matter how low the odds of getting caught, any more than it would be irrational for Ferraro to have sent the runner no matter how low the odds of his being thrown out. Even taking into account possible harm to one's reputation, cheating will still pay in cases where the probability of its detection, though not zero, is sufficiently low. Let us call these cases "golden opportunities." Finding a wallet full of cash in a deserted park is a golden opportunity. A person who returns the cash *merely* because he fears he might appear in a "Candid Camera" episode is being paranoid, not prudent. People often *do* confront opportunities in which the

---

*Ferraro is back with the Yankees now and still seems a little gun-shy. In a recent game he attempted to hold Willie Randolph at third after an extra-base hit, but Randolph ran past him and scored easily.

odds of being caught are low enough to make cheating rational, and most of them surely realize this.

The difficulty golden opportunities pose for the reputation argument may be seen clearly with the help of a simple example. Suppose there are two types of people in the world, honest and dishonest, and that each type makes up half the population. The former never cheat, the latter do so only when they confront a golden opportunity. These opportunities need not be foolproof. For argument's sake, suppose one dishonest person in fifty eventually gets caught.

Now suppose we need an honest person to carry out some task that will confront him with a golden opportunity. An applicant responds to our help-wanted notice. What do we learn by investigating his reputation? In this environment, 99 out of every 100 persons will have "good" reputations (50 of them genuinely honest, 49 of them cheaters who never got caught). Even if we discover that our applicant has a good reputation, we know that the odds are almost 50 percent (49/99) that he will cheat under sufficiently favorable circumstances. Since virtually the same odds (50/100) would apply to someone chosen at random, it clearly would not pay to incur significant expense to investigate the applicant's reputation. If dishonest persons behave rationally, most of them will escape detection. Thus, it appears, we have little chance of learning how people will behave in the one situation we care most about, namely, the golden opportunity.

Nor, if people act rationally, can we discover that someone is honest by observing what he does in situations where the detection of cheating is *not unlikely*. Unlike golden opportunities, these are situations where we frequently discover how a person has acted. For precisely this reason, however, it will not be rational to cheat in these cases. To observe that someone does not cheat would tell us only that he is prudent, not honest. By the very meaning of honesty, it appears that a reputation for not cheating cannot tell us very much. Not having a bad reputation is not the same thing as being known to be honest. The kinds of actions that are likely to be observed are just not very good tests of whether a person is honest.*

THE IMPLEMENTATION PROBLEM

These observations about reputation pose a puzzle. It is obvious that most people *think* reputations convey relevant information. If they really do not, however, then why do people care so much about them? Why, for example, do companies bother to interview references listed by job candidates? Or why does a homeowner investigate a firm's reputation before signing a contract to have her roof fixed? Must we suppose these behaviors are irrational? On the view that cheaters are efficient in their pursuit of self-interest, we seem forced to this conclusion.

It may still be possible, however, to breathe life into the reputation argument. The argument against it depends critically on the assumption that dishonest persons choose on the basis of rational calculation. In the preceding chapter, though, we saw ample grounds for questioning this assumption. Not even the most dedicated rationalist would insist that choices concerning food intake are governed strictly by rational forces. In addition to our powers of reason, we have our appetites to contend with, and we often eat even when we know it is not in our interests to do so.

For essentially parallel reasons, cheaters may not always pursue self-interest efficiently. For in cheating decisions, too, rational calculations play only an indirect role in motivation. A

---

*University of Chicago economist Lester Telser is also skeptical about the value of reputation, but for a different reason. The difficulty in his view is not that we rarely see events that test a person's character but that people have no character to test:

> . . . people seek information about the reliability of those with whom they deal. Reliability, however, is not an inherent personality trait. A person is reliable if and only if it is more advantageous to him than being unreliable. Therefore, the information about someone's return to being reliable is pertinent in judging the likelihood of his being reliable. For example, an itinerant is less likely to be reliable if it is more costly to impose penalties on him. . . . someone is honest only if honesty, or the appearance of honesty, pays more than dishonesty (1980, pp. 28, 29).

self-interested person sees the payoff from an opportunity to cheat, and the associated good feelings create an impulse to do so. Competing with this impulse, however, is an opposing one that arises from rational assessment of the odds of getting caught. If the odds are high enough, or sufficiently uncertain, the rational calculation will say cheating is not worth it. But this calculation does no more than summon a second set of feelings that compete with the impulse to cheat. It is by no means certain that these competing impulses will yield a prudent choice.

Once we grant the possibility that decisions to cheat may often be made on nonrational grounds, a logical basis arises for a significant link between a person's reputation and his true character. Suppose, for example, that dishonest persons cheat not only when confronted with golden opportunities, but frequently even in cases where there is a good chance of being caught. If, say, half of them are eventually caught, then we learn much more about a person when we learn he has a good reputation. He is now significantly more likely than a randomly chosen person to be honest. (In terms of the numerical example discussed above, the odds are now 67 percent, not 50 percent.)

At this stage, the link between reputation and character has become a theoretical possibility, nothing more. The mere possibility that a dishonest person may choose irrationally does not establish that he is likely to do so in a significant proportion of instances. More important, it does not establish that his errors are in the direction of cheating too *frequently*. In order for reputation to be a relevant clue to character, it is necessary that dishonest persons tend to cheat in situations where the odds militate against cheating. Otherwise, they wouldn't be caught often enough to earn bad reputations.

SPECIOUSLY ATTRACTIVE REWARDS

Experimental psychology provides compelling evidence for the existence of just such a tendency, one that derives from a tendency for immediate rewards to appear misleadingly attractive. The relevant evidence comes from experiments involving both humans and animals. These experiments show that not only does the size of a material reward or punishment matter, but so too does its timing.

Consider, for example, the pair of choices depicted in Figure 4.1. In situation *A,* subjects are asked to choose today between the following two rewards: (1) $100 to be received 28 days from now; or (2) $120 to be received 31 days from now. Here, most people respond in what seems like a rational manner by picking the second reward. (This response seems rational because there are no reasonably safe investments that yield 20 percent interest in three days. The second reward, in other words, is simply worth more than the first.)

In situation *B,* subjects are asked to choose between a different pair of rewards: (1′) $100 today; or (2′) $120 three days from now. The dollar amounts are the same as before, and the rewards are again three days apart. This time, however, most subjects choose the first reward. The inconsistency is that, for any interest rate for which reward (2) is more valuable than reward (1), reward (2′) must also be more valuable that reward (1′). And yet people choose differently in the two situations. In psychiatrist George Ainslie's terminology, the earlier payoff is said to be "specious" with respect to the later one.[3]

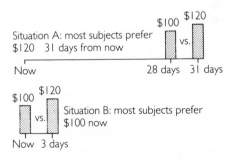

FIGURE 4.1 The Primacy of Immediate Reward

The behavioral psychologist's explanation for the inconsistency goes roughly as follows: With respect to the first pair of alternatives, the psychological reward mechanism regards each payoff as temporally remote. Something 28 days away seems virtually as far off as something 31 days away. One can't get immediate gratification anyway, so why not settle for the more valuable reward? In the second pair of alternatives, however, the immediacy of the first reward is, for many subjects, just too vivid to ignore. It floods their consciousness and overwhelms their judgment.

Psychologists discuss time-inconsistent choices in terms of Richard Herrnstein's "matching law." One of the matching law's properties is that the attractiveness of a reward is inversely proportional to its delay.[4] In this context, the term "delay" means the amount of time that will elapse before the reward is received. The matching law implies heavy discounting of distant future rewards, and accords near primacy to those that occur immediately. (The name of the law derives from its other main prediction, which is that individuals will divide their efforts between competing activities in such a way that their rewards per unit of effort are equally attractive—that is, so the rewards "match" one another.)

In Figure 4.2, the attractiveness-versus-delay feature of the matching law is illustrated for a reward that will be received on January 31. The attractiveness of the reward doubles each time the delay is cut by half. Thus, for example, its attractiveness on January 24, when there is a 7-day delay, is twice that on January 17, when there is a 14-day delay. As January 31 approaches, the attractiveness of the reward grows without limit. Some authors recognize the awkwardness of speaking about a boundlessly attractive reward, and note that none of the main conclusions of this literature would be altered if attractiveness approached some large, finite limit as delay approached zero.

Our concern here will be with all-or-nothing choices—such as, in Figure 4.1, the decision between the $100 and $120

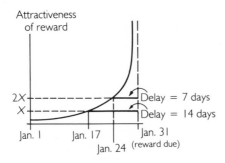

**FIGURE 4.2 The Attractiveness of a Reward Due
on January 31**

rewards; or, from our earlier discussion, the decision to cheat
or not. In such cases, the matching law predicts in favor of the
alternative with the most attractive reward *at the moment the
choice is made.*

When choosing between two rewards that would both be
received at the same time, the outcome does not depend on
when the decision is made. The larger of the two rewards will
be more attractive no matter how long the delay at the moment
of choice. The same cannot be said, however, when the larger
of two rewards is due at a later time. For a hypothetical person, Figure 4.3 plots the attractiveness of the two rewards from
the example in Figure 4.1. One curve denotes the attractiveness
of a $120 reward due on January 31, the other the attractive-
ness of a $100 reward due on January 28.

In this example, the two attractiveness curves happen to cross
on January 26. On that date, our hypothetical person would be
indifferent between the two rewards. Before January 26, he
would choose the larger reward. But between the 26th and the
28th, he would pick the smaller one. Again using Ainslie's terminology, the $100 reward is *specious* with respect to the $120
reward during the interval from January 26 to January 28.

Note that the inconsistency implied by the matching law is

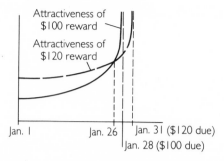

FIGURE 4.3   The Matching Law and Specious Reward

not the result simply of the fact that we discount future rewards. There is, after all, nothing irrational about *that*. In an uncertain world, a bird in the hand often really *is* worth two in the bush. Inconsistencies arise because of the specific *pattern* of discounting implied by the matching law. In rational discounting, the attractiveness of a reward gradually converges to a fixed value as its due date approaches. Under the matching law, by contrast, its attractiveness grows much more sharply, even if not without limit. Under rational discounting, preference reversals of the sort we see under the matching law simply cannot arise.

The time-discounting feature of the matching law, or some close variant of it, is one of the most robust regularities in experimental psychology. When a pigeon is given a chance to peck one of two buttons to choose between a morsel of food 30 seconds from now and a much larger morsel 40 seconds from now, it takes the latter. But when it chooses between the same morsel now and the larger morsel 10 seconds hence, it often picks the former. Rats behave the same way. So do cats, dogs, guinea pigs, and hogs. And so, much of the time, do humans. This feature is apparently part of the hard-wiring of most animal nervous systems.

•   •   •

THE EMOTIONS AS SELF-CONTROL DEVICES

This is not to say that material reward and delay feed mechanically into the matching law to produce a deterministic theory of human behavior.* On the contrary, people obviously have considerable control over the way they perceive the rewards from competing activities. So far as I know, no court of law has ever accepted a defense like, "I couldn't help stealing the money—there it was, and I was under the influence of the matching law." (Many societies, however, have laws against entrapment, and the matching law may be one reason why.)

The matching law does not say there is anything inevitable about choosing a specious reward. To see why, let us consider a variant of the cheating problem discussed in Chapter 3. This time, suppose cheating is difficult, but not impossible, to detect. If Smith gets away with it, he receives an immediate payoff. If he gets caught, however, he not only receives no current payoff, but he also acquires a bad reputation. His rational assessment tells him it is not a golden opportunity. He knows that people who refrain from cheating in these circumstances will develop good reputations and do better in the long run. But the prospect of the immediate payoff is tempting to him nonetheless.

If Smith is emotionally predisposed to regard cheating as an unpleasurable act in and of itself—that is, if he has a conscience—he will be better able to resist the temptation to cheat.

*It is clear, in any event, that a purely mechanical interpretation of the matching law leads to predictions that are contradicted by everyday experience. The matching law seems to predict, for example, that people would choose to experience pleasant events as soon as possible and to defer unpleasant ones as long as possible. George Loewenstein (1987) has shown, however, that most people prefer, on the one hand, to postpone intense, fleeting positive experiences (like "a kiss from your favorite movie star") and, on the other, to get unpleasant ones (like "a brief but painful electric shock") over with as quickly as possible. Loewenstein suggests that people want time to savor the prospect of the kiss and to minimize the time they spend dreading the electric shock. Once we recognize, however, that the *anticipation* of pleasure and pain often takes on much the same character as the actual experience, and thus becomes a reinforcement in and of itself, the observed behaviors are no longer clearly in conflict with the matching law.

If the psychological reward mechanism is constrained to emphasize rewards in the present moment, the simplest counter to a specious reward from cheating is to have a current feeling that tugs in precisely the opposite direction. Guilt is just such a feeling. *And because it too coincides with the moment of choice, the matching law does not discount it relative to the competing material reward.* If it is felt strongly enough, it can negate the spurious attraction of the imminent material reward.

Note that this observation does not contradict the matching law. Rather, it says that nonmaterial rewards and penalties may also matter. The matching law merely describes how the attractiveness of a reward—material or nonmaterial—tends to vary with its delay. Thus, although attractiveness tends to grow sharply as delay approaches zero, an imminent material reward is not always irresistible. It can be effectively countered by competing rewards, even nonmaterial ones, provided they too are imminent.

Even so, the matching law makes it apparent why a merely prudent person might often find it difficult to refrain from cheating when rational analysis says cheating doesn't pay. The problem is that the material gains from cheating come right away, the penalties only much later, if at all. If our psychological reward mechanism really does assign disproportionate weight to near-term rewards, a person who cares only about material rewards will cheat even when it is not prudent to do so.*

It is often prudent to refrain from cheating, as the tit-for-tat and reciprocal altruism theories have ably demonstrated. On such occasions, there will be advantage in being able to suppress the impulse to cheat. We can thus imagine a population in which people with consciences fare better than those without. The people who lack them would cheat less often if they could, but they simply have greater difficulty solving the self-

---

*Jon Elster has pointed out to me that the discounting pattern described by the matching law is not the only way specious intertemporal choices might arise. The principal claims of this chapter will also hold if people employ excessively high exponential rates of discounting.

control problem. People who have them, by contrast, are able to acquire good reputations and cooperate successfully with others of like disposition.

Similar reasoning will apply in the case of vengeance-seeking. Often it will be prudent to exact revenge even at considerable personal cost. This will especially be true when the action helps create a reputation that will deter acts of aggression. Perfectly rational persons with perfect self-control would always seek revenge whenever the future reputational gains outweigh the current costs of taking action.

The problem, as in the cheating example, is that the gains from a tough reputation come only in the future while the costs of vengeance-seeking come now. The matching law thus again suggests an impulse-control problem. A person may realize that it pays to be tough, yet still be tempted to avoid the current costs of a tough response. Being predisposed to feel anger when wronged helps solve this impulse-control problem. As with feelings of guilt, anger helps shift the relevant future payoffs into the current moment. In cases where reputational considerations weigh in favor of action, the angry person will be more likely to behave prudently than the merely prudent person who feels no anger.

It will likewise often be prudent to refuse a favorable transaction when the terms are starkly one-sided. By so doing, one can develop a reputation for being a tough bargainer, which will mean better terms in future transactions. In this case, too, we have future gains pitted against current costs and the resulting impulse-control problem. Here, someone who feels envious or resentful when he gets less than his fair share taps into the reward mechanism in the current moment, and on that account will be more likely to behave prudently. It is easier for a person to refuse an advantageous, but unfair, proposal if accepting it would make him feel bad.

Finally, love may also assist a person to follow a self-interested course. Future events that make it against one's interests to remain in a marriage are not the only contingencies people worry about. They also fear blundering out of a marriage that it pays to maintain. The matching law again helps explain why. A person may be tempted by the prospect of an extramarital affair, yet realize it would be better to keep his marriage intact. That the immediate rewards of the affair are specious makes them no less powerful. The gains from preserving the marriage, though more genuine, lie mostly in the future. It is an impulse-control problem, pure and simple.

As in the other examples, competing sentiments can assist in solving it. Strong feelings of affection for one's spouse tilt the psychological rewards of fidelity toward the present. People who experience such feelings are much better equipped to deal with temptation, even if not completely immune from it. And for this reason, they are more likely to achieve their long-range objectives.

The matching law tells us that the attractiveness of a reward increases sharply as its delay approaches zero. From this it follows that people who are concerned *only* about material rewards will often cheat (fail to retaliate, etc.) even when it is not rational to do so. The gains from cheating, again, come now while the costs come later, if at all. *Thus, when we see that a person has never been caught cheating, we have reason to believe that his behaviour is motivated, at least in part, by nonmaterial rewards.* And herein lies the kernel of truth in our belief that reputations matter.

On this view, the strength of the link between reputation and character will depend on the degree to which people find it difficult to resist immediate rewards. If impulse-control is only a minor problem, the inference will be weak. But if it is a serious one, then almost every merely prudent person (which is to say, people who care only about material rewards) will be caught cheating sooner or later.

DISCOUNTING AND RATIONAL CHOICE

Is it common for people's impulses to make them choose irrationally? Since at least the seventeenth century, philosophers have clearly believed so. Most people, according to Thomas Hobbes, are unlikely to observe the dictates of reason, because "of their perverse desire of present profit." John Locke emphasized the virtue of man's cultivating an ability "to deny himself his own Desires, cross his own Inclinations, and purely follow what Reason directs as best, tho' the Appetite lean the other way." Spinoza felt likewise: "In their desires and judgments of what is beneficial, they are carried away by their passions, which take no account of the future or anything else . . . no society can exist without the government and force, and hence without laws to control the unruly appetites and impulses of men." David Hume noted a "violent propension" in favor of immediate gratification, which he called the "source of all dissoluteness and disorder, repentence and misery."

Nineteenth-century economists were also aware of the impulse-control problem. As Stanley Jevons, for example, described it:

> To secure a maximum of benefit in life, all future events, all future pleasures or pains, should act upon us with the same force as if they were present, allowance being made for their uncertainty . . . But no human mind is constituted in this perfect way: a future feeling is always less influential than a present one.[5]

Böhm-Bawerk wrote of a "defect of the will," John Stuart Mill of "improvidence," and A. C. Pigou, in this century, of man's "faulty telescopic faculty." More recently, Robert Strotz[6] noted that people often alter their rankings of alternatives as time passes, even when the information they possess remains unchanged.

That idea that impulse-control problems are real and important is certainly difficult to reject from everyday experience. As every parent knows, they are the bane of the young child's existence. We invest much energy trying to teach our children to delay gratification, and only after several years do these efforts begin to bear fruit.

The advantage of passing up the small, early reward in favor of the larger, later one is a lesson not easily learned. Indeed, most adults continue to confront impulse-control problems of their own. The dieter spots the German chocolate cake on the dessert trolley and is sorely tempted. His rational assessment urges restraint. The weight he will gain, it tells him, is too big a price to pay for the fleeting moment of gastronomic pleasure. Yet, despite this calculation, he often gives in. And when he does, he almost invariably expresses regret.

Skeptics sometimes wonder whether these expressions are to be taken at face value.[7] Perhaps the dieter has forgotten how much he enjoyed the cake and is complaining now only because he is in the midst of the extra abstinence it required. Perhaps, in other words, the matching law applies in retrospect as well as in prospect: looking back soon after the event, the extra dieting may appear spuriously unattractive relative to the pleasures of the cake. One test of this possibility is to see how he feels, say, a year from now. By this standard, we are inclined to take the dieter's regrets as genuine. With both the pleasure of eating the cake and the pain of the extra dieting well behind him (and thus *both* heavily discounted), he will truthfully testify that eating the cake wasn't worth it.

Within the last decade, there has emerged a substantial scholarly literature on the topic of self-control.[8] The classical self-control problem is itself a commitment problem of the sort we have already seen. Virtually every author mentions the example of Homer's Odysseus, who was faced with having to sail past dangerous reefs where the sirens lay. Odysseus realized that once he was within earshot of the sirens' cries, he would be drawn irresistibly toward them and sail to his doom on the reefs. Able to foresee this temporary change in his preferences, he came up with an effective commitment device: he instructed his crewmen to strap him tightly to the mast and not to release him, even though he might beg them to, until they had sailed safely past.

Similar sorts of commitment devices are familiar in modern

life. Fearing they will be tempted to spend their savings, people join "Christmas clubs," special accounts that prohibit withdrawals until late autumn; and they buy whole-life insurance policies, which impose substantial penalties on withdrawals before retirement. Fearing they will spoil their dinners, they put the cashew jar out of easy reach. Fearing they will gamble too much, they limit the amount of cash they take to Atlantic City. Fearing they will stay up too late watching television, they move the television set out of the bedroom. These and countless similar behaviors may be viewed as attempts to avoid specious rewards identified by the matching law.

Even traditional problems of addiction are now viewed by some authors as direct consequences of the matching law.[9] These writers, and others, have argued that the tendency to give too much value to immediate rewards lies behind most problems with alcohol, tobacco, and other addictive drugs. By this view, for example, the alcoholic's difficulty is that the pleasure from drinking comes now, the pain only later. If the pain of a hangover came *before* the pleasure of intoxication, few people would ever drink too much. (Hence the efficacy of the drug disulfiram—Antabuse—which causes sudden feelings of nausea upon the ingestion of alcohol.)

One paper[10] surveyed the results of 60 published studies in support of the claim that shifting the timing of the alcoholic's payoffs can have a substantial effect on behavior. Drinkers for whom the prospect of ruined careers and shattered family relationships have had little deterrent effect often respond dramatically even to very small changes in current penalties and rewards, such as

- having to do a small amount of work before each drink,
- being placed in an isolation booth for a brief period after each drink, and
- being given small monetary payments for abstention.

Another study found, similarly, that increases in alcohol taxes lead consistently to significant reductions both in alcohol-related traffic fatalities and in deaths from cirrhosis of the liver.[11] The cirrhosis finding is especially provocative, for it suggests that increasing the immediate cost of drinking reduces alcohol consumption even among long-term, heavy abusers.

The addict's problem, apparently, differs in degree, not in kind, from one we all face—namely, how to accord distant penalties and rewards a more prominent role in our behavior. We are all addicts of a sort, battling food, cigarettes, alcohol, television sportscasts, detective novels, and a host of other seductive activities. That our psychological reward mechanism tempts us with pleasures of the moment is simply part of what it means to be a person. In the face of the behavioral evidence, it seems hardly far-fetched to suppose that rational assessments, by themselves, might often fail to assure behaviors whose rewards come mostly in the future.

It thus appears reasonable to conclude that a reputation for not cheating does, after all, convey substantial information about a person's character. Given the nature of our psychological reward mechanism, a person who is purely self-interested will sometimes give in to his temptation to cheat, even when he *knows* cheating does not pay. Because he does so, sooner or later he is likely to be caught. Knowing this, we can infer that a person who has *not* been caught is probably something more than a merely prudent person.

TIT-FOR-TAT REVISITED

In Chapter 2, we saw that the tit-for-tat strategy should always provide a better guide for behavior in repeated prisoner's dilemmas than the mediating emotions mentioned by Trivers. The computational demands of tit-for-tat are minimal and, unlike behavior driven by emotion, it does not run the risk of excessive or insufficient cooperation, retaliation, and so on.

We are now in a position, however, to see a fundamental difficulty with tit-for-tat. The problem is one of motivation, not computational complexity. A person might be able to calculate perfectly well that tit-for-tat was the right strategy, and yet be unable to summon the discipline to implement it. The retaliator, for example, must bear an immediate cost in the hope of a future material gain, and an angry person is better able to do that than a purely rational calculator. Although moral sentiments may sometimes lead to the wrong behaviors in purely material terms, they help solve the omnipresent impulse-control problem. This may well be a decisive advantage.

WHY EXCESSIVE DISCOUNTING?

The pervasiveness of impulse-control problems raises the question of how natural selection could have produced a psychological reward mechanism that gives so much weight to immediate material payoffs. Why wouldn't mutants whose reward mechanisms were more forward-looking have done better?

It is important to stress that the experimental literature does not say that immediate payoffs get *too much* weight in every situation. It says only that they always get *very heavy* weight. On balance, that was likely a good thing in the environments in which we evolved. When selection pressures are intense, current payoffs are often the *only* ones that matter. The present, after all, is the gateway to the future. Organisms that don't survive the current moment simply *have* no future. In highly competitive and uncertain environments, there must always have been a genuine advantage in concentrating most of one's attention on getting past the most immediate threats to survival.

If the choice were between a reward mechanism that gave heavy weight to current payoffs and one that gave uniformly greater weight to the future, it is thus easy to imagine why natural selection might have favored the former. Insufficient attention to even a few important situations in the present might spell disaster.

But why can't the reward mechanism discriminate more finely? That is, why can't it give more weight to future payoffs only in those cases where there would be particularly important advantages from doing so? In response to such questions, evolutionary biologists are quick to point out that natural selection is not free to cobble together just *any* desired combination of attributes. There are myriad constraints on the process, and the solutions we see in nature, while sometimes elegant, are more often much clumsier than those a purposeful engineer would have come up with. There may be sharp limits on the extent to which nature can fine-tune the reward mechanism. And, as noted, a mutant with a *uniformly* more future-oriented psychological reward mechanism might be unable to summon sufficient concern to deal forcefully with immediate threats.

Ainslie and Herrnstein suggest that heavy discounting might also have been favored because of cognitive limitations:

> The biological value of a low discount rate is limited by its requiring the organism to detect which one of all the events occurring over a preceding period of hours or days led to a particular reinforcer. As the discounting rate falls, the informational load increases. Without substantial discounting, a reinforcer would act with nearly full force not only on the behaviors that immediately preceded it, but also on those that had been emitted in past hours or days. The task of factoring out which behaviors had actually led to reinforcement could exceed the information processing capacity of a species.[12]

In sum, despite all of the obvious difficulties our strong present-orientation creates, it may simply be one of the constraints we are stuck with. Moral sentiments may be viewed as a crude attempt to fine-tune the reward mechanism, to make it more sensitive to distant rewards and penalties in selected instances.

MORAL SENTIMENTS WITHOUT PHYSICAL SYMPTOMS

On the foregoing account, we see that it may be possible for moral sentiments to have evolved even if there were no observable physical symptoms of them. For this to have happened, it is necessary that people have difficulty implementing behaviors they believe to be in their own interest. Absent such difficulty, we saw that there is little reliable connection between a person's observable behavior—his reputation—and his true character. And without that connection, the capacity to feel guilt could not have benefited a person by making him significantly more likely to acquire a good reputation.

A person's reputation is meaningful on the assumption that, given impulse-control problems, people with genuine moral sentiments are better able than others to act in their own interest. But the effect of these sentiments is not limited to situations in which the behaviors to which they refer—honesty, vengeance-seeking, fidelity, whatever—would be self-serving. The person controls his impulse to cheat, recall, by having a competing impulse that would create current psychological costs if he did cheat. Even though this competing moral sentiment may have originated because of its effects in situations where it was not rational to cheat, it does not discriminate on that basis. That is, the sentiment will be present not only where cheating does not pay, but also where it does.

People with good reputations can thus solve even nonrepeated prisoner's dilemmas. For example, they can cooperate successfully with one another in ventures where cheating is impossible to detect. Genuine altruism can emerge, in other words, merely on the basis of having established a reputation for behaving in a prudent way. Given the nature of psychological reward mechanism, it is no mean feat to have established such a reputation. People who manage to do so give some indication that they must be motivated, at least in part, by considerations other than material self-interest.

TWO PATHWAYS TO MORAL SENTIMENTS

We have now seen two possible pathways along which moral sentiments might have emerged. The first, described in Chapter 3, I will call the "sincere-manner" pathway. By that account, moral sentiments are accompanied by observable physical signs that allow outsiders to discern their presence. ("Smith seems sincere. Let's hire him.") In contrast, the second account—the "reputation" pathway—does not require any physical signs. By virtue of the practical difficulties of behaving prudently, reputation can emerge as an alternative means of identifying moral sentiments.

In many ways, the two accounts are similar. Both lead to genuinely altruistic behavior in the sense defined in Chapter 2. People who do not cheat when there is almost no possibility of getting caught would be better off by cheating and they know it. They refrain not because they fear the consequences of being caught, but because they would feel bad if they cheated.

The accounts are also similar in that both predict a stable mix of honest persons and opportunists in the population. In the sincere-manner case, recall, the costs of scrutiny assured that no population could consist entirely of cooperators. For in such a population it wouldn't pay to scrutinize people for the physical signs of sincerity, and defectors would therefore begin to prosper. Similar forces assure the same outcome in the reputation case. In any population that consisted almost entirely of cooperators, it would not pay to gather information about people's reputations, and defectors would thus fare better than cooperators. Opportunistic persons are an inevitable feature of the landscape under either account.

THE INFLUENCE OF CULTURE

Both accounts also suggest a coherent role for culture, something the accounts surveyed in Chapter 2 had trouble doing. Those accounts, recall, had difficulty explaining why opportunistic parents would participate in efforts to teach their children to cooperate when defection was impossible, or even very hard, to detect.

With the sincere-manner account, we do not have this difficulty. If there are visible signs of moral sentiments, then it can pay to cultivate them. These sentiments, once again, are almost surely not inherited in any very specific form. Definitions of honesty, notions of fairness, even the conditions that trigger anger, all differ widely from culture to culture. If people inherit anything at all, it is a receptiveness to training about the attitudes that are likely to serve them in life. Virtually every culture invests heavily in the moral training of its young. If people who successfully internalize these teachings are observably different from those who don't, it is no puzzle that parents cooperate enthusiastically in the training process.

Nor is there any difficulty seeing why parents might want to instill moral sentiments under the reputation account. For here, too, a person stands to benefit by the acquisition of these sentiments. Because they enable him to behave prudently in the face of contrary impulses, they facilitate the acquisition of a favorable reputation.

On conventional accounts, it is easy to see the utility of various religious beliefs for society as a whole. But the connection between these beliefs and the *individual's* material interests is often less clear. Both the sincere-manner and reputation accounts help suggest possible linkages. The threat of hellfire and damnation makes a person more likely to feel bad if she does the wrong thing. If such feelings are accompanied by physical signs, she stands to benefit for the reasons suggested in Chapter 3. Alternatively, they may help her solve the impulse-control problem, in which case she stands to benefit from a good reputation.

TWO DIFFERENT COMMITMENT PROBLEMS

The two accounts are also alike in that each views moral sentiments as practical devices for solving commitment problems. In the sincere-manner account, the commitment problem was how to make oneself want to be *honest* when the material incentives favor cheating. In the reputation account, by contrast, the commitment problem was to make oneself want to be *prudent* in cases where the long-term material incentives favor honesty. These two commitment problems could hardly be more different. Solving the first seems noble, the second merely expedient. The irony is that they are solved by precisely the same moral sentiments.

OPPORTUNISM, RELATIVELY SPEAKING

Both accounts of the emergence of moral sentiments speak of an equilibrium in which those who have them coexist with those who do not. In this equilibrium, the material payoffs received by the two types are the same.

Viewed in the context of traditional sociobiological models, this equality of payoffs is a tremendous victory for unopportunistic persons. Not only are they not driven to extinction, they are even able to do just as well, *in purely material terms,* as those who lie, cheat, steal, and so on.

Viewed from the vantage point of someone who believes that crime doesn't pay, however, the same equality of payoffs must seem disturbing. On this score, we will see evidence in later chapters that suggests a much more optimistic interpretation. Evolutionary models tell us that payoffs must be in balance between two strategies that differ in *relative* terms. Thus the accounts suggest only that there will be a niche for persons who are opportunistic, *relatively speaking.* They do not pin down what these people will be like in any absolute sense. Indeed, we will see evidence that extremely opportunistic persons fare very poorly in material terms. This evidence suggests that even to survive one must internalize a substantial measure of traditional moral teachings. People who achieve material success are not always paragons of virtue, true enough. But those who lack even a modicum of moral sentiments are much more likely to land in jail than atop the corporate ladder.

Another pitfall in discussing simple evolutionary models is

that some will take their equality of material payoffs to mean that the two types of strategies are a matter of social indifference. This, of course, could hardly be further from the truth. Society as a whole has a very clear interest in tipping the balance as much as possible in favor of the sentimentalists, and in later chapters I will examine a number of concrete steps whereby this might be accomplished.

The sincere-manner and reputation pathways are not mutually exclusive. The reputation pathway by itself could have accounted for the emergence of moral sentiments. Or it could have worked in tandem with the sincere-manner mechanism described in Chapter 3. That mechanism, after all, required only that there be some statistically reliable signal of trustworthiness. Either a sincere manner or a good reputation could serve that purpose.

The evidence we will examine favors the view that reputation and manner work in tandem. But for reasons I will discuss in the next chapter, the mechanics of natural selection make it unlikely that moral sentiments evolved *exclusively* along the sincere-manner pathway.

FIVE

SIGNALING

When a toad and his rival vie for the same mate, each faces an important strategic decision. Should he fight for her or set off in search of another? To fight is to risk injury. But to continue searching has costs as well. At the very least, it will consume time. And there is no guarantee that the next potential mate will not herself be the object of some other toad's affections.

In deciding between these alternatives, each toad's assessment of the other's fighting capabilities plays an important role. If one's rival is considerably larger, the likelihood of prevailing will be low, so it will be prudent to continue searching. Otherwise, it may pay to fight.

Many of these decisions must be made at night, when it is hard to see. Toads have therefore found it expedient to rely on various nonvisual clues. The most reliable of these turns out to be the pitch of the rival's croak. In general, the larger a toad is, the longer and thicker are its vocal cords, and thus the deeper its croak. Hearing a deep croak in the night, a toad may reasonably infer that a big toad made it. Indeed, experiments have shown that the common toad *(Bufo bufo)* is much more likely to be intimidated by a deep croak than a high-pitched one.[1]

The opportunities for cheating here are obvious. A mutant with longer and thicker vocal cords than those usually associated with toads his size will have an advantage. Potential rivals will overestimate his fighting capabilities, and be more likely to defer to him; for this reason he will leave a larger number of offspring. As with any other genes that help gain access to important resources, the genes for longer, thicker vocal cords will thus tend to spread in the toad population.

The process of escalating vocal cord size may continue through several iterations. Eventually, however, physical limitations will stand in the way of further increases. Other forces constrain the overall size of toads, and a toad's body can accommodate vocal cords only so large. Sooner or later, an equilibrium is reached in which all toads have larger vocal cords than before, but in which further increases in vocal cord size simply do not pay.

By the original standard, every toad now sounds larger than he really is. Once that happens, of course, the element of deception vanishes. What counts in the fight-or-search decision, after all, is the comparison of sizes, not the absolute sizes themselves. Once all toads have exploited the initial gains from having larger vocal cords, the pitch of each toad's croak is again a reliable basis for size comparisons. Except for that fact, it would have long since ceased to play any role in fighting decisions.

COMMUNICATION BETWEEN ADVERSARIES

It is useful to distinguish communications that take place between parties with common goals from those between parties who are potentially in conflict. Toads searching for mates obviously fall into the latter category, bridge partners into the former. When a bridge player uses the standard bidding conventions to tell her partner something, there is no reason for her partner not to take the message at face value. Neither player has anything to gain by deceiving the other. Communication here is a pure problem of information transfer. A message need only be decipherable. Error aside, its credibility is not in question.

Matters are distinctly different when the interests of would-be communicators are in conflict, or even potentially so. Suppose, for example, the bridge player whispers to the opponent on her left, "I always bid conservatively." What is the opponent to make of such a remark? It is perfectly intelligible. Yet, if all parties are believed to be rational, the relationship between them is such that the statement can convey no real information. If being known as a conservative bidder would be an advantage, that would be reason enough for a player to call herself one, true or not. The statement is neither credible nor incredible. It simply contains no information.

The signals we will be concerned with here are ones that take place between parties whose interests are at least potentially in conflict. We will be concerned, for example, with the signals transmitted between two parties who confront prisoner's dilemmas or other commitment problems. If the parties are self-interested, statements like "I will not defect" are problematic in the sense discussed for the opposing bridge players. They should convey no information.

But if the players are *not* purely self-interested, how can they communicate *that* to one another? Simply saying it obviously won't suffice. Indeed, many have questioned whether it is possible, even in principle, for adversaries to convey information about their intentions.[2]

We do know, however, that adversaries can communicate information that has strategic value. Toads, after all, are able to broadcast information of this sort. But they do not do it merely by saying "I am a big toad." The big toad's implicit claim is credible only because of the physical barriers that prevent the small toad from uttering a deep croak.

Some authors view the problem of communicating information about size and other physical attributes as fundamentally different from the problem of communicating information about intentions.[3] And yet intentions are often so clearly a function of capabilities that the utility of this distinction is not always clear. A toad may reasonably guess that a rival with a deep croak "intends" to fight if challenged. Seen in this light, intention is merely a rational prediction of what an individual with given attributes will do. Being emotionally predisposed to respond in a certain way is an attribute, no less of one than having a deep croak. For all practical purposes, an adversary who has discerned such an attribute has discerned its rival's intentions.

The toad example illustrates three properties of signals between potential adversaries: (1) they must be costly to fake; (2) they usually originate for reasons having nothing to do with signaling; and (3) if some individuals employ signals that convey favorable information about themselves, others will be forced to reveal information even when it is considerably less favorable. Each of these principles is important for our task of exploring how signals of intention—that is, clues to emotional predisposition—might have arisen. This task will be our main concern in Chapter 6. Here, I will state each principle in terms of its application in the toad example, and then try to offer an intuitive understanding of how it works by discussing its application in various other contexts.

THE COSTLY-TO-FAKE PRINCIPLE

For a signal between adversaries to be credible, it must be costly (or, more generally, difficult) to fake. If small toads could costlessly imitate the deep croak that is characteristic of big toads, a deep croak would no longer *be* characteristic of big toads. But they cannot. Big toads have a natural advantage, and it is that fact alone that enables deepness of croak to emerge as a reliable signal.

The costly-to-fake principle has clear application to signals between people. In Elmore Leonard's novel, *Glitz,* Vincent Mora employs it to demonstrate an aspect of his character to an adversary. Mora is a Miami detective whose girlfriend, Iris, has been murdered in Atlantic City. He is about to approach Ricky, a mob underling who might know something about her death. Mora realizes that Ricky would himself face death at the hands of his bosses if he revealed anything about their activities to an outsider. His only hope of getting any information out of him, therefore, is to present Ricky with an *immediate* threat to his life. (Again, the matching law!)

The implicit difficulty, however, is that Mora realizes that Ricky knows it would not be rational for an outsider to take a mob member's life. Mora's task is thus to convince him that he either is not rational or else is so tough that the threat of mob retaliation doesn't bother him.

Ricky's Eldorado is parked in front of a bar while he is inside collecting an extortion payment from the owner. As Mora waits for him to come out, he picks up a ten-pound chunk of masonry from under the boardwalk and tucks it under his raincoat. When Ricky emerges, Mora is leaning on the Eldorado. Ricky approaches him suspiciously.

> "Get away from the car."
>
> "Somebody smashed your window," Vincent said.
>
> "Where?" He came in a hurry now. Vincent nodded toward the driver's side and Ricky moved past him, intent. Vincent followed, walked up next to him.
>
> "What're you talking about? The window's okay."
>
> Vincent looked at it, his expression curious. He brought the chunk of masonry out of his raincoat to slam it in the same motion against the tinted glass and the window shattered in fragments. He turned to Ricky and said, "No, its's broken, see?"
>
> Ricky said, "You crazy?" With amazement. "You fucking crazy?"
>
> Vincent liked the question and liked the way Ricky stood there in a state of some kind of shock, those dead eyes showing signs of life for the first time, wondering. What is this? His expression, his pocked face made him appear vulnerable, sad, the poor guy wanting to know what was going on here, perplexed.

Mora puts Ricky behind the wheel of the Cadillac and has him drive to a desolate spot on the waterfront where, without even raising his voice, he has no difficulty discovering everything Ricky knows about Iris.

Mora's ploy with the chunk of masonry works because it is

not something just anyone could pull off. Most mild-tempered, dispassionate people simply couldn't have done it. The costly-to-fake principle gives Ricky good reason to suspect Mora really *is* extremely tough or crazy, or both. Note that for the signal to work it need not be *impossible* for a calm, rational person to have smashed the window, merely unlikely.

Examples from fiction obviously do not establish objective truths about human nature. They play the role of thought experiments, useful for testing our intuitions about how people behave. If the Leonard passage tells us something, it is because most readers have no difficulty imagining that, in Ricky's shoes, they too would have taken Mora's irrational threats seriously.

But the costly-to-fake principle is by no means limited to fictional accounts. It is also at work, for example, in Joe McGinnis's *Fatal Vision*. Captain Jeffrey MacDonald, an Army Green Beret physician, has been told he is suspected of having killed his wife and daughters. The Army has assigned him a military defense attorney. Meanwhile, however, MacDonald's mother recruits Bernard Segal, a renowned private attorney from Philadelphia, to defend her son. When Segal calls MacDonald in Fort Bragg, N.C., to introduce himself, his first question is about MacDonald's Army attorney:

"Are his shoes shined?"

"What?!" MacDonald sounded incredulous. Here he was, all but accused of having murdered his own wife and children, and in his very first conversation with the Philadelphia lawyer who presumably had been hired to set things right, the first question the lawyer asks is about the condition of the other lawyer's shoes.

Segal repeated the question. "And this time," he said later, "I could almost hear Jeff smiling over the phone. That was when I first knew I had a client who was not only intelligent but who caught on very quickly. He said, no, as a matter of fact, the lawyer's shoes were kind of scruffy. I said, 'Okay in that case, trust him. Cooperate with him until I can get down there myself.' The point being, you see, that if an Army lawyer keeps his shoes shined, it means he's trying to impress the system. And if he was trying to impress the system in that situation—the system being one which had already declared a vested interest, just by public announcement of suspicion, in seeing his client convicted—then he wasn't going to do Jeff any good. The unshined shoes meant maybe he cared more about being a lawyer."

The condition of the attorney's shoes was obviously not a perfect indication of his priorities in life. Yet they did provide at least *some* reason to suspect he was not just an Army lackey. Any attorney who wore scruffy shoes merely to convey the impression that he was not looking to get ahead in the Army actually *wouldn't* get ahead. So the only people who can *safely* send such a signal are those who really do care more about their roles as attorneys.

As a final illustration of the costly-to-fake principle, consider a degree with honors from an elite university. Employers are looking for people who are smart and willing to work hard. There are obviously a great many people in the world who have both of these traits, yet do not have an elite degree. Even so, employers are reasonably safe in assuming that a person who does have one is both smart and hard-working. For it is not obvious how anyone without that combination of traits could go about getting an elite degree with honors.

THE DERIVATION PRINCIPLE

A second important general principle illustrated by the toad example is that the trait that serves as a signal does not usually originate primarily for that purpose. This so-called "derivation principle," first described by the Nobel laureate ethologist Niko Tinbergen,[4] says that the original positive correlation between size of toad and depth of croak was purely incidental to the original functions of the toad's croak, whatever they might have been. It arose because toads with large bodies happened, for reasons entirely apart from signaling, to have larger vocal cords.

If that had not been the case, it is not clear how depth of croak could have evolved as a signal of size. Suppose size and depth of pitch had *not* been correlated to begin with. If a correlation is to emerge, mutations toward deeper croaks in large toads must be favored by natural selection. For that to happen, the first mutation toward slightly deeper pitch must benefit the particular large toad in which it occurs. Yet a lone large toad with a slightly deeper croak can hardly create a general impression that toads with deeper croaks are more formidable. The deepness of his croak is thus, by itself, no reason to expect him to leave more offspring than the large toads with normal croaks. A deep croak can function as a signal of size only when most large toads have one. But in order for the genes for the deeper croak to have spread, they would have to have benefited the first large toad in which they appeared. It is the first step in this process that is problematic.

An even clearer illustration of the derivation principle is the case of the dung beetle. This beetle gets its name from the fact that it escapes predators by looking like a fragment of dung. Almost certainly, however, that is not why it began looking the way it does. Evolutionary biologists emphasize that features forged by natural selection develop in tiny increments. At each stage, the new feature has to be more useful than the one it displaces. The nature of the process makes it clear that certain morphological features could not have arisen to serve the particular function we ultimately observe. The first increments in the dung beetle's evolution toward its current appearance, for example, could not very well have been selected for the ultimate role they were to play. For, as Stephen Jay Gould asks, ". . . can there be any edge in looking 5% like a turd?"[5]

More likely the beetle evolved to something near its current form for reasons completely unrelated to the current function of its appearance. Only when its appearance was *already* close enough to that of a dung fragment to fool its most nearsighted predators could natural selection favor changes *because* they made it an even better imitation.*

Note that the derivation principle is peculiar to the natural selection mechanism, which by its very nature cannot be forward looking. Natural selection cannot recognize that a series of steps would eventually lead to a fruitful result and then take the first of those steps unmindful of its current effects. If the first step doesn't accomplish something useful, the second step will never be reached.

The derivation principle does not apply to signals that result from the conscious actions of persons. These can be both purposeful and forward-looking. If an Army attorney wants to signal nonconformist attitudes about his work, he need not go through a tortuous process of letting his spitshine deteriorate bit by bit. He can simply refrain from shining his shoes in the first place; or, if they are already shined, he can scuff them up all at once. The derivation principle applies only to passive signals, especially ones that arise from natural selection. It does not apply to active, or purposeful, signals.

THE FULL-DISCLOSURE PRINCIPLE

A third important principle illustrated by the toad example I will call the "full-disclosure" principle. It says that if some individuals stand to benefit by revealing a favorable value of some trait, others will be forced to disclose their less favorable values. This principle helps answer the initially puzzling question of why the smaller toads bother to croak at all.[6] By croaking, they tell other toads how small they are. Why not just remain silent and let them wonder?

---

*Dawkins (1986) argues against Gould's point by observing that very small changes are sometimes enough to fool some predators under some circumstances. But, uncharacteristically, Dawkins seems to miss the essence of Gould's claim. Gould clearly has in mind a change so small as to make the beetle look no more like a dung fragment than like a host of other things that bear not even the slightest resemblance to one. If that change fooled even a single predator, then the beetle must have already looked *almost* like a dung fragment to that predator to begin with. But then how did it get to *that* point? Surely by a series of small morphological changes that had nothing whatever to do with its ultimate resemblance to the dung fragment.

Suppose all toads with croaks pitched higher than some threshold level did, in fact, remain silent. Imagine an index from 1 to 10 that measures the pitch of a toad's croak, with 10 being the highest, 1 the lowest; and suppose, arbitrarily, that toads with an index value above 6 kept quiet. It is easy to see why any such pattern would be inherently unstable. Consider a toad with an index of 6.1, just above the cutoff. If he remains silent, what will other toads think? From experience, they will know that, *because* he is silent, his croak must be pitched higher than 6. But how much higher?

Lacking information about this particular toad, they cannot say exactly. It generally will be possible, however, to make a statistical guess. Suppose toads were uniformly scattered along the pitch scale. With the croaking threshold at 6, experience would then tell that the average index for toads who remain silent is 8 (halfway between 6 and 10). Any toad with an index less than 8 would, by the fact of his silence, create the impression that he is smaller than he really is. Our toad with an index of 6.1 would therefore do far better to croak than not.

Thus, if the threshold for remaining silent were 6, it would pay all toads with an index less than 8 to croak. If they do, of course, the threshold will not remain at 6. It will shift to 8. But a threshold of 8 will not be stable either. With the cutoff at that level, it will pay all toads with an index less than 9 to croak. *Any* threshold less than 10 is for similar reasons destined to unravel. This happens not because the small toads *want* to call attention to their smallness by croaking. Rather, they are forced to do so in order to keep from appearing smaller than they really are.

The full-disclosure principle derives from the fact that potential adversaries do not all have access to the same information. In the toad case, the asymmetry is that the silent toad knew exactly how big he was, while his rival could only make an informed guess. Similar asymmetries give rise to a host of important signals between people.

They help explain, for example, why corporations might

guarantee even relatively low quality products. The asymmetry here is that producers know much more than consumers about how good their products are. The producer who knows she has the best product has a strong incentive to disclose that information to consumers. A credible means of doing so is to provide a liberal guarantee against product defects. (This device is credible because of the costly-to-fake principle—a low-quality product would break down frequently, making it too costly to offer a liberal guarantee.)

Once this product appears with its liberal guarantee, consumers immediately know more than before, not only about *its* quality, but about the quality of all remaining products as well. In particular, they know that the ones without guarantees cannot be of the highest quality. Lacking any other information about an unguaranteed product, a prudent consumer would estimate its quality as the average level for such products. But this means consumers will underestimate the quality of those products that are just slightly inferior to the best product.

Consider the situation confronting the producer of the product that is second best. If he continues to offer no guarantee, consumers will think his product is worse than it really is. Accordingly, he will do better to offer a guarantee of his own. But because of his product's slightly lower quality, the terms of his guarantee cannot be quite so liberal as those for the best product.

With the second-best product now guaranteed, the class of remaining unguaranteed products is of still lower average quality than before. The unraveling process is set in motion, and in the end all producers must either offer guarantees or live with the knowledge that consumers rank their products lowest in quality. The terms of the guarantees will in general be less liberal the lower a product's quality. Producers clearly do not want to announce their low quality levels by offering stingy warranty coverage. Their problem is that failure to do so would make consumers peg their quality levels even lower than they really are.

Note that Tinbergen's derivation principle does not apply in the case of product guarantees. Unlike the toad's croak or the dung beetle's basic appearance, product guarantees didn't originate for some purpose unrelated to the signaling of product quality. They are an active signal, not a passive one. This distinction is important, again, because some of the signals we will later discuss likely emerged through natural selection, others through purposeful action.

An illuminating application of the full-disclosure principle is the difficulty it predicts for government policies that try to restrict the amount of information corporations can demand of job applicants. Consider, for example, the legislation that prohibits employers from asking about marital status and plans for having children. Before the enactment of this legislation, employers routinely solicited such information, particularly from female job candidates. The information is roughly correlated with the likelihood of withdrawal from the labor force, and the employer's motive in asking for it was to avoid investing in the hiring and training of workers who would not stay long. Since the demographic information is costly to fake (few people would refrain from marrying in order to appear less likely to drop out of the labor force), it can serve as a signal between parties whose interests might be in conflict. The purpose of the legislation was to prevent employers from favoring job candidates on the basis of marital status.

In order for it to achieve this, however, it is not sufficient merely to prohibit employers from asking about demographic categories. For if a woman realizes that her own particular situation places her in the most favored hiring category, she has every incentive to *volunteer* the relevant information. This sets up the familiar unraveling process whereby all but the least favorable information will eventually be volunteered freely by job candidates. The candidate who fails to volunteer information, however unfavorable, is simply assumed to be in the least favorable category. If the legislation were to achieve its desired intent, it would somehow have to prohibit job candidates from volunteering the information at issue.

People and things possess attributes and these, in turn, often exist in hierarchies. Some attributes are, by consensus, better than others. To be trustworthy is better than to be untrustworthy, hard-working better than lazy, and so on. The general message of the full-disclosure principle is that lack of evidence that something resides in a favored category will often suggest that it belongs to a less favored one. Stated in this form, the principle seems transparently simple. And yet its implications are sometimes far from obvious.

For example, it helps resolve the long-standing paradox of why new cars usually lose a large fraction of their economic value the moment they are driven from the showroom. How is it, exactly, that a new car purchased for $15,000 on Wednesday could command a price of only $12,000 in the used car market on Thursday? Clearly the car does not lose 20 percent of its value within 24 hours merely because of physical depreciation.

Economists struggled for years to make sense out of this curious pattern. In an uncomfortable departure from their characteristic assumptions about human nature, some even speculated that consumers held irrational prejudices against used cars. George Akerlof, however, suggested that mysterious superstitions might not be necessary. In his "The Market for 'Lemons,' " one of the most widely cited economics papers in the past several decades, he offered an ingenious alternative explanation (which became the first clear statement of the full-disclosure principle).[7]

Akerlof began with the assumption that new cars are, roughly speaking, of two basic types—good ones and "lemons". From the outside, the two types look alike. But the owner of any given car knows from experience which type hers is. Since prospective buyers cannot tell which type is which, good cars and lemons must sell for the same price. We are tempted to think the common price will be a weighted average of the respective values of the two types, with the weights being the proportions accounted for by each type. In the new car market, in fact, this intuition proves roughly correct.

In the used car market, however, things work out differently. Since good cars are worth more to their owners than lemons are to theirs, a much larger fraction of the lemons finds its way quickly into the used car market. As buyers notice the pattern, the price of used cars begins to fall. This fall in price then reinforces the original tendency of owners of good cars not to sell. In extreme cases, it may happen that the *only* used cars for sale will be lemons.

Akerlof's insight was to realize that the mere fact that a car was for sale constituted important information about its quality. This is not to say that having a lemon is the only reason that prompts people to sell their cars. Even if it were just a minor reason, however, it would still be sufficient to keep the owner of a good car from getting full value for it in the second-hand market. And that may be all that is needed to initiate the by now-familiar unraveling process. Indeed, it is a safe presumption that trouble-free cars rarely find their way into the used car market except as a result of heavy pressure from external circumstances. ("Going overseas, must sell my Volvo station wagon.")

Akerlof's explanation thus vindicates our intuition that physical depreciation is an insufficient reason for the sharp price differential between new and used cars. The gap is much more plausibly understood as a reflection of the fact that cars offered for sale, taken as a group, are simply of lower average quality than cars not offered for sale.

SIGNALS OF MORAL SENTIMENTS

Even though it will often be the purpose of moral sentiments to facilitate cooperation, each encounter presents opportunities for exploitation. There is advantage in merely seeming to be honest, or merely seeming to be a vengeance-seeker. Signals of moral sentiments are clear examples of communication between potential adversaries. Any satisfactory account of their emergence must thus be consistent with the constraints imposed by our theoretical understanding of such communications.

The costly-to-fake principle, for example, must surely govern the ultimate form taken by signals of moral sentiments. Statements like "I am honest" just will not suffice. In the case of the reputation pathway to moral sentiments, the costly-to-fake principle operates through the matching law discussed in Chapter 4. Recall that in order for a merely prudent person to develop a reputation for not cheating, it would have been necessary somehow to abandon the short-term emphasis of the psychological reward mechanism, a step with obvious costs. In the case of the sincere-manner pathway to moral sentiments, our task in the next chapter will be to explain why imposters cannot inexpensively simulate the physical symptoms of emotional predispositions. It will turn out that there are good reasons why it might prove very costly indeed for a person to subject all expression of emotion to conscious control.

In our attempts to understand how moral sentiments are communicated between people, we will also need to make use of the distinction between active and passive signals. Physical symptoms of moral sentiments, again, are in the passive category and are thus subject to the derivation principle. This principle tells us that it is extremely improbable for the physical symptoms of moral sentiments to have originated *because* of their signaling effects. The first small mutation toward a given symptom in the bearer of a sentiment would not have created the impression of a general relationship between the symptom and the behavior. So it is difficult to see how natural selection could have favored the symptom on account of any signaling role. As with the account of the toad's croak, the derivation principle leads us to prefer an explanation in which the sentiments began by serving some purpose unrelated to their physical symptoms.

The reputation account sketched in Chapter 4 suggests precisely such an explanation. For by that account, a small mutation in the direction of a moral sentiment can be useful even if not accompanied by any observable physical symptom. If it makes even a marginal contribution to the development of a reputation for behaving prudently, the emerging sentiment will be favored by selection. It happens, as we will see in the next chapter, that there is also an incidental link between states of emotional arousal and observable physical symptoms. While this connection probably did not *cause* the emergence of moral sentiments, neither did it impede them. Once the incidental connection between a sentiment and its symptoms becomes recognized by outsiders, selection pressures can bear not only on the sentiment itself but on its symptoms as well.

Unlike passive signals, active signals are not subject to the derivation principle. This suggests the possibility that signals of moral sentiments may sometimes be the result of purposeful action. One basis for such a signal might be the relationship between moral sentiments and the costs or benefits of membership in specific groups. For example, perhaps sympathetic people generally enjoy employment as social workers, whereas unsympathetic people would tend to find it highly burdensome. In such cases, the groups people decide to join will convey statistically reliable information about their moral sentiments.

This notion seems borne out in the practice whereby many affluent couples in New York City recruit governesses for their children. The care of children is one of those tasks in which trustworthiness is of obvious importance, since it is very difficult to monitor the caretaker's performance directly. The very reason for needing someone else to look after them, after all, is that you are not there to do so yourself. Apparently experience has persuaded many New Yorkers that the local labor market is not a good place to recruit people who perform reliably without supervision.

The solution many of these couples have adopted is to advertise for governesses in Salt Lake City newspapers. They have discovered that persons raised in the Mormon tradition are trustworthy to a degree that the average New Yorker is not. The signal works because someone who merely wanted to *appear* trustworthy would find it unpalatable, if not impossible, to have remained in the Mormon tradition. That tradition involves continuing, intensive moral enculturation, an experience most purely opportunistic persons would find too taxing to endure. Like the deepness of a toad's croak as a signal of its size, membership in the Mormon tradition is a good signal of trustworthiness because it would be so costly for an opportunistic person to simulate.

The full-disclosure principle will also influence our understanding of how moral sentiments are communicated to potential adversaries. It suggests, for example, that it will generally be difficult to exempt oneself from the signaling process entirely. For if, say, the expression of emotion is a reliable clue to the *presence* of these sentiments, its lack of expression will then be an indication of their *absence*. Where size mattered, even the smallest toads were forced to participate in the croaking contest. Likewise, where moral sentiments are important, failure to convey them will summon an uncharitable interpretation of one's position.

The full-disclosure principle will apply to reputation as well as to physical symptoms. It suggests why it might once have been more difficult than it is now for opportunists to soften the effects of a bad reputation. In the current environment, where mobility is very high, an opportunist would be attracted to the strategy of moving to a new location each time he got caught cheating. But in less mobile times, this strategy would have been less effective. For when societies were more stable, trustworthy people had much more to gain by staying put and reaping the harvest of the good reputation they worked to develop. In the same sense that it is not in the interests of the owner of a good car to sell, it was not in the interests of an honest person to move. In generally stable environments, movers, like used cars, were suspect. Nowadays, however, there are so many *external* pressures to move that the mere fact of being a newcomer carries almost no such presumption.

These examples illustrate the workings of three general principles that govern the transmission of information between people whose interests are potentially in conflict: the costly-to-fake, derivation, and full-disclosure principles. Passive signals that arise from natural selection must conform to all three, whereas active signals are exempt from the derivation principle. Our concern in the next chapter will be with physical symptoms of moral sentiments. Since these symptoms are likely to have originated in passive form, and since they clearly involve communication between potential adversaries, all three principles will apply.

SIX

TELLTALE CLUES

Anyone can tell at a glance that the intentions of the two dogs in Figure 6.1 are not the same.

The dog on the left is in what Charles Darwin called the "attack posture."[1] It approaches with its head raised, its tail erect and rigid, the hairs on its back and neck bristled. It walks upright, its ears are pricked, and its eyes have a fixed stare. "These actions . . . follow from the dog's intention to attack his enemy and are thus to a large extent intelligible."[2]

When a dog approaches its master, however, virtually every element of its bearing is reversed. Instead of walking upright, the dog sinks into a crouch. Its tail is lowered and wagging from side to side. Its hackles lie flat. Its ears are drawn backwards and its lips hang loosely. Its eyes no longer appear round and staring.

FIGURE 6.1   The Attack Posture and Its Antithesis
[*Source:* Darwin, 1873 (1872), pp. 52, 53]

THE PRINCIPLE OF SERVICEABLE ASSOCIATED HABITS

Darwin used these drawings to illustrate two of the three principles by which he accounted for the expression of emotion in man and animals. The first is his "principle of serviceable associated habits":

> Certain complex actions are of direct or indirect service under certain states of the mind, in order to relieve or gratify certain sensations, desires, etc.; and whenever the same state of mind is introduced, however feebly, there is a tendency through the force of habit and association for the same movements to be performed, though they may not then be of the least use.[3]

This principle might have been better named the "principle of serviceable associated *movements*," for it applies not only to habitual behaviors but also to those governed by instinct or inborn neural circuits.

Note how the posture adopted by the dog in the left panel of Figure 6.1 is suited for combat in every particular. Even the erect hairs on his neck and back serve this purpose, making him appear larger, and thus more likely to intimidate his opponent. Each element of the dog's posture is under the direct control of his central nervous system. For the hairs to stand erect, nerve impulses must travel from the dog's brain along his spinal column to the skin of the neck and back, where they activate tiny, nonstriated muscles that surround each follicle. The task of coordinating all the impulses that make up the attack posture is indescribably complex.

In carrying it out, nature relies on various shortcuts. In this case, the necessary coordinating mechanisms in the dog's brain evolved by natural selection, just as its fur did. The attack posture is hard-wired, instantaneously triggered by the emotions experienced during conflict. A dog that had to summon this posture through willful coordination of the relevant muscle groups would be woefully unequipped to deal with sudden threats.

Because of the natural advantage inherent in instinctual and habitual (nonwillful) patterns of response, Darwin reasoned, these patterns will be reliably associated with specific states of mind.[4] That is, they will be reliable signals of the states of mind that provoke them. Darwin did not have Tinbergen's derivation principle (see Chapter 5) consciously in mind when he wrote about the canine attack posture. But it is clear that his principle of serviceable associated habits is in harmony with it, since in no way does it contemplate that the dog's posture emerged *because* of its role as a signal of intention.

THE ANTITHESIS PRINCIPLE

A second principle illustrated in Figure 6.1 is Darwin's "principle of antithesis":

Certain states of the mind lead . . . to . . . movements which were primarily, or may still be, of service; and . . . when a directly opposite state of mind is induced, there is a strong and involuntary tendency to the performance of movements of a directly opposite nature, though these have never been of any service.[5]

Each detail in the right-hand panel of Figure 6.1, for example, stands in exaggerated contrast to the corresponding detail in the attack posture, even though, as Darwin put it, "not any of them, so clearly expressive of affection, [is] of the least direct service to the animal."[6]

Darwin rejected the notion that antithetical movements could have originated from any purposeful attempt to communicate opposing states of mind. Rather, he argued, they arose because opposing intentions are so often associated in practice with opposing actions. When we want an object to move to the left, we push it to the left; when to the right, we push to the right. We often make these same movements even in contexts where we know they will have no effect. Darwin describes the familiar gestures of the novice billiards player who wants his errant shot to veer slightly to one side: "[W]hen a man sees his ball traveling in a wrong direction, and he intensely wishes it to go in another direction, he cannot avoid . . . unconsciously performing movements which in other cases he has found effectual."[7] And even the most casual baseball fan will never forget Carlton Fisk's vivid body English in the sixth game of the 1975 World Series, as he successfully coaxed his long drive down the left field line to remain in fair territory.

Because opposing muscle groups are so often associated with opposing objectives, Darwin felt there was a natural tendency for opposing frames of mind to evoke opposing muscle movements. He seemed well aware that once a complex of movements originated under the antithesis principle, natural selection might enhance its usefulness as a signal of intention. But he realized that the signaling role was not necessary for its emergence. The antithesis principle, like the principle of serviceable associated habits, is thus completely consistent with Tinbergen's derivation principle. As required by Tinbergen, the signaling role of antithetical movements is not responsible for their emergence.

THE PRINCIPLE OF DIRECT ACTION OF THE NERVOUS SYSTEM

Darwin's third and final principle for the expression of emotion was the "principle of direct action of the nervous system":

When the sensorium [perceptual system] is strongly excited nerve force is generated in excess, and is transmitted in certain directions, dependent on the connection of the nerve cells, and, as far as the muscular system is concerned, on the nature of the movements which have been habitually practised.[8]

In modern terms, Darwin's excessive nerve force would be called a state of extreme arousal. One common manifestation is an uncontrollable trembling of the muscles. Darwin recognized that because such trembling is of no real use, and often even harmful, it could not be accounted for by his principle of serviceable associated habits.

Of course, it would not have been like him to believe that excessive nerve force was without explanation. Because the stresses that confront an individual are highly varied, so too are its needs for energy. Sometimes there is imminent peril, other times complete safety. Energy is a scarce resource, and the most successful organisms will be those that deploy it when likely to do the most good. The arousal mechanism, which regulates the individual's readiness for action, evolved under the pressures of energy scarcity. Using sensory information, the individual evaluates each situation in terms of its goals. On the basis of this evaluation, its arousal mechanism focuses attention and regulates the release of energy appropriate for each circumstance.

A strong threat to survival, for example, evokes the emotion of intense fear. Fear, in turn, stimulates the autonomic nervous system, which innervates the nonstriated, or involuntary, muscles and organs, triggering a rise in adrenaline, heart rate, blood pressure, blood sugar and a host of other changes that we now call the "fight or flight" response. A person who is fighting or fleeing for his survival has no reason to hold anything back.

But there will be many times when the best response to a frightening stimulus is neither to fight nor flee. In these cases, energy reserves are fully mobilized with nowhere to go. Darwin recognized that the natural result is for the excess nervous energy to spill over into its usual channels, hence the trembling muscles of the frightened person.

An important feature in this scheme is that excessive nerve force does not spill over at random. Rather, it discharges preferentially into the nerve pathways that are least under control of the will. We now know, of course, that there are virtually no nerve pathways that are not at least partly subject to conscious manipulation. The accomplished yogi, for example, can regulate body temperature, pulse rate, blood pressure, and other metabolic processes that in most people are well beyond purposeful control. Even untrained people, with effort, are often able to suppress deeply habituated movements and actions. Yet there remains a clear hierarchy among pathways in the nervous system, with some much more susceptible to conscious control than others. In Darwin's scheme, arousal will be first and most freely expressed by discharges along pathways least subject to conscious control.

Because arousal tends to manifest itself along these pathways, the resulting physical symptoms will convey statistically reliable information about underlying emotional states. To the extent that there are no truly involuntary nerve pathways, the connection between symptoms and states of mind will not be perfect. But the symptoms will nonetheless be informative in at least a probabilistic sense.

Note that, under Darwin's third principle, the connection between the emotion and its symptoms is again purely incidental. As with his first two principles, his principle of the direct action of the nervous system results in expressions of emotion that exist independently of their ability to convey information to outsiders. That is, like his first two principles, his third also satisfies Tinbergen's derivation principle. Darwin's three principles thus provide us with the explanation we need (see Chapter 5) for how observable symptoms of the emotions could have emerged independently of their ultimate usefulness as signals of intention.

Before examining symptoms of specific emotions in detail, it will be useful to review the basic thread of the argument thus far. Our fundamental concern, once again, is about why people often behave in ways patently contrary to their own material interests. Why, for example, does the prospect of guilt deter people from cheating even when they are certain they cannot be detected?

The commitment model suggests that emotional predispositions to behave in such ways can help solve prisoner's dilemmas, bargaining problems, and various other commitment problems. In order for the emotions to perform this service, outsiders must be able to discern their presence. Tinbergen's derivation principle implies that observable physical symptoms of the emotions probably did not originate *because* of their role as symptoms. The derivation principle thus suggests that the original usefulness of the emotions must not have depended on their physical symptoms. There must either have been some other means by which outsiders could identify them, or they must have served some other purpose.

We saw in Chapter 4 that the emotions may indeed serve some other purpose. Psychological rewards are dispensed in accordance with the matching law, which often favors behavior that conflicts with long-term self-interest. When the odds of getting caught are high, a person may realize it is not prudent to cheat, yet may cheat anyway because the gains come now, the costs only much later. We also saw how guilt and other emotions might mitigate this timing problem, by translating future costs and benefits into the present moment. That is, we saw that moral sentiments might have originally been (and might still be) useful for helping to solve impulse-control problems.

If so, then a logical basis exists for discerning emotional predispositions independently of any physical symptoms that may accompany them. The mere fact that a person consistently behaves prudently will be a signal to outsiders that he is more than a merely prudent person.

With this summary account of the origins of the emotions and their expression in mind, let us turn now to the details of the expressions themselves.

FACIAL EXPRESSIONS

The muscles of the face are subject in varying degrees to voluntary control. Studies of brain-damaged patients show that voluntary and involuntary control of the facial muscles often originate in different parts of the brain. People with damage in the pyramidal neural systems, for example, cannot smile on command the way normal people can, yet they laugh normally when something amuses them. Injury to other specific brain sites has precisely the opposite effect: victims can smile voluntarily, but show no reaction when they feel mirthful.[9] Because many of the facial muscles are not subject to voluntary control, and because the face is so visible, facial expressions are an especially important vehicle for emotional expression.

Facial expressions characteristic of specific emotions are recognized in virtually every culture. The list of universally recognized expressions includes those for anger, fear, guilt, surprise, disgust, contempt, sadness, grief, happiness, and probably several others. As we have already seen, there will often be advantage in pretending to feel an emotion one does not. If all the facial muscles were perfectly subject to conscious control, facial expressions would be robbed of their capacity to convey emotional information. And yet people everywhere believe that facial expressions have precisely this capacity.

In his 1985 book, *Telling Lies,* psychologist Paul Ekman summarizes the results of nearly three decades of research he and his colleagues have conducted on the physical symptoms of emotion. Ekman stresses that the key to detecting the genuineness of a facial expression is to focus on the muscles that are least subject to conscious control. For obvious reasons, he calls these the *reliable* facial muscles. In terms of our discussion in Chapter 5, reliable facial muscles can produce signals of emotion that are costly (difficult) to fake.

Figure 6.2 portrays the major muscle groups that control facial expressions. By asking experimental subjects to produce deliberate movements in specific facial muscles, it is possible to learn which muscle groups are hardest to control. Aspects of the following three groups prove especially difficult: the *quadratus menti* (chin muscle), the *pyramidalis nasi* (muscles at the bridge of the nose, or pyramidal muscles), and the *occipito frontalis*

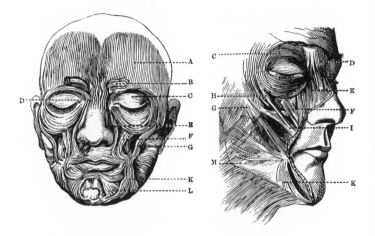

A. Occipito-frontalis, or frontal muscle
B. Corrugator supercilii, or corrugator muscle
C. Orbicularis palpebrarum, or orbicular muscles of the eyes
D. Pyramidalis nasi, or pyramidal muscle of the nose
E. Levator labii superioris alaeque nasi

F. Levator labii proprius
G. Zygomatic
H. Malaria
I. Little zygomatic
K. Triangularis oris, or depressor anguli oria
L. Quadratus menti
M. Risorius, part of the Platysma myoides

FIGURE 6.2   The Major Facial Muscle Groups
[*Source:* Darwin, 1873 (1872), p. 24]

and *corrugator supercilii* (frontal, or forehead, and brow muscles). For example, only about 10 percent of us can deliberately pull the corners of our lips downward without moving our chin muscles. Yet almost all of us do so automatically when we experience sadness or grief.[10]

In Figure 6.3, notice Woody Allen's eyebrows. Note, in particular, how each is most elevated at the center of his brow. Now sit in front of a mirror and try to duplicate this expression. If you are like 85 percent of the population, you cannot.[11] The oblique configuration of the eyebrows, together with the particular pattern of furrows in the forehead, involves movements of the pyramidal, frontal, and corrugator muscles that

---

*Ekman and his colleagues believe the same expression is also associated with feelings of guilt, although the difficulties in designing an experiment to test that view are apparent.

FIGURE 6.3 The Normally Reliable Frontal, Corrugator, and Pyramidal Muscles [Photograph by Philippe Halsman]

most of us are unable to summon voluntarily. And yet this same pattern is produced readily when we experience feelings of sadness, grief, or distress.* Woody Allen is one of a small minority of persons who are either born with, or later acquire, voluntary control of this expression.

Figure 6.4 shows the characteristic expression of fear or terror. The eyebrows are raised and pulled together, another combination of the pyramidal, corrugator, and frontal muscles that is difficult to control. Fewer than 10 percent of us can produce this expression voluntarily.[12] The raised upper eyelid and tensed lower eyelid are also characteristic of the expression of

FIGURE 6.4   Fear
[*Source:* Darwin, 1873 (1872), p. 299]

fear. But since the orbicular muscles, which move the eyelids, are relatively easy to control, these features may drop out of the expressions of persons trying to conceal their fear.

In Figure 6.5, we see the characteristic expressions for anger and surprise. The brow and eyelid muscles involved in these expressions are relatively easy to control, making them less reliable indications of the underlying emotional states. A more accurate indication of anger, at least in its milder forms, is a subtle narrowing of the lips. As Ekman describes it:

The red area becomes less visible, but the lips are not sucked in or necessarily pressed. This muscle action is very difficult for most people to make, and I have noted it often appears when

FIGURE 6.5   Anger and Surprise
[*Source: (left)* Leo de Wys, Inc.; *(right)* The Bettmann Archive]

someone starts to become angry, even before the person is aware of the feeling.[13]

In Darwin's account, the open-mouthed expression that often goes with both surprise and fear is explained partly by the fact that breathing is done much more quietly through the mouth than the nose. Quiet breathing makes it easier to hear and to escape detection, and is thus surely a "serviceable associated habit" for a person in danger.

MICROEXPRESSIONS

Even when a facial expression involves muscles that are relatively easy to control, the actual fact of control may require time to accomplish. Some of the most reliable clues to emotion thus come from the so-called "microexpression." This is a complete facial expression that correctly conveys the underlying emotion, but only for a fleeting instant. As soon as it appears it vanishes, replaced by some other expression more nearly in accord with the emotion the subject wishes to portray. Microexpressions, or fragments thereof, do not always occur when someone is trying to mask an emotion. But when they do, they are extremely reliable.

THE EYES

Folk wisdom places great emphasis on the eyes as a clue to how a person feels. A furtive glance and difficulty making eye contact, for example, are widely regarded as symptoms of guilt. As Darwin wrote:

> My correspondents almost always unanimously answer in the affirmative to my query, whether the expression of guilt or deceit can be recognized amongst the various races of man; and I have confidence in their answers, as they generally deny that jealousy can thus be recognized. In the cases in which details are given, the eyes are almost always referred to. The guilty man is said to avoid looking at his accuser, or to give him stolen looks. The eyes are said "to be turned askant" or "to waver from side to side," or "the eyelids to be lowered and partly closed . . . "[14]

Ekman is critical of Darwin's interpretation on the grounds that eye movements are relatively easy to control. He cites several examples of notorious liars who had no difficulty maintaining a steady gaze even in the midst of the most perfidious deceptions.[15] As noted in Chapter 1, Adolf Hitler was said to have been such a person.

If the point here is that a steady gaze is not a *perfect* indication of trustworthiness, it is of course well taken. But the same criticism applies to *all* of the other clues to emotion. None is perfect. It is well documented that the eyes have a natural tendency to dart about quickly during states of extreme arousal. Rapid eye movements are adaptive in this state because they help detect sudden changes throughout the visual field. Even if subject to conscious control, they are still another item on the list of things the would-be deceiver has to worry about.

•　　•　　•

OTHER SYMPTOMS OF AROUSAL

In addition to facial expressions, other physical symptoms are also useful in detecting changes in arousal. Again referring to the eyes, elevated arousal has consistently been shown to produce pupillary dilation, something that is extremely difficult to manipulate consciously. It is associated as well with increased frequency of blinking, which is itself subject to imperfect control.

Heightened arousal is also linked with the vague symptom known as "brightness" of the eyes. Darwin mentions this symptom as yet another manifestation of guilt, describing an episode involving one of his children:

> In one instance, the expression was unmistakably clear in a child two years and seven months old, and led to the detection of his little crime. It was shown, as I record in my notes made at the time, by an unnatural brightness of the eyes, and by an odd, affected manner, impossible to describe.[16]

Another frequently mentioned sign of guilt is facial blushing. It seems to be triggered by the sensation of extreme self-consciousness, and is thus closely associated with embarrassment and shame. We know that a blush results when the capillaries of the face and neck suddenly dilate, and that blushing occurs more frequently in women than in men. But the actual mechanism that triggers this response is not well understood.

Darwin's account of blushing begins with an observation that the attention of a self-conscious person would naturally focus on his or her face. He then describes the relationship between attention and sensation, noting examples in which a sharp new pain obliterates a smaller existing one, and of how sensations of any sort may be lessened by focusing the mind on something else. Since the various nerves that innervate a specific body part are in close physical proximity in the brain, he speculated that focusing attention on a body part may sympathetically excite the nerves that govern vasodilation and other autonomic processes in the same body part.

Darwin was well aware of the belief that symptoms of guilt prevent people from cheating. He mentions his informant Dr. Burgess, "who believed that blushing was designed by the Creator, in 'order that the soul might have sovereign power of displaying in the cheeks the various internal emotions of the moral feelings,' so as to serve as a check on ourselves, and as a sign to others, that we were violating rules which ought to be held sacred."[17] Darwin was also surely aware that the individualistic emphasis of his natural selection mechanism seemed to favor cheating and other forms of opportunistic behavior. But the implicit tension between the Creator's objectives and those of natural selection was a subject he simply did not pursue in *The Expression of Emotion in Man and Animals.**

Whatever the source of emotions like guilt, and whatever the mechanism by which they induce people to blush, we do know that blushing is one of the most difficult facial clues to control. Indeed, conscious attempts at control are much more likely to intensify than inhibit it.

Increased perspiration is another symptom of heightened arousal that is difficult to inhibit. The extra flow of perspiration reduces the galvanic resistance of the skin, one of the central measures of arousal recorded by polygraph machines. Changes in galvanic skin response are clearly of little use to an observer equipped only with the five senses. But special monitoring equipment is not always necessary. Few of us who witnessed President Nixon's televised speech just before the climax of the Watergate scandal will ever forget the large drop of per-

---

*In *The Descent of Man* (1871, Chapters 4 and 5), he sketched a preliminary account of how conscience and other moral sentiments might have sprung from a general sense of sympathy. He argued that sympathy, in turn, was useful because it made a person better able to function in groups. In his autobiography, however, Darwin described humanity as a learned, not inherited, trait: "I can say in my own favor that I was as a boy humane, but I owed this entirely to the instruction and examples of my sisters. I doubt indeed whether humanity is a natural or innate quality. 1882/1983, p. 11. If this passage reflects his final position on the matter, he seems to have concluded that cultural indoctrination is required to overcome our inherited selfish tendencies.

spiration that dangled accusingly from the end of his nose before tumbling onto the pages of his prepared text.

States of heightened arousal are also associated with a reduction in the flow of saliva. The person who swallows frequently and has trouble enunciating sharp consonants thus betrays an inner state of agitation. We know, too, that it is difficult for a person with a sharply diminished flow of saliva to whistle. A person who whistles freely thereby gives indication that he does not feel excessively nervous. In a recent John MacDonald novel,[18] the stalwart Travis McGee made clever use of this association. Disguised as a department store deliveryman, his task was to apprehend a dangerous killer. To put him off guard, McGee whistled as he approached the house where the fugitive was hiding. McGee was nervous, of course, but summoned the saliva he needed by biting the inside of his lip.

Mouth dryness was even used as a primitive lie detector in some ancient societies. Rice was placed in the suspect's mouth and if it came out dry he was assumed to be lying.

THE VOICE

Another reliable indication of increased arousal is elevated pitch of the voice. In roughly 70 percent of experimental subjects, pitch becomes higher when the subject is emotionally upset.[19] It goes up, for example, when subjects tell lies. It is not clear, however, that this response is a symptom of guilt per se. Generally, it seems to signify fear or anger and thus, in the lying subject, may correspond to fear of detection. There is also evidence that the cadence of speech increases with both anger and fear, and falls with sadness; and that the pitch of the voice also falls with sadness. Recent technical advances in quantifying specific aspects of the pitch and timbre of the voice promise to shed new light on whether each specific emotion registers a characteristic signature.[20]

Would-be deceivers may also reveal themselves through pauses and errors of speech. These are of course a normal part of everyone's speech, but their duration and timing will often differ in the apprehensive person. For such clues to be interpreted accurately, the observer must know something about the person's normal speech pattern. Thus, for example, while stammering may be a sure sign of discomfort in one person, it may be a regular feature of the speech of another.

BODY LANGUAGE

Because the face and voice are the objects of greatest scrutiny, would-be deceivers must focus their attention on trying to control clues from these sources. But there are additional signals of emotion, including gestures, posture, and other forms of body language. Some researchers have argued that because efforts at control focus on the voice and face, these other clues are especially valuable.[21]

The so-called "emblem" is one of the clearest of the body-language clues. An emblem is a gesture that conveys specific meaning—such as a shrug of the shoulders to indicate ignorance or helplessness, or the joining of the thumb and index finger to indicate "OK" or approval. Emblems often differ from culture to culture. A gesture similar to what Westerners would call "waving goodbye," for example, means "come here" in India.

Many emblems are clearly expressive of emotion, such as those for anger or contempt. The French, for instance, express contempt by thrusting one fist in the air, restraining the biceps with the other hand. Americans, by contrast, will sometimes gesture contemptuously with the middle finger. Within any given culture, the meaning of such emblems is clear to almost everyone.

People who are trying to inhibit the expression of an emotion will rarely present its emblem in the usual way. But they will sometimes partially display, and then quickly alter, the emblem of an emotion they wish to inhibit. Or they may display it in an unconventional way.

In one particularly provocative experiment, Ekman filmed a professor in the process of conducting a hostile interrogation of graduate students whose career prospects depended heavily on their ability to remain in his good graces.[22] The experiment was designed to invoke anger and contempt for the professor, emotions that the students would naturally wish to hold in check. When Ekman later told one of the subjects that she had put her outstretched middle finger on her knee pointing in the direction of the professor, neither she nor the professor could believe it. Yet evidence of such partial emblems (partial here because not presented in the usual conspicuous manner) was unmistakably clear in the films of the interviews.

Other mannerisms also provide useful clues to emotion. Imprecise gestures of the hands and facial features, for example, often accompany the normal flow of speech. The use of these gestures, or "illustrators," varies widely across cultures and from person to person within any culture. But if the normal pattern for a particular individual is known, deviations from it are sometimes a good indication of elevated arousal. In particular, the speech of persons engaged in deceit tends to be accompanied by fewer illustrators. With their attention focused on carrying out their deception, they apparently lack the capacity to orchestrate their usual gesture patterns.

SELF-DECEPTION

If liars believe they are doing the right thing, observers will not be able to detect symptoms of guilt because there will not be any. With this notion in mind, Robert Trivers suggests that the first step in effective deception will often be to deceive oneself, to hide "the truth from the conscious mind the better to hide it from others."[23] He describes an evolutionary arms race in which the capacity for self-deception competes for primacy against the ability to detect deception.

Extensive research shows that self-deception is indeed both widespread and highly effective. People tend to interpret their own actions in the most favorable possible light, erecting complex belief systems riddled with self-serving biases.[24]

Some observers take our obvious skill at self-deception to

mean that we are free to convey misinformation at will. On this view, there would be no reliable clues to deceit, and deception would be universal. This interpretation implicitly rests on the traditional belief that guilt, while socially useful, is disadvantageous to the individual. (See Chapter 2.) It focuses exclusively on the *costs* to people of betraying their inner feelings, and thus overlooks the commitment model's claim that guilt might *benefit* the individual in some way. We saw, for example, that being known to have the capacity to feel guilt would make someone an attractive partner for ventures that require trust (Chapter 3); and that it might help overcome impulse-control problems associated with the present-orientation of the psychological reward mechanism (Chapter 4).

We can't have it both ways. To be a perfect self-deceiver will help us get away with cheating, of course. But by the full-disclosure principle discussed in Chapter 5, it will also eliminate the advantages that might result from being known to have the capacity to feel guilt. Failure to show evidence of belonging to a favorable category, recall, creates the presumption of belonging to a less favorable one.

We saw in Chapter 3 that the relative advantage from being able to cooperate successfully declines with the share of the population that has this ability. If almost everyone had the capacity for perfect self-deception, few people would be able to cooperate successfully, and the advantage to being an *imperfect* self-deceiver would then be decisive. Natural selection would begin to favor individuals with diminished capacities for self-deception.

These observations tell us that there is advantage in self-deception only up to a point. Once it becomes sufficiently widespread, it becomes self-defeating. The only stable outcome will be one in which at least some people have less than perfect capacity for self-deception.

Extensive research has identified a multitude of statistically reliable clues to the emotions people feel. We have seen that these clues are unlikely to have originated because of their ability to transmit information. By Darwin's account, they emerged for completely independent reasons. But given that they exist, for whatever reasons, they obviously can come under selection pressures *because* of their signaling role. We know, after all, that individual differences in emotional responsiveness are at least partly inherited.[25] If, for example, trustworthiness and a tendency to blush go together, and if being known to be trustworthy is advantageous, selection pressures can clearly affect both the tendency to blush and the emotion that triggers it.

One point in favor of the commitment model is that it accords in detail with many of the important constraints imposed by the theory of natural selection. This is hardly conclusive evidence in its favor, since it was constructed with these requirements clearly in mind. It is always possible to comply with all known theoretical constraints by constructing a sufficiently complicated story. And yet the commitment model is very simple, well within the grasp of any intelligent high school student. It does not purchase consistency at the expense of parsimony.

On the strength of its ability to accommodate a variety of important constraints in a relatively simple way, the commitment model seems at least to merit additional consideration. I have attempted to confront it with as much varied evidence as possible, some of it original, most of it the work of others. The results of this effort, while by no means conclusive, have increased my confidence in the model. Our agenda for the coming chapters will be to review this evidence.

SEVEN

PREDICTING
COOPERATION

The major elements of the commitment model's account of the strategic role of the emotions are now in place. At its core lies the commitment problem, as embodied in various forms of the prisoner's dilemma and other common strategic interactions (such as the cheating, deterrence, bargaining, and marriage problems discussed in Chapter 3). These problems are widespread, and there are large material payoffs available to those who solve them. Solutions require commitments to behave in ways that are contrary to self-interest, and the emotions are one way of effecting these commitments. But by themselves they are not sufficient. There must also be some means for outsiders to discern their presence.

We saw two different ways the inference might occur. The first is reputation. Under the self-interest model, reputation should hardly matter, because we so rarely witness what people actually do in situations that test their character. Opportunists have an obvious interest in *appearing* honest (or vengeful, or loving), and this should severely limit what we can learn from their observable behavior. In Chapter 4, however, we saw that this view of reputation overlooks known properties of the human psychological reward mechanism. The opportunist may *want* to appear in a certain way, but there remains the problem of carrying it off. The difficulty, recall, is that the material rewards from opportunistic behavior often come now, the costs only in the future. Because of the tendency of the reward mechanism to discount the future too heavily, someone who cares only about material rewards will find it a formidable task even to pretend to be unopportunistic.

The second way of discerning emotional predispositions is through physical and behavioral clues. If these signals were completely under a person's control, they would obviously reveal nothing useful. If a signal is to be reliable, it must be costly to fake. As we saw in Chapter 6, there appear to be many such signals of emotional predisposition. Facial expressions, the voice, posture, and the like are not perfect measures of arousal by any means, but they do convey statistically reliable information. The question remains, however, whether they really work in the situations contemplated by the commitment model.

THE RELIABILITY OF CLUES TO EMOTION

How reliable are the various clues to emotion? And how good is the average person at interpreting them? We know that even under the best of circumstances, our ability to identify specific emotions is imperfect. Even the experienced polygraph expert, who has access to all sorts of detailed information the rest of us lack, makes frequent mistakes.[1]

Two recent articles survey the results of sixteen published studies that evaluate lay observers' success at detecting deception.[2] In all but two of the sixteen, accuracy was significantly better than chance.[3] None of the subjects in these studies had access to any technical equipment. They relied only on their own senses, and made use of the sorts of clues described in Chapter 6. They were "more likely to perceive as deceptive those messages that are characterized by less gazing, less smiling, more postural shifts, longer response latencies, slower speech rate, more speech errors, more hesitations during speech, and higher pitch."[4] The researchers note that "[a]lthough there are more clues that reliably predict perceptions of deception than actual deception, overall the correspondence between cues to actual deception and the cues that are used in perceivers' judgments is substantial."[5]

Certain personality traits seem to predict skill at spotting lies.[6] Gregarious persons, those who perceive human nature as complex, those who feel socially anxious, and especially "high self-monitors"—people who are very conscious of both their own self-presentation and the self-presentation of others in social situations—all perform better than average. The so-called Machiavellian personality type is very adept at lying but, surprisingly, does not perform significantly better than others at detecting lies.

While accuracy in distinguishing truth from falsehood is statistically better than chance in most studies, and while some individuals are extremely good at it, average accuracy levels are not very high in absolute terms. In thinking about what this means for the commitment model, we must bear in mind that all of the studies were designed to test only whether deception could be detected in a fleeting encounter involving a perfect stranger. Many did not even involve face-to-face interaction, but instead required subjects to rely only on video-taped presentations by potential deceivers.

Needless to say, these are hardly ideal conditions for testing people's abilities to detect symptoms of emotion. As we have seen, many of the relevant clues are subtle, and what is a reliable signal in one person will not be in another. It takes time to recognize a person's normal pattern of speech, gesturing, and other mannerisms, and the experimental studies simply did not provide that opportunity. The research on deception tells us that reliable clues to emotional states exist, but that the average person is not highly skillful at interpreting them on short exposure.

The commitment model does not say that important decisions about whom to trust need be made on the basis of impressions gathered during a single, brief encounter.* In order

---

*As I stressed in Chapter 1, a person who has a given moral sentiment will be influenced by it even during fleeting encounters. The issue here is not whether it will influence behavior in such encounters but whether others will have sufficient opportunity to discern it.

for moral sentiments to help solve commitment problems, it is necessary only that outsiders be able to discern their presence at reasonable cost. If that can be accomplished in a single encounter, as at least some of the experimental evidence suggests, so much the better. But the mechanism can function even if much more extensive exposure is required.

AN EXPERIMENTAL TEST

Are cooperators indeed recognizably different? Or do they appear more or less the same as defectors? My Cornell colleagues Tom Gilovich and Dennis Regan, both psychologists, and I have conducted a series of experiments designed to answer these questions.* Our experiments involved volunteer subjects who played a simple prisoner's dilemma game with one another. Many were students recruited from courses in which the prisoner's dilemma is an item on the syllabus. Others were given a preliminary briefing about the game, much like the description of it that appears in Chapter 2.

Following this briefing, the volunteers were told that they would play the game with each of two other people. The payoff matrix, shown in Table 7.1, was the same for each play of the game. Volunteers were told that the games would be played for real money, and that none of the other players would learn

TABLE 7.1. Payoffs for the Prisoner's Dilemma Experiment

		PLAYER X	
		COOPERATE	DEFECT
YOU	COOPERATE	$2 for you $2 for X	$0 for you $3 for X
	DEFECT	$3 for you $0 for X	$1 for you $1 for X

*The results I report here are preliminary. Gilovich, Regan, and I will discuss the details of this work in a forthcoming technical paper.

how their partners responded in each play of the game. (More below on how confidentiality was maintained.)

Volunteers were told that the purpose of the experiment is to determine whether people can predict whether their partners will cooperate or defect. Before beginning play, each group of three was given approximately thirty minutes to get acquainted. During this period, they were free to discuss any subjects they wished. They were free even to make agreements with one another regarding play of the game.

Following this thirty-minute period, each subject was taken to a separate room and asked to fill out a form indicating his response (cooperate or defect) to each of the other two players. In addition, subjects were asked to predict how each of their partners would respond. They were also asked to record a number from 50 to 100 indicating how confident they felt about each of these predictions. A response of 50 meant that the prediction was no better than chance, one of 100 that they were completely confident of it. Intermediate numbers could be used to indicate intermediate degrees of confidence.

After the subjects had filled out their forms, the results were tallied and the payments disbursed. Each subject received a single payment that was the sum of three separate amounts: (1) the payoff from the game with the first partner; (2) the payoff from the game with the second partner; and (3) a term that was drawn at random from a large list of positive and negative values. None of these three elements could be observed separately, only their sum. The purpose of the random term was to make it impossible for a subject to infer from his total payment how any of the other subjects had played. It prevented both the possibility of inferring individual choices and also of inferring even group patterns of choice. Thus, unlike earlier prisoner's dilemma experiments, ours did not enable the subject to infer what happened even when each (or none) of his partners defected. (More on these earlier studies in Chapter 11.) We explained to subjects that even though they were free to make promises not to defect, the anonymity of their responses would render such promises unenforceable.

Our experimental design offers several advantages over previous studies. Recall that in the deception studies discussed earlier, subjects interacted with one another only fleetingly, and in many cases had to make evaluations on the basis of merely having watched video tapes. In our design, by contrast, subjects interacted face-to-face in small groups for a period of thirty minutes. This feature of our experiment served two purposes. First, it provided an opportunity for the subjects to develop rapport with one another. This is important, because the commitment model stresses that cooperation is based on affect, not reason. Extensive interaction is also important because it allows subjects a better opportunity to size one another up. If there are indeed statistically reliable clues that predict behavior in these circumstances, it should be much easier to discern them in a more protracted period of interaction. Thirty minutes still isn't very long, but is considerably more than subjects had in most earlier studies.

The other major advantage of our experimental design is that the random component of subjects' payoffs eliminated any need for a defector to fear reprisal from his partners. In earlier studies, which lack this feature, subjects could not be sure that the dominant strategy was to defect. Put another way, these earlier studies did not confront subjects with a true prisoner's dilemma.

PRELIMINARY FINDINGS

To date, we have conducted experiments involving a total of 61 pairwise interactions.* Since each person predicted the choice his or her partner would make, we thus have a total of 122 predictions. With the subjects' permission, we taped many of their conversations, during which they invariably made promises to cooperate. (Why would anyone say, "I'm going to

---

*The odd number resulted because two of our preliminary groups contained four people, and one contained only two, instead of the usual three.

defect"?) If we may extrapolate this experience to the groups whose conversations we did not tape, this makes for a total of 122 promises to cooperate. Of these, 83 were kept, the remaining 39 broken. Thus, despite the fact that our random payoff term assured confidentiality, more than two-thirds of our subjects did not play the dominant strategy. This percentage lies in the range of results found in previous studies. In view of the added step we took to assure anonymity, it provides even stronger evidence of the inadequacy of the self-interest model.

Our subjects predicted cooperation and defection rates of 79.5 percent and 20.5 percent, respectively, whereas the actual rates were 68 percent and 32 percent. Because our general concern here is with whether a cooperative predisposition can yield material rewards, the data of greatest interest are those pertaining to the accuracy of the predictions concerning specific players. (See Table 7.2.) Of the 97 who were predicted to play cooperatively, 73, or 75.2 percent, actually did so. Although our subjects were overly hesitant about predicting defection, the predictions they did make were remarkably accurate: of the 25 people predicted to defect, 15, or 60 percent, actually did so. Given that the overall rate of defections was less than one in three, this is a very strong performance indeed. The likelihood that such a high overall accuracy rate would happen by chance is less than one in one hundred.

TABLE 7.2. Predicted *vs.* Actual Behavior in a Prisoner's Dilemma

| | | ACTUAL RESPONSES | | |
		COOPERATE	DEFECT	TOTAL PREDICTED
PREDICTED RESPONSES	COOPERATE	73	24	97
	DEFECT	10	15	25
TOTAL ACTUAL		83	39	122

Patterns in the confidence figures that subjects recorded for their predictions were also supportive of the commitment model. These figures, recall, are the numbers between 50 and 100 that indicate the level of confidence the subject feels in each prediction. Subjects were usually much more confident in their estimates than subsequent experience warranted. Even so, the patterns we found were broadly consistent with the view that people can make meaningful character judgments even on the basis of brief personal interaction. In keeping with their implicit estimate of the base rate of cooperation, subjects were more confident of their predictions of cooperation (average confidence level = 87) than of their predictions of defection (78.4). More important, they placed greater confidence in the predictions that subsequently proved correct (88.6) than in those that proved incorrect (76.5).

The average confidence values for each of the four types of outcomes are reported in Table 7.3. The numbers in the upper left and lower right cells, for example, are the average confidence figures for the two types of correct predictions. Those in the upper right and lower left cells are the corresponding values for the two types of incorrect predictions. The odds of such a supportive pattern having emerged purely by chance are less than 5 percent.

While these preliminary findings are supportive of the commitment model, they should not be interpreted as evidence of stable personality types called cooperators and defectors. On

TABLE 7.3. Average Confidence Values for Accurate and Inaccurate Predictions

ACTUAL RESPONSE OF SUBJECT X

		COOPERATE	DEFECT	OVERALL AVERAGE
RESPONSE	COOPERATE	90	78	87.0
	DEFECT	73	82	78.4

the contrary, we found that at least some of our subjects did not consistently follow either strategy: 13 of them (21 percent) cooperated with one of their partners but defected on the other. The remaining 48 followed a single strategy in both of their games, but this obviously does not imply that they would do likewise in every situation.

Indeed, in two closely related experiments, we found that the tendency to cooperate depends very strongly on how the interactions between subjects are structured. In one variation, subjects were permitted to interact for only 10 minutes instead of thirty, and were prohibited from making promises to cooperate. In a second variation, they were allowed to interact for the full thirty minutes, but again could not make agreements about how to play. Overall cooperation rates were lower in the first variation (37 percent) than in the second (61 percent), and in both cases were lower than in the basic version of our experiment (68 percent). Also as expected, predictive accuracy was substantially lower in both variations than in the basic experiment.

A pattern observed in all three versions of the experiment, but much more pronounced in the basic version, was for subjects to behave the same way they predicted their partners would. In the basic version, for example, 83 percent of the subjects who predicted their partners would cooperate also cooperated themselves. Similarly 85 percent of the subjects who predicted defection also defected themselves.

One possible interpretation of our findings is that people decide to cooperate or defect at least partly on the basis of the quality of their interactions with specific individuals. If, for example, a pair of subjects has a smooth, friendly interaction, each may be more likely to feel personal regard for the other, and be motivated by that feeling to cooperate. Alternatively, those who for whatever reason fail to establish rapport may tend to be wary that their partners will defect, and may therefore be more likely to defect themselves. In future experiments we will investigate these possibilities by having subjects fill out exit questionnaires in which they describe their reasons for their responses.

The notion that pleasant interactions might prompt cooperation is consistent with the basic message of the commitment model, in which sympathy plays such a prominent role. The self-interest model, by contrast, says that behavior in prisoner's dilemmas should be independent of the quality of interaction. No matter whether an encounter was bumpy or smooth, the dominant strategy, in purely material terms, is to defect.

To forestall possible confusion, I should stress that the point of our experiments was not to see whether cooperators do better in prisoner's dilemma games. Indeed, the structure of the game is such that they necessarily do worse. The benefit to being a cooperator, if there is one, lies in being able to recognize other cooperators and interact *selectively* with them. In our experiment, of course, there was no opportunity for selective interaction. Each subject had to play the game with each of the other two players assigned to his or her group. But since our subjects predicted their partners' performance considerably better than chance, we know that many of them could have avoided being exploited had they been given the opportunity to do so.

TOO STRICT A TEST?

Although these preliminary findings are suggestive, they are far from conclusive. Unlike real-world experience, our experiment did not let us see how people behave under varied and stressful circumstances. Even if it did, there would remain the difficulty of interpreting individual differences in expressions, mannerisms, and gestures. The latter difficulty, as we saw in Chapter 6, is that a pattern that signals deceit in one person will be perfectly innocent in another.

With such difficulties in mind, we may say that our prisoner's dilemma experiment constitutes a "strict" test of the commitment model. (A strict test of a hypothesis is one that, if passed, supports it but, if failed, gives no real cause to doubt it. For example: We can test the claim that Smith has an unusually good memory by asking her first to read pages 1–5 of a phone book, close the book, then report the 563rd name and phone number on the list. If she succeeds, we know she has a good memory but, if she fails, we cannot say she does not.) For obvious reasons, strict tests are perennial favorites among researchers: a pet hypothesis has a chance to win support, but nothing is really lost if it doesn't.

In order for the commitment mechanism to work, recall, it is necessary only that people be able to make statistically reliable character inferences at reasonable cost. While it would obviously be helpful if that could be done quickly, instant assessments are not essential. Inability to make them does not necessarily imply failure with more extensive information. Thus, even if, contrary to our preliminary findings, people were not, in fact, very adept at identifying defectors in brief encounters, we would be left to wonder whether more extensive contact would have helped.

OUR THOUGHT EXPERIMENT REVISITED

The real question, then, is this: Is it possible (if necessary after an extended period of acquaintance) to learn something about the likelihood that a person will behave opportunistically? If so, then predispositions to eschew self-interest will emerge and prosper under the terms of the commitment model. Otherwise, the model fails.

The basic question is very much like the one we considered in the simple thought experiment in Chapter 1: Do you know someone you believe would be unlikely to cheat you even if he could do so with no possibility of being detected? Assuming you do, note again how difficult it is to offer factual evidence in support of your belief. You cannot rationally have made this inference from experience, because if this person had previously cheated you in a similar situation, you could not have known about it. Once again, a "yes" answer in this thought experiment means you believe you can fathom the inner motives of at least some other people.

The prisoner's dilemma experiment lends support to our intuition that we can identify unopportunistic persons. That we can, in fact, do this is the central premise upon which the commitment model is based. From this premise, it logically follows that unopportunistic behavior will emerge and survive even in a ruthlessly competitive material world. We may thus concede that material forces ultimately govern behavior, yet at the same time reject the notion that people are always and everywhere motivated by material self-interest. And as we will see in the coming chapters, this perspective helps accommodate a variety of evidence that the self-interest model cannot.

EIGHT

BECOMING MORAL

The message of the commitment model is in close accord with what eighteenth-century moral philosophers had to say about the motives for moral action. David Hume, for example, believed that morality was based on sentiment, not logic, and that the most important sentiment was sympathy. Sympathy also played an important role in Adam Smith's more elaborate scheme, in which the central motivating force was each person's desire to please an "impartial spectator."

But the role of sentiment was to suffer considerably at the hands of the great materialist thinkers of the nineteenth and twentieth centuries. Even the humane moral philosophy of John Rawls, so influential in our own time, is derived from a quintessentially rationalist thought experiment in which self-interest is the primary human motive. In this landmark treatise, *A Theory of Justice,* people are asked to decide upon the rules of social justice by imagining themselves in an "original position" in which they lack knowledge of their own specific talents and abilities. Rawls accords no appreciable role to sentiments such as sympathy, charity, or envy in the choices made by his social contractors.

The decline of the role of sentiment was also influenced by the ascendancy of behaviorism in psychology. The behaviorists, according to their critics, viewed the child's mind as a *tábula rasa,* a blank slate upon which experience was free to engrave whatever messages it would.* They saw right and wrong

---

*This is perhaps an unfair caricature because even the most purely environmental theories included "a principle of drive, or motivation, that embodied the final form taken by the instinct doctrine, although disguised in a new vocabulary" (Herrnstein, 1972, p. 24).

not as innate, intuitive concepts, but ones to be learned through careful environmental reinforcement.

Behavioral scientists now understand that biology constrains what experience and conditioning can accomplish. We now believe, for example, that the fundamental structure of language is an inherited part of each person's neural circuitry.[1] And we are beginning to realize what many twentieth-century composers did not, namely, that not just any musical structures can produce pleasurable sensations in the human nervous system.

The attractions of narrow rationalism have also begun to decline. Philosophers such as Derek Parfit have stressed that people have, and profit by having, much broader concerns than the ones identified by conventional self-interest theories of rational behavior.[2] We are returning to the notion that people are emotionally predisposed to form communities, and to seek nurturance in cooperative relationships with others.[3]

The climate was thus ripe for psychologist Jerome Kagan's provocative 1984 book, *The Nature of the Child,* in which he argues that emotion, much more than reason, lies behind our moral choices. This is of course the same conclusion that emerges from the commitment model. But Kagan has reached it by a different route, by his direct observations of the behavior of children. The evidence he offers is an important source of indirect support for the commitment model, and is therefore worth careful examination.

THE CHALLENGE TO STRICT BEHAVIORISM

But before examining that evidence, it will be useful to look briefly at the forces that have led to abandonment of the strict behaviorist paradigm. Much of the intellectual power of behaviorism came from experiments carried out in the laboratory of its foremost practitioner, B. F. Skinner. Skinner and his colleagues demonstrated that rats and other laboratory animals can be taught an extraordinary repertoire of complex behaviors by the use of simple punishments and rewards. From these experiments, they generalized that virtually all behavior in every species was the result of similar environmental conditioning.

During the 1960s, however, a series of experiments carried out by psychologist John Garcia and his collaborator Robert Koelling produced what eventually proved an insurmountable challenge to Skinner's scheme. The Garcia experiments subjected each of four groups of genetically identical rats to a standard form of Skinnerean avoidance conditioning. Rats in the first group were given water to drink and, while drinking, were punished with a mild electric shock. The punishment was preceded by a signal in the form of a noise and flashing light. Exactly as predicted by the behaviorist model, the rats quickly learned to avoid the punishment by ceasing to drink as soon as the signal was given. They acquired the classical "avoidance response."

For the second group of rats, the signal consisted of adding a distinctive flavor to the water, and the punishment was to bombard them with X rays, causing nausea. Like the first group, this group also quickly developed the expected avoidance response.

With the third and fourth groups, the signal and punishment pairs were interchanged: the third group got a noise and light signal followed by the artificially induced nausea, while the fourth got the distinctive flavor followed by the electric shock. The startling result was that none of the rats in these two groups developed an avoidance response.

Rats apparently have no difficulty learning to associate a noise and light with an electric shock, or a distinctive flavor with nausea. Garcia and Koelling argued that the rat's brain evolved to be especially receptive to such associations. A causal relationship between nausea and the most recent novel taste is, after all, inherently plausible. Physical pain, similarly, is frequently linked both to sounds and changes in the visual field. By contrast, a causal connection between novel taste and nonabdominal physical pain is inherently implausible. Nor are there likely to have been many circumstances in nature where a non-food stimulus triggered feelings of nausea. Because some types of association are so implausible, the rat's brain can save capacity by not even considering them. Any rat that devoted scarce cognitive resources to investigating such relationships would probably not have survived for long.

The Garcia experiments contradicted the conventional behaviorist wisdom in another important respect by showing that the ability to make plausible associations is relatively insensitive to the time lag between stimulus and result. The rats made the association between taste and nausea, for example, despite time lags of up to 75 minutes. By the prevailing behaviorist theory, which held that larger gaps between stimulus and reinforcement would produce sharply weaker patterns of association, this was an inexplicably long interval.

It is perhaps an understatement to say that behaviorists were not receptive to these new claims. None of the leading academic psychology journals would publish accounts of the Garcia experiments. Only after much delay were they finally published in then-obscure outlets.[4] One prominent learning theorist of the day called Garcia's findings "no more likely than birdshit in a cuckoo clock."[5]

Despite such vituperative resistance, the Garcia experiments slowly produced a revolution among learning theorists. It soon became clear that their findings applied not only to rats but to humans as well. Martin Seligman coined the term, "Sauce Béarnaise phenomenon," to describe "prepared" or "directed" learning, our general tendency to learn some associations much more readily than others.[6] Several hours after eating filet mignon with his then-favorite sauce, Seligman became violently ill. Despite the long time interval between eating and becoming ill, despite a large number of other novel stimuli that occurred during that same time interval, and despite the fact that he later discovered that his symptoms were really the result of a stomach flu, Seligman reports that he has never again been able to eat Sauce Béarnaise. The very same week of Seligman's illness, the first of the Garcia papers appeared in print.

DEVELOPMENT AND SPECIFIC BRAIN COMPETENCIES

The brain has specific competencies that develop at specific times. Armed with this knowledge, post-behaviorists have made great progress toward understanding the developmental patterns we see in children. The usefulness of the new orientation is clearly illustrated in Kagan's account of "separation distress," the anguished response of an infant whose parent has just left the room. Separation distress is rarely observed before 7 months of age. Most infants below that age will continue to play normally when a parent leaves the room. But sometime between the ages of 7 and 15 months, an abrupt change occurs: the parent's sudden absence will provoke the child to cry.

One popular explanation of this change was that the child cries because she has finally learned that she is in greater danger when her parent is away. Another explanation was that it takes at least 7 months for the infant to become firmly enough attached to its primary caregiver to experience concern about his or her disappearance. But these explanations seem to miss something important:

[N]either . . . can account for the fact that the timing and the form of appearance of separation distress . . . are very similar for children blind from birth, and for children raised in American nuclear families, in kibbutzim in Israel, in Barrios in Guatemala, in Indian villages in Central America, in orphanages, or in American daycare centers. Why should all these infants, growing up under such different conditions, learn a conditioned fear reaction to caregiver departure at the same age? It also strains credibility to assume that despite the extraordinary variation in the amount of time infants spend with their mother across these different settings, the developmental function for the emotional relation to the caregiver is similar.[7]

We might also wonder why the transition in behavior is so abrupt. Our intuitive understanding of emotional attachment is that it is established gradually. Gradualism should apply as well to learning about pain and danger. If infants gradually develop emotional attachment, if they gradually learn that the caregiver's absence implies greater danger, why then doesn't their response to the caregiver's departure also emerge gradually? That is, why don't the infants start off being only a *little* distressed when the caregiver leaves?

Kagan believes the onset of separation distress results from the maturation of the competence to retrieve images from memory and compare them with the present. This competency matures abruptly at around 8 months. Before it appears, the child is unable to find a toy that he has just seen placed beneath a cloth in front of him. Once the toy disappears from view, it is as if it had ceased to exist. With the maturation of memory retrieval, however, the child can suddenly find the toy with no difficulty.

Without the capacity to retrieve stored mental images and compare them with the present, the child is unable to perceive the discrepancy between the caregiver's presence and absence, and thus has no basis for becoming distressed when the caregiver leaves the room. Once she develops that capacity, however, she becomes aware that there has been a change. Because of her *existing* attachment to the caregiver, it is a change that matters. Being able to do nothing about the discrepancy results in her distress.

EMOTIONAL COMPETENCY AND MORAL BEHAVIOR

The revisionist account of separation distress, which emphasizes the emergence of innate competencies in the central nervous system, answers many of the questions the behaviorist accounts cannot. Kagan employs a similar strategy for probing the role of the emotions in moral behavior. He combines careful observation of the behavior of children in richly varied settings with our emerging knowledge of the developmental patterns of specific cognitive and affective capabilities.

Moral philosophers have long noted the wide differences in specific moral norms, both across cultures and over time within any single culture. In most Western cultures, for example, the wrongness of lying typically depends much less than in many Eastern cultures on the context in which a lie occurs. In Japan, where the maintenance of social harmony is often a more important ethical goal than truthfulness, a person has a moral duty to lie in many social situations. In the ancient Greek city-states, loyalty to one's place of residence was of much greater importance than in modern urban societies. And the right of each citizen to pursue a better life, so taken for granted in twentieth-century liberal democracies, did not even exist in most ancient societies, which often saw nothing ethically indefensible about the enslavement of "barbarians."

Circumstances of time and place play an obvious and important role in determining which virtues of character will be most valued in any particular society: a society under constant military threat will emphasize physical courage; a rich society will emphasize charity toward needy persons; one that is poverty-stricken and disease-ridden will encourage detachment; and so on. The behavior called for by a society's celebrated virtues will require effort, Kagan argues, but will generally be within the capacity of most citizens.

His principal claim is that, while specific moral norms are enormously varied and complex, they are supported by a limited number of simple, highly uniform emotional capacities. Stressing that his labels are less important than the underlying concepts, he lists the following five basic categories of unpleasant emotion:

- anxiety (as, for example, over physical harm, social disapproval, or task failure);

- empathy (especially with those in need or those at risk);
- responsibility (especially for causing harm to others);
- fatigue / ennui (following repeated gratification of a desire);
- uncertainty (especially from poorly understood discrepant events and inconsistency of beliefs).

These categories interact to produce the related feelings of guilt and shame. For example, when a person knows he is responsible for an action that harms others, but no one else knows it, he feels guilt. If others do know, he feels both guilt and shame. If others wrongly believe he has harmed another, he feels only shame.

The similarity of these basic affective states across time and location is vividly illustrated in these two accounts of the feeling of guilt, the first from an adult living in modern western Kenya:

> You remain unhappy because you have something in your heart that will draw you to a shadow of being afraid of something that you have done to someone else. Because you will charge yourself according to your heart that you were not right at that time.[8]

The Kenyan's account is similar in essence to the one written by David Hume a continent apart and more than two hundred years earlier:

> When you pronounce any action or character to be vicious, you mean nothing, but that from the constitution of your nature you have a feeling or sentiment of blame from the contemplation of it.[9]

The desire to avoid the various unpleasant affective states, in Kagan's scheme, is the principal motivating force behind moral behavior. People will try to avoid actions, motives, and qualities that make them feel afraid, sorry for those less privileged, anxious, bored, fatigued, or confused. The specific actions or circumstances that trigger these emotions will depend heavily on cultural context. But the motivating emotions are always and everywhere the same.

THE ROLE OF STANDARDS

A careful examination of the stages by which children begin to behave morally produces impressive support for the claim that moral behavior is driven by a small set of underlying emotions. The first important step is the emergence of standards, which happens sometime after the middle of the second year. In one experiment, fourteen-month-old and nineteen-month-old children were allowed to play in a room that contained numerous toys, some of which were conspicuously damaged or flawed. None of the fourteen-month-olds paid special attention to the damaged toys. Yet more than half of the older children became clearly preoccupied with them. These children "would bring a flawed toy to their mother, point to the damaged part, stick a finger in the place where the animal's head had been removed, or, if they had language, indicate that something was wrong by saying, 'Fix' or 'Yucky.' "[10]

The older children do not respond this way to just any deviations from normality. If a shirt has an extra button, for example, they may look a little longer at it, but there is none of the emotional coloration so obviously present in their reaction to a shirt with a missing button. The source of the child's concern appears to be her recognition that the action that caused the missing button was improper.

It would be pointless to deny that one source of the child's emerging standards is the parental feedback emphasized by behaviorists. Many of these children, after all, have repeatedly been exposed to parental disapproval on occasions when they have damaged their toys or clothing.

At the same time, however, there is clear evidence that behaviorist reinforcement cannot be the *only* source. Indeed, there are numerous familiar instances in which a child's behavior persists despite determined efforts to discourage it. Almost every child, for example, reacts with obvious interest, and often deep concern, when she sees someone whose face is deeply disfigured. In the interest of sparing the disfigured person's feelings, most parents do all they can to discourage such behavior, usually to little avail.

Another source of standards is the child's emerging capacity to empathize. Children very early display the familiar tendency to identify another person's feeling with their own.[11] The two-year-old child, who has herself experienced physical discomfort many times, is able to infer that other children experience it under largely the same circumstances. This appreciation, moreover, is not emotionally neutral. It generally summons a clear expression of concern for the other child.

Another source of standards is the example of peer and adult behavior. The child apparently has an untutored tendency to feel anxious when he is unable to perform a task that others can do: "When a woman approaches a child, picks up some toys, acts out some brief sequences that are difficult to remember or to implement, and then returns to her chair, children from diverse cultural settings will immediately cry or protest."[12]

Noting the unlikelihood that children in all of these diverse settings had been punished for failure to imitate others in the past, Kagan dismisses behavioral conditioning as a cause of their distress. Instead, he argues that the child simply "invents an obligation to duplicate the adult's actions."[13] Indeed, it is easy to see how an emotional predisposition to imitate the behavior of people in superior positions might be adaptive, even if bound to lead to occasional frustration.

That the behavior of others is a strong, and innate, source of standards appears clear. Infants only a few hours old, for example, will carefully duplicate the facial expressions of their mothers, down to such details as tongue movements and the blinking of the eyes.[14] Even for ostensibly mature adults, peer behaviors remain an important source of standards. Failure to follow them has the capacity to stir unpleasant feelings even when the activity is one that all prior training and conditioning have opposed. In a 1970 film, for example, the

> veteran student of human nature Allen Funt . . . placed his telephone number in a help-wanted advertisement, then arranged

personal interviews with those who responded. We are shown an
interviewee as he is directed to a small office in which several
other persons are already seated, apparently waiting. To the
experimental subject, the others appear to be fellow interview-
ees, but we know they are really confederates of Mr. Funt.
Responding to no apparent signal, the others abruptly rise from
their seats and begin taking off their clothing. We are shown a
close-up of the experimental subject, his face a mask of appre-
hension as he surveys what is happening. A few moments pass,
then he, too, rises from his chair and proceeds to disrobe. At no
point in the process does he ask any of the others why they are
removing their clothing. As the scene ends, we see him standing
there, naked alongside the others, apparently waiting for some
clue as to what happens next.[15]

The flip side of anxiety over being unable to perform a task
is the joy a child feels when he masters it. Children all over the
world display the so-called "smile of mastery" in situations where
they could not possibly have been conditioned to do so by prior
punishments and rewards. It is summoned by a feeling of
intrinsic reward, something basic in almost every child's innate
emotional repertoire.

Of the various sources of the child's standards, only one—
adult punishment and reward—fits the traditional behaviorist
description of the process of moral learning; and, as we will
see, even it may depend strongly on the presence of an innate
emotional competency. The other sources of standards differ
markedly from the simple carrot-and-stick mechanisms of the
strict behaviorists.

The two-year-old child has all the cognitive and affective
equipment she needs for the development of standards, yet is
clearly not a morally mature person. It is one thing for the
child to appreciate that a specific action or event violates a
standard, quite another for her to be fully responsible for her
own behavior. To achieve moral maturity, additional competencies are necessary, some cognitive, some affective.

In the affective realm, the child must be able to make a connection between the actions she performs and her evaluation of herself. This skill usually comes during the third or fourth year. Once the child equates the performance of bad actions with a bad evaluation of self, and good actions with a good evaluation of self, she has a powerful motive to perform good actions.

In addition to the affective capacity for self-condemnation, mature moral behavior requires cognitive capabilities that most two-year-olds lack. In order to experience feelings of guilt, for instance, it is necessary for the child to be able to infer that she is *responsible* for having violated a standard. The ability to make such an inference will depend, in turn, on her ability to perceive that she had the option of having behaved differently. By the fourth year, almost all children are able to assess personal responsibility for at least some of their actions. But because the causal connections are often exceedingly complicated, the process of moral maturation normally continues throughout adulthood.

STANDARDS AND EMOTION

The most important feature of Kagan's argument, in terms of its relevance to the validity of the commitment model, is that standards evoke an emotional response. A standard, he emphasizes, is thus different from a convention, such as "Always drive on the left side of the road in England." Both standards and conventions are norms, but conventions lack emotional coloration. It is prudent that we all stick to the same side of the road, but no one feels intense emotion about it. Which side we choose is fundamentally arbitrary. With standards, however, there is an emotional conviction that the choice really matters.

The fact that standards evoke an emotional response is of course what accounts for their motivational significance. People will risk life and property in defense of a standard, but will do little on behalf of a convention. It is thus easy, Kagan says, to understand why many parents are so concerned about what their children see in movies and on television.

> Although many parents may not be able to explain why they believe in the correctness of certain standards, deep probing would, I suspect, reveal the connection that the child who witnesses too much aggression, dishonesty, sexuality, and destruction will stop experiencing the emotions of fear, anxiety, and repugnance that sustain the standards for these acts. Most adults fear—correctly, I might add—that when emotional reactions to socially undesirable responses cease, the standard will become arbitrary and less binding.[16]

The difficulty is not that rational analysis is unnecessary for moral behavior, but that the rationalists give short shrift to other sources of motivation. The status of rational analysis, in Kagan's scheme, is much the same as its status in the dieter's decision about whether to eat dessert. (See Chapter 4.) In both cases, it is but one among many inputs that produce the feeling states that directly motivate behavior.

AN INDIRECT TEST OF THE ROLE OF EMOTION

In support of his thesis that moral behavior is driven by the emotions, Kagan has examined the emergence of such behavior in children. Critical to this process is the acquisition of standards. He has shown that most of the ways children acquire standards—empathy and concern about peer behavior, for example—are clearly linked to the development of specific emotional competencies. As noted, only one—adult punishment and reward—appears completely consistent with the behaviorist scheme.

The fact that specific emotional competencies emerge concurrently with specific steps toward moral behavior is clearly supportive of Kagan's thesis. In purely logical terms, however, it does not prove that the emotional competencies play a causal role. We would be much more inclined to accept the thesis if it could also be shown that *failure* to develop the relevant emotional competencies *prevents* the emergence of moral behavior.

Since the competencies at issue are virtually universal, this kind of test is inherently difficult to carry out. There is one body of research, however, that is at least indirectly relevant. It pertains to the so-called psychopathic personality, a behavioral syndrome that sociologist Lee Robins describes as follows:

> We refer to someone who fails to maintain close personal relationships with anyone else, who performs poorly on the job, who is involved in illegal behaviors (whether or not apprehended), who fails to support himself and his dependents without outside aid, and who is given to sudden changes of plan and temper in response to what appear to others as minor frustrations. These characteristics must be chronic and more or less typical of the whole life history up to the point of diagnosis.[17]

The populations of prison offenders and of psychopaths are not identical. Many prisoners do not fit the typical definitions of psychopathy and many psychopaths are not currently in prison. Even so, a diagnosis of psychopathy is the strongest predictor we have of the likelihood of being convicted of a criminal offense. In addition, even criminal offenders who are not classified as psychopathic tend to deviate in the direction of psychopathy along every measured dimension of personality. It seems fair to assert that psychopaths and near psychopaths comprise a sample that lacks the normal pattern of moral behavior discussed by Kagan.

Is there any indication that psychopaths also display the diminished emotional competencies predicted by his thesis? Harvey Cleckley's discussion of the psychopathic personality points in precisely this direction.[18] He emphasizes the frequency with which psychopaths lack feelings of guilt or empathy, two particularly important sentiments in Kagan's scheme. The difficulty here is that we lack concrete tests for the presence of such feelings. Perhaps researchers deny guilt and empathy in psychopaths merely because psychopaths fail to behave morally. If so, their reports provide no new information on the validity of the claim that emotions are the driving force behind moral behavior.

There is one collection of experiments, however, that identifies an objectively measurable deficiency in the emotional competency of the psychopath. Working with standard definitions from the clinical literature, Robert Hare and Michael Quinn divided a sample of Canadian prison inmates into three categories: (1) clearly psychopathic, (2) marginally psychopathic, and (3) clearly nonpsychopathic.[19] They then subjected volunteers from each category to the following simple conditioning experiment. First, the subjects were connected to a polygraph-like device that measured heart rate, blood vessel constriction, and galvanic skin response. The volunteers wore headsets into which Hare and Quinn would repeatedly send 10-second tones of either low, medium, or high pitch. Following the low pitch, nothing happened; the medium pitch was followed by a slide of a nude female projected onto a screen; and following the high pitch, subjects received a mild electric shock.

All three measures of arousal in nonpsychopathic volunteers conditioned in the expected manner. That is, the respective tones preceding the electric shock and the nude photograph produced changes in heart rate, blood vessel constriction, and galvanic skin response prior to the actual occurrence of the stimulus. Heart rate and blood vessel constriction conditioned similarly for the two psychopathic groups.

But for galvanic skin response, the most sensitive of the three measures of emotional arousal, psychopaths showed no conditioning at all. It rose briefly during the actual shock or photograph, but showed not even the slightest change during the tones that preceded those stimuli. Similar findings have been reported in several other studies.[20] In these experiments, we see at least tentative evidence that diminished emotional competency is associated with chronic inability to conform to conventional standards of moral behavior.

How do we know it is diminished emotional competency, not a more generalized inability to learn, that makes punishment and reward ineffective sources of standards for the psychopath? A voluminous literature reports that psychopaths do just as well as others on traditional tests of intelligence.[21] But as Hare points out, the psychopaths in these studies are typically ones who have been caught and institutionalized for their antisocial behavior.[22] On the plausible assumption that psychopaths who do not get caught (or who get caught less often) are cleverer than the ones who do, it follows that psychopaths are *more* intelligent, on the average, than nonpsychopaths. The intelligence studies make clear, at any rate, that the asocial behavior of psychopaths is not the result of a general incapacity to learn.

In the absence of emotional conditionability, no amount of adult punishment and reward seems sufficient to induce a person to behave morally. Perhaps even adult reinforcement, the most ostensibly behaviorist of the various sources of standards, must itself be supported by innate emotional competencies.

IMPULSIVENESS AND CRIMINALITY

Recall from Chapter 4 the idea that the emotions help mitigate the tendency toward impulsiveness associated with the matching law. Virtually every author on the subject of criminal behavior has noted impulsiveness as a common characteristic of offenders, whether pyschopathic or not.[23] The association between impulsiveness and criminal behavior has also been supported in numerous quantitative studies.[24] One study of seventh graders even showed that tests of impulsivity in simple psychomotor tasks are predictive of future delinquency.[25]

In Chapter 4, we saw that certain emotions may help curb impulsivity, by translating future costs and benefits into the present moment. On this view, the widespread and chronic impulsiveness of criminal offenders may also be interpreted as support for the claim that emotional competencies underlie moral behavior. This claim, if correct, provides independent support for the commitment model's interpretation of why people so often fail to pursue material self-interest.

Humans are by far the most flexible of the earth's inhabitants. The power of experience and conditioning are greater for us than for any other species. Yet we must reject the notion that there are no bounds on our conditionability. Our flexibility is in part limited by simple design constraints. One way of economizing on scarce neurological hardware is to replace flexibility with simple rules of thumb, as in the case of rats who refuse to consider causal associations between electric shocks and novel flavors. There is no longer any question that human behavior comes under similar influences. The "moral sense" spoken of by eighteenth- and nineteenth-century philosophers is apparently not merely a metaphor.

But evolutionary design constraints are not the only plausible reason for limited flexibility. For even if additional neurological capacity were available free of charge, we would not always do better to have it. We have seen, in particular, that perfect flexibility would often make it impossible to solve the commitment problem. In the specific moral behaviors discussed by Kagan, there may thus be powerful advantages in having one's hands tied by emotional predispositions. And this may help explain why, as he puts it, "feeling, not logic, sustains the superego."[26]

NINE

FAIRNESS

The self-esteem of professional economists derives in no small measure from their belief that they are the most hardheaded of social scientists. In their explanations of human behavior, only self-interested motives will do. A prominent case in point is Richard A. Posner, formerly of the University of Chicago Law School, now judge of the U.S. Court of Appeals, Seventh District. Posner won his justly deserved professional reputation as a pioneer in law and economics, an emerging field in which economic analysis helps clarify important concepts of law. His text, *Economic Analysis of Law,* has become a standard reference.

Material costs and benefits reign supreme in Posner's world. People do, of course, care strongly about material payoffs, and his approach has produced genuine insights about behavior. Buoyed by the success of the cost-benefit framework, Posner's followers have grown increasingly skeptical of nonmaterial motives. Ones that conflict with the quest for material gain are viewed with particular suspicion. Posner speaks, for example, with thinly veiled contempt about woolly legal notions like "fairness" and "justice," which he calls "terms which have no content."[1]

The Posnerians are indeed hardheaded, only not in the sense they mean. On issues like fairness, they think of themselves as tough-minded, but in fact they are merely stubborn, for they refuse to acknowledge compelling evidence that fairness is an extremely powerful source of human motivation.

The rationalists complain that fairness is a hopelessly vague notion. And yet, as we will see, there is a reasonably simple definition that captures much of what people seem to mean by it. More important, we will see that concerns about fairness often motivate costly actions. The traditional self-interest model, which ignores these concerns, once again provides woefully inaccurate predictions about what people actually do.

DEFINING FAIRNESS

Fairness almost always refers to the terms of a transaction (not necessarily an economic one) that occurs between people. To give the notion of fairness a working definition, it is thus useful first to introduce some simple terminology concerning transactions.

A transaction occurs when two parties exchange something. A gives B a dollar, B gives A a pineapple. When a transaction takes place voluntarily, it is conventional to assume both parties benefit. In the illustrative example, we infer that the pineapple is worth more than a dollar to A (else he would not have bought it), less than a dollar to B (else he would not have sold it).

In any transaction, there is a "reservation price" for both the buyer and seller. For the buyer, it is the most he would have paid. Had he been charged more, he would have walked away from the transaction. The seller's reservation price is the smallest amount he would have accepted.

The "surplus" from any transaction is the difference between the buyer's and seller's reservation prices. In the pineapple example, if these reservation prices are, say, $1.20 and $0.80 respectively, the resulting surplus is 40 cents.

The traditional economic model says that exchange will occur if, and only if, there is a positive surplus—that is, if and only if the buyer's reservation price exceeds the seller's. Whenever an exchange does occur, the total surplus is divided between the buyer and seller. For the particular values assumed in the pineapple illustration, the surplus was allocated equally, both parties receiving 20 cents, or 50 percent of the total.

In the self-interest model, the reservation price for one party to a transaction is defined independently of the circumstances of the other. It makes no difference to the seller, in the traditional theory, whether the buyer is rich or poor: nor is the buyer assumed to care how much the seller might have paid for the thing he is now trying to sell. It is as if we imagined people who conduct all of their business with vending or purchasing machines. Each transactor is viewed in isolation, facing a take-it-or-leave-it decision that depends only on what the product itself is worth to him.

Using the notions of reservation price and surplus, we can construct the following operational definition of a fair transaction: *A fair transaction is one in which the surplus is divided (approximately) equally. The transaction becomes increasingly unfair as the division increasingly deviates from equality.* Simple as this definition seems, it is not always easy to apply. The most immediate problem is that reservation prices are often difficult to discern in practice. The art of bargaining, as most of us eventually learn, is in large part the art of sending misleading messages about them.

Much of the time, though, we will have at least a rough idea of what the relevant reservation prices are. But even if they are known precisely, not every transaction in which the surplus is divided evenly will necessarily seem fair. Psychologist Daniel Kahneman and economists Jack Knetsch and Richard Thaler have investigated people's attitudes about fairness in a variety of specific economic transactions, and in at least one instance their findings seem at odds with the simple fairness definition I suggest above. Specifically, they asked a large sample of subjects whether the landlord had acted fairly in the following scenario:

A landlord rents out a small house. When the lease is due for renewal, the landlord learns that the tenant has taken a job very close to the house and is therefore unlikely to move. The land-lord raises the rent $40 more than he was planning to.[2]

In this hypothetical example, the tenant's reservation price for the apartment has increased by virtue of the sudden increase in the value of its location. A $40 per month increase in rent would thus be fair, under my definition, if the increased value of the location were as little as $80 per month. And yet more than 90 percent of the subjects interviewed by Kahneman et al. responded that the landlord's action was unfair.[3] A richer theory of fairness would have to encompass attitudes about the role played by each party in generating the total surplus. People in the survey may have felt, for example, that the landlord was not entitled to a rent increase because he had not con-tributed in any way to the larger surplus. In any event, pre-vailing attitudes about fairness apparently do not require *every* surplus to be divided equally.

Some people may object to my proposed definition on the grounds that the seller's reservation price might be high for what they consider unjust reasons. It might be high, for example, simply because the seller knows that others are willing to pay a lot for it, even though it is a product he doesn't particularly need or even care about. This objection, however, seems directed more to the system of property rights under which the object was acquired than to the fairness of the price at which it sells. People who accept that the seller is entitled to sell the object in the first place will generally concede that it is fair to charge a price that many buyers would gladly pay. (Otherwise, a third party with no interest in the product could buy and quickly resell it at a profit.) Thus, for example, if the opening of a nearby subway stop made an apartment's location *generally* more valuable, most people would concede that at least some increase in rent would be fair.

Kahneman, Knetsch, and Thaler develop a more richly detailed theory of fairness than the simple account I sketch here, one that accommodates many of the subtle distinctions present in people's notions of fairness. My concern is less to accommodate these distinctions than to explore why it might be advantageous to care about fairness in the first place. But even my simple definition seems to accord reasonably well with many of our popular perceptions of fairness. My claim, in any event, is not that it is a particularly compelling definition but that, despite its obvious difficulties, it leads easily to a theory of behavior that clearly outperforms the self-interest model.

Suppose we assume that buyers care strongly about fairness as defined. In particular, suppose they have a strong aversion to receiving less than 50 percent of the surplus. (Many people, of course, will feel no difficulty about receiving *more* than half. But as we will see, a surprisingly large number choose a 50–50 split over one that gives them a larger share.) My simple definition of fairness, coupled with the assumed aversion to unfairness, yields a "fairness model" with the following specific prediction: *People will sometimes reject transactions in which the other party gets the lion's share of the surplus, even though the price at which the product sells may compare favorably with their own reservation price.*

In the self-interest model, of course, this can never happen. There, the division of the surplus simply plays no role in determining whether a transaction will take place. It will occur provided each party gets some positive share of the surplus, no matter how small. When Posner says fairness "has no content," this feature of the traditional model must be at least in part what he has in mind. Yet, as we will presently see, concerns about fairness repeatedly cause people to reject transactions with positive surplus.

THE COMMITMENT MODEL AND CONCERNS ABOUT FAIRNESS

Now, Posner and other rationalists would hardly deny that people *say* they care about fairness. But hardheaded economists treat such statements as mere verbiage, devoid of any power to predict behavior. They are committed to the view that beliefs about fairness will not prompt costly actions. It is one thing, they feel, to endorse fairness, but quite another to incur real costs on account of it.

There is seductive power in this view. After all, it really is *not* rational to refuse to buy something simply because the terms of the transaction are unfair. If it is selling for less than it is worth to you, your best bet is to swallow whatever aversion to unfairness you might have and buy it anyway.

But the rationalist view misses something important. In particular, the commitment model suggests that a self-interested person might do better if he *did* care about fairness. The reason is that people who don't are likely to be ineffective bargainers. The basic argument for this claim, recall, was introduced in Chapter 3. To recapitulate, suppose a person is given the following ultimatum: she can either accept a transaction in which she gets only 1 percent of the surplus or else reject it entirely. If she doesn't care about fairness, she will obviously accept. Any positive share of any surplus, she realizes, is better than none. The difficulty, of course, is that being *known* to feel that way is likely to affect the terms she gets in negotiations with others.

Imagine a board of directors that knew it was dealing with a union whose members did not care about fairness. It could then employ the following strategy: First, it could adopt a corporate charter under which only the fully assembled board is empowered to authorize wage increases. Next, it could meet and vote a wage equal to the union's "reservation wage" plus some small, token amount. (The employment transaction is in this respect like any other—both the buyer and seller have reservation wages. Their difference is the total surplus to be shared. The board's offer thus claims virtually all of this surplus for the owners of the firm.) Finally, the board members could disperse for extended vacations, making it impossible to reconvene. By so doing, they make it impossible to negotiate further. The union members must either accept the offer or refuse it. If they care only about absolute wealth, not about fairness, they will accept it.

By contrast, people who are known to care strongly about fairness are not vulnerable to stratagems of this sort. They will reject even profitable transactions when the terms are too heavily stacked against them. If the board of directors knew it was dealing with workers who felt that way, it would see nothing to gain by committing itself to one-sided wage offers.

The rationalist may object that this illustration is simplistic—that it ignores the fact that even someone who does not care about fairness may refuse profitable, but one-sidedly unfavorable, offers as a bargaining tactic. A truly rational person should be willing to accept losses now for the sake of establishing a reputation as a tough negotiator, thereby to receive more favorable terms in the future.

This objection has obvious force. Yet it faces two serious difficulties. First, it ignores the implementation problems inherent in strategies that trade current costs against future benefits. Recall from Chapter 4 that the psychological reward mechanism is strongly attuned to penalties and rewards that occur in the present moment. People may calculate that it would be rational to make sacrifices now to secure gains in the future and yet lack the motivation to carry out this strategy. For this reason, a person who assigns *intrinsic* value to the current sacrifice will have a clear advantage. A worker who dislikes working under an unfair contract, even when the alternative is worse in material terms, will be much more strongly motivated to endure the hardships of a strike or lockout. An added bonus is that if he is known to feel that way, he is much less likely to have to endure them.

A second difficulty with the rationalist's objection is that there are many situations where long-term strategic considerations simply play no role. Many transactions occur only once and involve actors who have no way of knowing how their partners have behaved in the past. In these situations, the issue of reputation is irrelevant.

Fortunately, reputation may not be the only way to solve the commitment problem. As we saw in Chapter 6, behavioral clues often reveal inner emotional states. Perhaps people who are concerned about fairness for its own sake are observably different from others. If so, the concern for fairness, and the willingness to act irrationally that follows from it, can yield material benefits even in one-shot bargaining encounters.

There are thus logically coherent reasons why the Posnerian rational actor might do worse than people who are willing to bear costs in the name of fairness. The question remains, however, whether people actually are willing to bear such costs. The evidence on this question could hardly be less equivocal.

ULTIMATUM BARGAINING EXPERIMENTS

Even though reservation prices are often difficult to determine in practice, it is possible to design experiments that remove all uncertainty about them. German economists Werner Guth, Rolf Schmittberger, and Bernd Schwarze have followed this strategy in a series of provocative studies.[4] One of their experiments, the so-called "ultimatum bargaining game," provides an elegant test of the self-interest model.

The game is played a single time by pairs of subjects who do not know one another. Player 1 in each pair is given a sum of money and asked to divide it between himself and player 2. He must propose an allocation, which player 2 must then either accept or refuse. If he accepts, they divide the money as proposed. If he refuses, however, neither player gets any money at all. Thus, for example, if player 1 proposes to divide $10 by allocating $3 to player 2 and the remaining $7 to himself, player 2 can either accept, in which case player 1 gets $7 and he gets $3; or he can refuse, in which case each gets nothing. Player 1's proposal is an ultimatum, hence the name of the game.

All of the relevant reservation prices and surpluses are transparently clear in the ultimatum bargaining game. The total surplus is simply the amount of money the two players have to divide. Player 2's reservation price, as reckoned by the traditional self-interest model, is the smallest possible positive amount, namely one cent. Since this is obvious to both players, the "rational" strategy for player 1 is also clear: he should offer player 2 a penny and keep the rest for himself. It is similarly rational for player 2 to accept—he knows they will not be playing this game repeatedly, so there is no point refusing the offer in hopes of establishing a tough reputation. The experimenters have neatly contrived a pure one-shot bargaining problem with which to test the rational theory of bargaining.

The findings from one version of their experiment are reproduced in Table 9.1. As indicated there, player 1 rarely employed the rational strategy. That is, he almost never proposed an extremely one-sided division. A 50–50 split was the most common allocation proposed, and in only 6 of 51 cases did player 1 demand more than 90 percent of the total. On the occasions when player 1 did claim an egregiously large share for himself, player 2 usually responded not as a Posnerian rationalist, but in the manner predicted by the fairness model. In five of the six cases where player 1 claimed more than 90 percent, for example, player 2 chose to settle for nothing.

TABLE 9.1. The Ultimatum Bargaining Game

	ACTUAL	PREDICTED BY RATIONAL CHOICE MODEL
Average percentage of total demanded by player 1 (*N*=51)	67.1	99 +
Percentage of proposed 50–50 splits (*N*=13)	25.5	0
Percentage of total proposals rejected by player 2 (*N*=11)	21.5	0
Average percentage demanded by player 1 in rejected proposals (*N*=11)	85.3	100
Average percentage demanded by player 1 in accepted proposals (*N*=40)	61.0	99 +
Percentage of player 1 demands greater than 90% (*N*=6)	11.8	100

Source: Guth et al., 1982, Tables 3–5.

The Guth experiments leave several issues incompletely resolved. One problem is that player 2 was rarely put to a severe test: most of the time, player 1 made a reasonably fair proposal, which player 2 then accepted. It would be nice to know more about how people behave when presented with an unfair ultimatum. Another difficulty concerns possible spillovers in future interactions. Even though the game was played only once between subjects who did not know one another, some subjects may nonetheless have shown restraint because of concern about future costs. Occasionally, for example, player 2 may have been a person player 1 hoped to get to know in the future. Or perhaps player 1 feared player 2 would somehow find a way to retaliate for a one-sided proposal. Player 1's main concern might have been purely selfish, merely to forestall player 2's rejection; or, more charitably, he might have thought it "right" to show restraint.

Light is shed on all of these issues by a series of experiments conducted by Kahneman, Knetsch, and Thaler.[5] To learn more about how people respond to unfair proposals, Kahneman et al. began by asking subjects to divide $10 in a very similar ultimatum bargaining game. Their design differed from that of Guth et al. in that they asked player 1 to limit his choice to pairs from the following list:

> $9.50 for player 1, $0.50 for player 2
> $9.00 for player 1, $1.00 for player 2
> $8.50 for player 1, $1.50 for player 2
>
> · · ·
>
> $5.00 for player 1, $5.00 for player 2

From the same list, they asked player 2 to indicate the least favorable division he would accept. Thus, even in the majority of cases where player 1 makes a fair proposal, it still possible to determine the limits of player 2's tolerance. The findings for one of their samples are summarized in Table 9.2. As indicated, player 2 was willing to accept an average penalty of almost 26 percent of the total surplus rather than participate on the short end of a one-sided bargain.

TABLE 9.2. Minimum Acceptable Offers in Ultimatum Bargaining

Total to be divided ($N=43$)	$10.00
Average amount offered by player 1	$4.76
50–50 offers	81%
Average minimum acceptable offer for player 2	$2.59

Source: Kahneman et al., 1986a, Table 1.

Kahneman et al. used another simple experiment to explore the motivation for making fair offers. Player 1 was asked to divide $20 between himself and an anonymous player 2. He was limited to these two choices: (1) $10 for each; or (2) $18 for himself, $2 for player 2. This time, player 2 did not have the option of rejecting player 1's proposal. Player 2 got either $2 or $10, depending solely on player 1's choice. Assurance was given that player 2s would not learn the identities of player 1s.

Out of 161 subjects, 122, or 76 percent, proposed the even split. Since the design of the experiment completely eliminated both fear of rejection and any threat of retaliation, Kahneman et al. conclude that an intrinsic concern about fairness was the primary motive for these allocations.

Similar uncertainty surrounds player 2's motives for rejecting a one-sided offer. An obvious possibility is that he wishes to punish player 1 for being greedy. Or perhaps he just wants to avoid participating in an unfair transaction. To find out more about what drives player 2, Kahneman et al. conducted a second stage to the preceding experiment. In the followup stage, subjects selected from the first stage were placed in groups of three. Each group contained at least one subject of each type from the first stage—that is, one who picked the even split *(E)*, and another who chose the uneven split *(U)*.

The third member of each group was then given the following choice: He could either divide $12 evenly with *U*, or else divide $10 evenly with *E*. Most of the subjects (74 percent) chose to split $10 with *E*. Most people, in other words, were willing to incur a cost of $1 in order to punish *U* and reward *E*. Of the subjects who had themselves chosen the $10–$10 split in the first stage, an even larger percentage (88 percent) chose this more costly option in the second stage. Kahneman et al. conclude that the motive for rejecting unfair offers must be at least in part to punish those who make them.

There are a number of recent studies that have produced findings similar to the ones discussed above.[6] None of these findings, needless to say, is very sympathetic to the Posnerian view of fairness.

FAIR PRICES IN THE MARKETPLACE

The power of concerns about fairness to motivate costly action is not limited to contrived bargaining games. It applies as well in the case of ordinary products traded in the marketplace. To explore people's attitudes about fair prices, Thaler administered the following pair of questions to two groups of participants in an executive training program.[7] The first group responded to the version with the passages in parentheses, the second to the ones in brackets.

> You are lying on the beach on a hot day . . . For the past hour you have been thinking about how much you would enjoy a nice cold bottle of your favorite brand of beer. A companion gets up to make a phone call and offers to bring back a beer from the only nearby place where beer is sold, (a fancy resort hotel) [a run-down grocery store]. He says that the beer might be expensive and so asks how much you would be willing to pay for the beer. He says he will buy the beer if it costs as much or less than the price you state, but if it costs more than the price you state he will not buy it. You trust your friend, and there is no chance of bargaining with the (bartender) [storeowner]. What price do you state?[8]

Note that the price sought in these questions is the potential buyer's reservation price for the beer. The self-interest model states unequivocally that this figure should not depend on who is selling the beer. And yet the median response for the resort hotel group ($2.65) was over a dollar more than for the grocery group (1.50). Both beers will be consumed on the same beach on the same hot day by the same thirsty people. The only difference lies in where the beer is purchased. Having the beer is worth $2.65 to the median respondent in the resort hotel group, and yet the median respondent in the grocery store group would refuse to pay even $2 for it.

Thaler emphasizes that concerns about fairness seem to be the driving force here. And sure enough, the simple fairness model accommodates these findings without difficulty. The resort hotel, having higher operating costs than the grocery, has a correspondingly higher reservation price for its beer. Even though it charges a higher price, it thus does not command a larger share of the surplus. In terms of our simple definition, a fair price at the resort hotel is higher than at the grocery. Contrary to the self-interest model, the identity of the seller is apparently not a matter of indifference to the buyer.

There is evidence that the attitudes reflected in these responses make themselves felt in the pricing decisions of profit-seeking firms. The most conspicuous examples have to do with seasonal and other demand-related variations in prices. To appreciate the force of these examples, it is necessary first to consider what the self-interest model has to say about costs and prices during peak demand periods.

Ski resorts, which experience considerable variations in demand, provide a convenient context for this discussion. As every skier is well aware, crowds at ski resorts are heaviest during holiday weekends. Ski operators obviously know this, too, and their initial investments in both total acreage and lift capacity are chosen with these peak demand periods clearly in mind. The result is that, during slack times, there is much more capacity than required. The slopes are nearly empty and lift lines virtually nonexistent.

On the basis of such observations, economists say that visitors during peak times are responsible—in the causal sense— for almost all of the costs associated with the ski area's capacity. For if it were not for these holiday weekend users, the area could provide adequate service with much smaller capacity. By contrast, if some visitors during uncrowded periods were to stay away, the ski resort would save nothing on capacity costs, which simply do not depend on the size of the off-peak crowds.

Economic theory says also that users who are responsible for a given cost should be the ones to pay for it. This means that virtually all of the capacity costs of the resort should be borne by holiday weekend users. Now, ski resorts usually do charge somewhat higher prices during holiday periods. But the price differentials are usually small, certainly much smaller than predicted by the traditional economic theory of cost allocation. Also contrary to the traditional theory, long lift lines and crowded slopes are all but universal during holiday periods.

The reluctance of ski operators to boost their holiday prices apparently has to do with customer perceptions of fairness. Sad to say, the average skier is unfamiliar with the economic theory of how costs should be apportioned across periods of varying demand. It is natural for most people to focus on the fact that the lifts cost the same to operate no matter what day of the season it is. Much less salient is the issue of who is responsible for a resort having the capacity it does. This perception about costs leads the typical skier to believe it unfair for the ski operator to charge a dramatically higher price during holiday weekends.

But if excess demand is so high during these weekends, why do ski operators *care* what skiers think about fairness? Why not just raise the rates anyway and earn the extra revenues? Even if ski operators could earn more on holiday weekends, it does not necessarily follow that their best overall strategy is to raise peak rates. They must be concerned that high holiday prices may alienate visitors who ski not only on holiday weekends but during slack periods as well. In the words of one ski industry consultant, "If you gouge them at Christmas time, they won't come back in March."[9]

"Insufficient" price variation is by no means peculiar to the ski industry. Similar economic reasoning dictates sharp price premiums for haircuts on Saturday mornings, and yet most barbershops still charge the same price at all hours of the week. Tickets to the Super Bowl, the World Series, championship prize fights, the U.S. Open, Rolling Stones concerts and a host of other sporting and entertainment events are invariably in short supply. The most popular restaurants in big cities require several weeks notice for reservations on a Saturday night. Hit plays are sold out months in advance. And true to their name, movie blockbusters draw queues several city blocks long. Pricing patterns in all of these instances differ substantially from the ones predicted by the self-interest model. And in every case, concerns about fairness appear to explain much of the discrepancy. The rationalist, who disdains concerns about fairness, has no satisfactory explanation for these widespread pricing patterns.

WAGES AND PROFITS

Concerns about fairness influence not only the prices we pay but also the wages we receive. On the average, firms with higher profit rates pay higher wages. Economists have been aware of this correlation for many decades.[10] The difficulty is that the self-interest model states unequivocally that profit rates should *not* affect wages. Workers, under the self-interest model, are supposed to be paid the value of what they produce. Those who produce a lot should get high wages, and vice versa. This should be true no matter whether their employers' profits are above or below average.

The logic behind the self-interest model's prediction seems compelling. If a firm paid less than the value of what a worker produced, it should eventually lose him to a competitor. And if it paid more, it would earn lower profits than if it hadn't hired him in the first place. The self-interest model would predict that if highly profitable firms paid more, workers from less profitable firms would apply to them in droves; and that the resulting movements would tend to equalize wages, thus eliminating any correlation with profit rates. Because the self-interest model states so clearly that profit rates should not matter, many economists who study wage movements simply omit any mention of profits. The problem, which refuses to go away, is that profits clearly do matter.

Here, too, the incompatibility between theory and observation seems to have something to do with concerns about fairness. Recall that the employment transaction resembles others in that both parties have their respective reservation prices. For the worker, it is the lowest wage he would accept before going off in search of work elsewhere. For the firm, it is the highest wage it could pay before becoming unprofitable. Everyone concedes that the unusually profitable firm has the ability to pay higher wages. The difference between the two reservation prices, which is the total surplus available for the firm and its workers to divide, will thus increase with the firm's profitability.

Although the more profitable firm has the ability to pay higher wages, the self-interest model perceives no motive for it to do so. The fairness model, however, suggests one. Note that if the firm with a strong market position pays only as much as other firms do, it will garner a disproportionate share of the total surplus—an "unfair" share in terms of my simple definition. Thus, if workers care strongly about the fairness of the labor contract, as other evidence suggests, they will require a wage premium for working for the more profitable firm. The other side of this coin is that they are often content to work for less when the employer has lower than average profits. The fairness model implies that workers are willing to give up income in the name of fairness, and it is this willingness that forces the more profitable firm to pay higher wages.

The correlation between wage and profit rates shows no signs of going away. It will continue to embarrass economists who insist that concerns about fairness never translate into costly actions.

FAIRNESS AND STATUS

Concerns about fairness are also reflected in the sacrifices workers must make in order to occupy high-ranked positions among their coworkers.[11] The argument in support of this claim rests on two simple assumptions: (1) most people prefer high-ranked to low-ranked positions among their coworkers; and (2) no one can be forced to remain in a firm against his wishes.

By the laws of simple arithmetic, not everyone's preference for high rank can be satisfied. Only 50 percent of the members of any group can be in the top half. But if people are free to associate with whomever they please, why are the lesser-ranked members of groups content to remain? Why don't they all leave to form new groups of their own in which they would no longer be near the bottom? Many workers undoubtedly do precisely that. And yet we also observe many stable, heterogeneous groups. Not all accountants at General Motors are equally talented; and in every law firm, some partners attract much more new business than others. If everyone prefers to be near the top of his or her group of coworkers, what holds these heterogeneous groups together?

The apparent answer is that their low-ranked members receive extra compensation. If they were to leave, they would gain by no longer having to endure low status. By the same token, however, the top-ranked members would lose. They would no longer enjoy high status. If their gains from having high rank are larger than the costs borne by members with low rank, it does not make sense for the group to disband. Everyone can do better if the top-ranked workers induce their lesser-ranked colleagues to remain by sharing some of their pay with them.

Not everyone assigns the same value to having high rank. Those who care relatively less about it will do best to join firms in which most workers are more productive than themselves.*

---

*The term "rank" here is used to denote rank in the firm's productivity distribution. Thus, for example, a "high-ranked" worker is one who is more productive than most other workers in the firm.

As lesser-ranked members in these firms, they will receive extra compensation. People who care most strongly about rank, by contrast, will want to join firms in which most other workers are less productive than themselves. For the privilege of occupying top-ranked positions in those firms, they will have to work for less than the value of what they produce.

Workers are thus able to sort themselves among a hierarchy of firms in accordance with their demands for within-firm status. Figure 9.1 depicts the menu of choices confronting workers whose productivity takes a given value, M. The heavy lines represent the wage schedules offered by three different firms. They tell how much a worker with a given productivity would be paid in each firm. The average productivity level is highest in firm 3, next highest in firm 2, and lowest in firm 1. The problem facing persons with productivity level M is to choose which of these three firms to work for.

Workers who care most about status will want to "purchase" high-ranked positions like the one labeled "A" in firm 1. In such positions, they work for less than the value of what they produce. By contrast, those who care least about status will elect to receive wage premiums by working in low-ranked positions like the one labeled "C" in firm 3. Workers with moderate con-

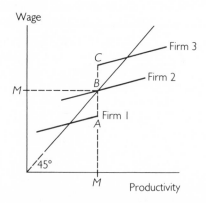

FIGURE 9.1   The Wage Structure When Local Status Matters

cerns about local rank will be attracted to intermediate positions like the one labeled *"B"* in firm 2, for which they neither pay nor receive any compensation for local rank.

Note also in Figure 9.1 that even though not every worker in each firm is paid the value of what he or she produces, workers taken as a group nonetheless do receive the value of what they produce. The extra compensation received by each firm's low-ranked workers is exactly offset by the shortfall in pay of its high-ranked workers.

The self-interest model, by contrast, says that *every* worker is paid the value of what he or she produces. Yet in every firm and occupation for which the relevant data are available, high-ranked workers are paid less than the value of what they produce, while low-ranked workers are paid more. The difference, in large measure, represents the price a high (low)-ranked worker pays (receives) for the position he or she occupies in the firm's internal hierarchy.

This egalitarian pattern of wages within firms has often been justified by noneconomists in the name of fairness. But there is a specific sense in which this justification ought to be intelligible even to flint-eyed commentators like Richard Posner. Suppose, contrary to fact but in line with the predictions of the self-interest model, that all workers were paid the value of what they produce. The top-ranked workers in each firm would then enjoy their positions of high rank free of charge; and bottom-ranked workers, in turn, would suffer the disutility of low rank without compensation. High local rank is something of value whose existence is made possible solely by the willingness of others to endure low local rank. By any accepted meaning of the term fairness, it is not fair for one person to benefit free of charge from a cost borne by another. Any rationalist who accepts the preceding statement must thus also accept that the wage structure implied by the self-interest model is not fair. It is one in which all of the surplus goes to the high-ranked workers.

How large are the wage deviations that occur in the name of

fairness? The answer will be different for different occupations. In occupations in which coworkers do not associate closely with one another, people will not be willing to pay much for a high-ranked position. After all, the comparisons that most matter are those between people who interact most intensively. The price paid for high rank (and received for low rank) will be highest in occupations where coworkers work closely together for extended periods.

The self-interest model says that a worker's wage should go up by a dollar each time she adds a dollar to the value of the firm's production. The fairness model, by contrast, predicts that the wage will rise by less than a dollar for each extra dollar of value produced. It says further that the difference between productivity and pay will increase with the extensiveness of interaction between coworkers.

Table 9.3 presents estimates of the rates at which earnings rise with productivity for three occupations. The occupations are listed in increasing order of closeness of interaction. Real estate salespersons, who have the least intensive contact, pay the lowest amounts for high-ranked positions. At the other end of the spectrum, research chemists, who work together in close-knit groups for extended periods, pay very large sums indeed. In the sample studied, the most productive chemists accounted for over $200,000 more in revenues each year than their least productive colleagues, yet received only slightly

TABLE 9.3. Pay *vs.* Productivity for Three Occupations

OCCUPATION	EXTRA EARNINGS PER EXTRA DOLLAR OF PRODUCTION	
	ACTUAL	PREDICTED BY SELF-INTEREST MODEL
Real estate sales	$0.70	$1.00
Automobile sales	$0.24	$1.00
Research chemists	<$0.09	$1.00

Source: Frank, 1985, Chapter 4.

higher salaries.[12] Auto salespersons do not associate nearly as intensively as chemists but, unlike real estate salespersons, they do spend their working hours together in the same location. Just as predicted, the price of high-ranked positions for auto salespersons lies between those of the other two occupations.

Here again, the self-interest model fails, and by a wide margin. And once more, concerns about fairness appear to play a central role.

None of the evidence discussed in this chapter says that material costs and benefits are unimportant. On the contrary, the commitment model's main emphasis is that rational behavior does not always prevail because it so often stands in the way of material gain. An intrinsic concern about fairness will sometimes motivate people to act irrationally. But in so doing, it can also steer them into situations that are materially advantageous.

Not all of the actions people undertake in the name of fairness have this benign property. They will surely not have it when popular perceptions of fairness are erroneous, as they often appear to be. If people had greater economic sophistication about how to assign responsibility for capacity costs, for example, I believe their perceptions of fairness would often change. Ski operators would become free to shift more of their costs onto peak-period users, which, in turn, would cut holiday crowds and reduce capacity requirements. In the end, skiers as a group would benefit. Similar benefits could be had in many other industries if misperceptions of fairness did not prevent prices from varying with the intensity of demand.

In many circumstances, however, popular perceptions of fairness and the underlying realities appear one and the same. We may feel certain, for example, that no amount of economic education will alter the fact that top-ranked workers must share part of what they produce with their lesser-ranked coworkers.

Nor will greater economic sophistication prevent a worker from choosing a wage cut in preference to a job in which the employer claims virtually all of the employment surplus.

Whether perceptions are accurate or not, it is clear from the evidence that concerns about fairness strongly affect people's behavior. Posnerians and others who insist that fairness has no content are talking about a world that does not exist.

TEN

LOVE

Many people believe selfless love is the motivating force behind intimate personal relationships. The worldly economist, however, takes a predictably less sentimental view. In his landmark *A Treatise on the Family,* University of Chicago economist Gary Becker writes, "An efficient marriage market develops 'shadow' prices to guide participants to marriages that will maximize their expected well-being."[1] In Becker's scheme, people with stable, well-defined preferences act in purposeful ways to choose mates that best promote their material interests.

The materialist view of human relationships is by no means confined to economists. On the contrary, it has become a hot import item in other social sciences. Increasing numbers of psychologists, sociologists, political scientists, anthropologists, and other behavioral scientists have begun to view intimate relationships as purposeful exchanges in which each party receives something of value.

Sociologist Michael Hannan, for example, writes that "Becker's stark economic conception of actions cuts through the romantic mist that so often blinds social scientists to the hard choices faced by families and their members."[2] Sociologists George Homans[3] and Peter Blau[4] penetrated that mist decades earlier, and their work on "exchange relationships" continues to have wide influence among sociologists and social psychologists. Psychologist Harold Kelley, himself a pioneer of the cost-benefit school,[5] writes that a "person remains in [a] relationship as long as the pros outweigh the cons."[6] Ellen Berscheid, a leading psychologist in the field of interpersonal relations, writes that the degree of emotional involvement in a relationship is a function of "facilitative interconnections" and "meshed interchain sequences."[7] And in a passage that could easily have been lifted from Adam Smith, a prominent book on equity in personal relationships begins by saying that "Man is selfish. Individuals will try to maximize their outcomes."[8] Psychologist Daniel Goleman nicely summarizes the continuing trend: "In recent years, the mainstream of psychological research has looked at love almost as if it were a business transaction, a matter of profit and loss."[9]

The view that personal relationships are like ordinary goods and services has drawn bitter criticism.[10] Most critics simply reject the materialistic orientation of the rational choice framework. I will argue, however, that the exchange model is much more effectively challenged on its own terms. We can shed its most troublesome aspects without abandoning the assumption that material payoffs play a pivotal role in shaping behavior. But before laying out the details of the argument and evidence, it will be helpful first to look at some of the reasoning that motivates the economic approach to personal relationships.

THE MARKET FOR RELATIONSHIPS

The materialist view of relationships is hardly new. We see it, for example, in the familiar practice whereby people rate the attractiveness of persons of the opposite sex by assigning them numbers between 1 and 10. These attractiveness ratings, or something essentially like them, are the shadow prices in Becker's efficient marriage market. If participants follow the rule of thumb, "Marry the most attractive person who will have you," the result will be assortative mating. The 10s will pair with other 10s, the 9s with other 9s, and so on.

At one level, many of us want to say it is a gross insult to suppose that the countless rich dimensions of a person could thus be captured on a single numerical scale; or that such a number could somehow represent the essence of what transpires between people in love. Many of us may also lament the inflated role played by physical appearance, especially in environments where people do not know one another well. And yet no one would deny that some people are generally more sought after as potential marriage partners, and would remain so even in environments with perfect information.

Most people want mates who are kind, caring, healthy, intelligent, physically attractive, and so on. Everyone will assign his or her own weights to each of these qualities. But given a set of weights, there is at least a rough sense in which it is meaningful to speak of the overall attractiveness of a person. The concept of an overall attractiveness rating makes it clear that an implicit tradeoff exists between the various traits people value. For example, two people may be regarded as equally attractive even though one is less physically attractive, but more intelligent, than the other.

The coin of the realm in the relationship market is each person's own overall attractiveness rating. This is the "endowment" with which she or he shops for a mate. Some elements of this endowment are acquired, others inherited. It is possible, for example, to make oneself a more attractive person by becoming better informed, or by cultivating a more caring and gracious posture toward others. At the same time, however, there are obvious limits beyond which such traits as intelligence or physical appearance cannot be manipulated. Elevator shoes and shoulder pads may help in some settings, but are of little use at the beach. Inevitably, the distribution of endowments in the relationship market will display painful inequities.

The same is true, of course, of the distribution of cash incomes that support participation in markets for ordinary goods and services. Most economists make no claims of fairness on behalf of the distributions of endowments in any of the markets they study. Instead, their claims focus on efficiency, and take roughly this form: *For a given distribution of endowments, free trade between self-serving individuals will maximize welfare.* By "maximize welfare," economists mean that no alternative arrangement exists that would improve one person's lot without simultaneously injuring others.

Becker's marriage market purports to be efficient in this specific sense. There is no claim that it is fair. But if we set aside our concerns about the distribution of endowments, we discover that it nonetheless metes out a certain rough justice. A given endowment in the marriage market, after all, can purchase only so much: to marry someone with a pretty face, one must be willing to settle for fewer of the other desirable traits. There is thus a genuine advantage in being someone who cares more about inner traits of character than about straight noses or smooth complexions. For with a given endowment, such a person can "purchase" a mate who is more thoughtful, intelligent, and caring. By comparison, someone who is more concerned about mere physical appearance must settle for less of these qualities.*

The economic details of the search for prospective marriage partners are interesting in their own right, often involving the signaling issues we encountered in Chapter 5. As with the toad that had to estimate the size of his rivals in the dark, the problem here, too, is that many key traits are difficult to observe. In the relationship market, the crafty searcher will look for behavioral signals that reveal them. In Chapter 5, we saw that for a signal to be effective, it must be costly to fake. Someone who is looking, say, for a highly disciplined partner might thus do well to take special interest in people who run marathons in less than two and a half hours.

Even the degree of interest a person shows in a prospective

---

*This conclusion rests on the conventional view that a preference for a smooth complexion is somehow less worthy of respect than a preference for thoughtfulness. On the alternative view that preferences for various attributes are equally worthy of respect, the same conclusion obviously would not follow. Indeed, one could just as easily say that there would be advantage in not caring about intelligence, because then one would get a more physically attractive mate.

partner will sometimes reveal a lot. Groucho Marx once said he wouldn't join any club that would have him as a member. To follow a similar strategy in the search for a relationship would obviously result in frustration. And yet Marx was clearly onto something. There may be good reasons for avoiding a seemingly attractive searcher who is too eager. If this person is as attractive as he or she seems, why such eagerness? Such a posture will often suggest unfavorable values for traits that are difficult to observe. The properties of effective signals thus make it clear why coyness, within limits, is so adaptive in the market for relationships.

The same properties tell us something about the institutional arrangements under which people search for partners. An oft-decried difficulty of modern urban life is that heavy work schedules make it hard for people to meet one another. In response, commercial dating services offer to match people with ostensibly similar interests and tastes. Participants in these services are thus spared the time and expense of getting to know people with whom they have few interests in common. They also avoid uncertainty about whether their prospective partner is interested in meeting someone. And yet, while marriages do sometimes result from commercial dating services, the consensus appears to be that they are a bad investment. The apparent reason is that, without meaning to, they act as a screening device that identifies people who have trouble initiating their own relationships. To be sure, sometimes a participant's trouble is merely that he is too busy. But often it is the result of personality problems or other, more worrisome difficulties. People who participate in dating services are indeed easier to meet, just as the advertisements say. But signaling theory says that, on the average, they are less worth meeting.

LOVE AS AN IRRATIONAL FORCE

The exchange model of close personal relationships leaves many outsiders scratching their heads. Can the exchange theorists possibly be serious? Their views certainly do stand in sharp contrast to traditional views about love. In his novel *Clea*, for example, Lawrence Durrell offers this picture:

> It may be defined as a cancerous growth of unknown origin which may take up its site anywhere without the subject knowing or wishing it. How often have you tried to love the "right" person in vain, even when your heart knows it has found him after so much seeking? No, an eyelash, a perfume, a haunting walk, a strawberry on the neck, the smell of almonds on the breath—these are the accomplices the spirit seeks out to plan your overthrow.[11]

In the same vein, Douglas Yates tells us, "People who are sensible about love are incapable of it." Pascal, too, was no friend of the rationalists when he wrote, "The heart has its reasons which reason knows nothing of."

Our traditional notions of love, in short, could hardly be any less compatible with the cool, deliberative tones of the self-interest model. Yet, despite bitter objections from traditionalists, the economist's approach continues to flourish.

THE PREDICTIVE POWER OF THE SELF-INTEREST MODEL

How are we to reconcile traditional views of love with the continuing inroads of the exchange model? Despite widespread discomfort with the cost-benefit approach, it has prospered on the strength of its ability to predict and explain behavior. One of its predictions is that families with a given income will have fewer children as the market value of the mother's time increases. Precisely this relationship has been found in numerous studies.[12] It also successfully predicts that women with high earning power will be more likely to divorce, as will women who live in states with generous welfare benefits.[13] And it successfully predicts that men with higher incomes tend to marry at younger ages.[14] The traditionalists, by contrast, say merely that people marry and have children because of love. With some justification, the exchange theorists find such pronouncements distressingly vague.

The market model not only makes detailed predictions about behavior, it even offers practical insights for the lovelorn. A colleague once told me about a close friend who complained that her love life was mysteriously perverse. "Why is it," she asked, "that the people I fall in love with are never interested in *me*, whereas the ones who do fall in love with me are never the ones *I* care about?" My colleague knew the woman well, and felt free to offer this candid assessment: "You're an 8 constantly chasing after 10s," he explained, "and constantly being chased by 6s." By the woman's own account, this one-sentence "analysis" proved more helpful than years of psychological counseling had.

If, as the traditional view insists, irrationality is an essential ingredient of the emotion of love, why does the self-interest model tell us so much about what people *do* in love relationships? The commitment model suggests not that the self-interest model is wrong, but that it leaves out something important. A ruthless application of it implies important limitations on the ability of self-seeking actors to achieve material objectives in love relationships. As in earlier chapters, the difficulty again stems from the commitment problem: being known always to pursue self-interest often forecloses valuable opportunities, ones that can be exploited only in the presence of a commitment to forego maximum advantage.

A SIMILAR PROBLEM IN THE RENTAL HOUSING MARKET

The nature of the difficulty is very clearly illustrated by a similar problem encountered in the market for rental housing. That market shares several important features with the informal market for marriage partners. Both are characterized by incomplete information on both sides of the exchange. Just as it takes time and effort to meet people and get to know them, so it takes time and effort to discover which dwellings are available and what they are like. For the landlord's part, it takes time to interview tenants to discover how responsible they are and how much rent they will pay.

Because time and other resources are scarce, it generally will not make sense to visit each vacant apartment or to interview every potential tenant. By visiting only a small sample, apartment-seekers can get an approximate idea of what types of units are available at what prices. Landlords, similarly, can get some idea of the distribution of available tenants without interviewing everyone.

Based on their estimates of the relevant distributions, landlords and tenants can sensibly choose thresholds for terminating their searches. Once a sufficiently good tenant or apartment comes along, it will not pay to look further. The threshold that defines "good" here will naturally depend on circumstance. Apartment seekers with free time on their hands, for example, will want to search longer than others. Similarly, landlords who rent furnished apartments with many breakable items will want to spend more time interviewing.

Whatever the circumstances of any particular searcher, once he encounters his threshold quality level, it will be rational to stop looking. This will be true even though, in the tenant's case, there is *certain* to be a better apartment for less rent available somewhere; and even though, in the landlord's, there is sure to exist some other tenant who is both more responsible and willing to pay more.

The match between tenant and landlord does not stop with their having found one another. The standard practice includes the additional step of signing a lease, a formal contract that fixes the rent and other terms for a specific period. Why this commitment? If both parties were sure they had found the best possible match, a lease would not be necessary. The tenant would have no incentive to leave, nor would the landlord ever want him to. The problem is that neither party has any such assurance. Having agreed to move in, the tenant might stumble onto a much better deal, acceptance of which would force the landlord to begin his costly search anew. The tenant faces a parallel risk.

On the tenant's side, it is not merely the costs of search that are in jeopardy. Often he will wish to tailor the dwelling to his own tastes. The costs of paint, curtains, and other custom furnishings will be well worth it to him if he can stay for an extended period. But he will not be willing to make these investments without the protection afforded by a lease.

Both the landlord and the tenant realize that they would strike a less favorable bargain if each were to remain free to pursue his own interests. The tenant would not be willing to pay as much rent without the security of a lease, nor would the landlord be willing to accept as little. They each thus have a clear material incentive to limit their options. They face a commitment problem of the familiar sort. The landlord does not *want* to be able to remove his tenant the moment a better one comes along. The tenant, similarly, does not want to be able to leave if a better apartment turns up. Unrestricted rational choice would result in a worse outcome for both of them. A lease is not a perfect way of solving their commitment problem, but it works well enough.

THE COMMITMENT PROBLEM IN THE RELATIONSHIP MARKET

The parallels between the rental housing market and the market for personal relationships are clear. The exchange model views each participant in the relationship market as searching for the best partner his or her endowment will command. Information about prospective partners is notoriously incomplete, much more so than in the rental housing market. Even if a person knew exactly what he or she was looking for, many of the relevant traits would remain exceedingly difficult to discover.

The implication is that exhaustive search, even if physically possible, would be economically wasteful. As in the rental housing market, searchers in the relationship market employ limited samples to get some idea of the distribution of potentially available partners. Signals of the sort discussed earlier may play an important role. On the basis of their estimates of the relevant distributions, searchers then choose a threshold quality level. A match occurs, finally, with the pairing of two searchers who meet or exceed one another's thresholds. As in the rental housing case, each party will generally feel sure that there is a better partner out there somewhere. But again, it simply does not pay to look further.

At this point, each party has a strong motive for making a commitment to the relationship for an extended period. For here, even more than in the rental housing case, each has a compelling interest in making investments whose success depends on the relationship's survival. The rearing of children is the most obvious one, but there are also many others. They will wish, for example, to accumulate joint property, much of which would be difficult or impossible to divide if they were to separate. It is easy enough to replace the missing half of a record collection, but what can take the place of a painting each has come to treasure?

Just as most societies have rental leases, most also have formal marriage contracts. The terms of these contracts vary widely. Some, such as Ireland's, make it all but impossible to divorce. Most others are much more liberal, but almost all impose nontrivial penalties. In view of the clear reasons marriage partners have for wanting to limit their own future options, it is easy to see why so many societies have adopted this institution.

Even so, two important forces limit what can be accomplished by the formal marriage contract. The first is the natural desire to let people terminate irretrievably broken marriages. Our mutual interest in making long-term investments does not dictate that we prevent *all* forms of marriage termination, only those that involve opportunistic switching of marriage partners. The problem is that any contract lenient enough to allow termination of hopeless marriages cannot at the same time be strict enough to prevent opportunistic switching. By varying the strictness of the contract, we serve one goal only at the expense of the other.

The second limitation involves enforcement. The state can do only so much to alter the behavior of persons who do not want to remain in their marriages. It can fine them, it can make them endure bureaucratic red tape, it can even make it illegal to divorce. But it cannot force them to live under the same roof in a mutually supportive manner.

We confront essentially the same limitation in the labor market. Often it would pay corporations to invest heavily in job training, provided they could be sure workers would remain for extended periods. Nonetheless, we do not permit long-term, binding labor contracts. A warehouse can be leased for 99 years, but a worker cannot be leased for 99 seconds. If the circumstances that led people to sign the warehouse lease were to change, only property would be at stake. We would still be willing to enforce the original contract, even if its terms suddenly became highly burdensome to one of the parties. We are not willing, however, to insist that someone continue at a job that has been made repugnant by altered circumstances. Nor would there be any practical legal means to do so. Virtually all employees enjoy sufficient discretion on the job to make a nuisance of themselves without violating any rules; and as a result, employers have no material incentive to force them to stay on against their will. It is the same, in effect, with marriage contracts.

The difficulty that confronts the exchange model of intimate relationships may thus be summarized as follows: Because search is costly, it is rational to settle on a partner before having examined all potential candidates. Once a partner is chosen, however, the relevant circumstances will often change. (A more attractive partner may come along, a partner may become disabled, and so on.) The resulting uncertainty makes it imprudent to undertake joint investments that would otherwise be strongly in each party's interest. In order to facilitate these investments, each party wants to make a binding commitment to remain in the relationship. But practical difficulties stand in the way of their doing so through the legal system.

LOVE AS A SOLUTION TO THE COMMITMENT PROBLEM

Fortunately, the problem can be attacked in another way. The alternative approach is emotional rather than legalistic. It is epitomized in the Aztec Two-Step song lyric, "There'll always be a faster gun, but there'll never be another one like you." The worry that people will leave relationships because it may later become rational for them to do so is largely erased if it is not rational assessment that binds them in the first place. Objective personal characteristics may continue to play a role in determining which people are initially most attracted to one another, as much evidence suggests. But the poets are surely correct that the bond we call love does not consist of rational deliberations about these characteristics. It is instead an intrinsic bond, one in which the person is valued for his or her own sake. And precisely therein lies its value as a solution to the commitment problem.

If your wife married you merely because you offered the most favorable exchange possibilities, she would quickly leave you if Tom Selleck bought the house next door and announced his availability. (Even if Selleck then left *her,* she could still get a lucrative book contract out of the experience.) But if she married you because she loved you, there would be at least a reasonable chance she would remain. This assurance frees people to undertake the joint investments that make up such an important part of successful marriage relationships.

Just as love may act as a carrot by causing people to *want* to remain in relationships, it may also act as a stick by punishing them for leaving. More specifically, bonds of affection may accomplish this by means of a complementary relationship with guilt. As noted, to break a promise to a stranger elicits guilt in most people. But even stronger guilt feelings are induced by breaking a promise to a friend. And guilt will be most strongly summoned by disloyalty to a beloved person. With this in mind, it is no mystery that the transactions that most require trust so often involve people who love one another.

LOVE AND THE IMPLEMENTATION PROBLEM

Relationships based on selfless love enjoy an additional advantage over those based on rational exchange, one that stems from the nature of human motivation. Recall from Chapter 3 that rational assessment is merely one of many inputs into the psychological reward mechanism. Rational calculations often lose out to other, more basic forms of reinforcement. We saw, for example, that part of the motivation to eat involves biochemical forces that are little connected to the material payoffs from food intake. The overweight person may know it is in his interest to eat less, but must nonetheless contend with his appetite.

Sexual motivation is little different. Arousal is mediated partly, but only partly, by rational forces. Although many people are apparently reluctant to admit it, much of the rest is simply hard-wired. Biologists John Krebs and Richard Dawkins note the smug superiority many people express when they see an animal respond mechanically to some environmental stimulus.[15] We are amused, for example, by the male stickleback's aggressive response to a red mail van that enters his field of vision. Essentially similar responses, however, clearly lurk within us:

Humans are apt to feel superior to sticklebacks aroused to anger by mail vans or to sexual activity by pear-shaped dummies. We

think them "stupid" to be "fooled" by such crude approxima-
tions, since we assume that they, in some sense, "think" that the
mail van really *is* a male stickleback, just because it is red. But
a little reflection on our own species helps us to sympathize. A
man may be sexually aroused by a picture of a naked woman. A
Martian ethologist, observing this, might regard the picture as
"mimicking" the real thing, and assume that the man was "fooled"
into "thinking" it was a real woman. But nobody who is aroused
by such a picture is actually fooled into thinking it *is* the real
thing. He knows very well that it is a pattern of printer's ink on
paper; it may even be a rather unrealistic caricature; yet it has
enough visual stimuli in common with the real thing to have a
similar effect on his physiology. We should not ask whether the
stickleback "thinks" the mail van really is a rival, nor whether
he is so "stupid" as to be incapable of distinguishing a mail van
from a stickleback. Very probably he can distinguish them very
well, but both make him see red! His nervous system is aroused
by them to the same emotion, even though it is perfectly capable
of seeing the difference between them.[16]

A purely rational person who married solely because of
exchange possibilities might willingly pledge fidelity, fully aware
of all he stands to lose if he reneges. But because of the nature
of the reinforcement mechanism, he may still feel sorely tempted.
Recall from Chapter 4 that the attractiveness of a material reward
is inversely proportional to its delay, with the result that small,
immediate rewards are often speciously chosen over larger, more
distant ones. With the illicit affair, the difficulty is that the
rewards occur right away. Its costs, by contrast, are both
uncertain and in the future, and are therefore heavily discounted by the matching law. (See Chapter 4.) The problem of
avoiding specious sexual rewards confronts even the most
determinedly rational marriage partner. The behavior called
for by material self-interest may be perfectly clear. The difficulty is in implementing it.

The person whose marriage is based on love has an inherent
advantage in solving this problem. Love for one's partner

imposes an additional cost on the affair, one that is experienced right away. Because the emotional cost of betraying a loved person occurs in the present moment, there is at least some chance it can outweigh the immediate attractions of the affair. The purely rational materialist, who does not experience this immediate cost, will have greater difficulty implementing his pledge.

Similar implementation problems arise in connection with other vicissitudes of married life. Western marriage vows commonly include a pledge to remain with the relationship through thick and thin. One's partner may develop a serious physical illness, or suffer from temporary bouts of deep depression. Even a pure rationalist would want to wait out such difficulties in order to reap the expected return on long-term investments in the marriage. Here again, however, the behavior dictated by reason need not coincide with the behavior favored by the reinforcement mechanism. In the midst of a rocky period, the costs come now, the rewards only later. The pure materialist will thus find it much harder to ride out times of marital difficulty, even when he knows that future rewards make it rational for him to do so.

Both the commitment and implementation problems suggest why relationships motivated purely by material self-interest might be less successful, even in material terms, than those motivated by irrational love. Perhaps Shakespeare anticipated these arguments when he wrote

> Love is not love
> Which alters when it alteration finds,
> Or bends with the remover to remove;
> O, no! it is an ever-fixed mark,
> That looks on tempests and is never
> shaken.[17]

The question remains, of course, whether people really are motivated by feelings of the sort Shakespeare described. Do people in love relationships really set aside material self-interest? There is evidence that many do.

EXCHANGE-ORIENTATION AND SATISFACTION

In a 1977 study, psychologists Bernard Murstein, Mary Cerreto, and Marcia MacDonald examined the relationship between concerns about exchange and the satisfaction people report from their marriages. Their first step was to measure how "exchange-oriented" a sample of people felt about their marriages. Here, being exchange-oriented means to believe it important "that every positive or negative action by one individual should be met by a similarly weighted action by the recipient."[18] At one pole of the exchange-orientation is the person who feels bad when he does his spouse a favor and is not rewarded in some specific way. At the other is one who simply does not keep a running mental tally of such exchanges.

Murstein et al. measured exchange-orientation by asking subjects to report the extent to which they agree with such statements as "If I do the dishes three times a week, I expect my spouse to do them three times a week," and "It does not matter if the people I love do less for me than I do for them." Their survey consisted of 44 items, responses to which were aggregated into an exchange-orientation index for each respondent. An index of marital adjustment was also constructed from responses to a questionnaire.

As expected under the commitment model, Murstein et al. found that exchange-orientation was significantly negatively correlated with marital satisfaction for both men and women.* A similar study found that direct reciprocation of a partner's benevolent act served not to increase, but to reduce, the initiating partner's satisfaction.[19]

---

*The correlation coefficients for men and women were $-.63$ and $-.27$, respectively.

Such findings are clearly troublesome for the exchange model. Indeed, they flatly contradict one of its most cherished prescriptions for a happy marriage:

> The idea that exchange is the basis of intimate relationships may even have the effect of impairing such relationships. For example, the recommendation, which seems to be growing in popularity, that prior to a marriage a contract be drawn up that specifies in detail what each partner expects frrom the other, should, if followed, tend to undermine the relationship.[20]

Troubling as they are, however, these findings do not prove that irrational love is what motivates successful marriage partners. A rationalist might object, for example, that people who are not exchange-oriented on the Murstein et al. test are just not very discriminating. Perhaps these even-tempered folk would feel content irrespective of their objective circumstances. Or the rationalist might complain that how happy people *say* they are is not much related to how satisfied they really are. A more powerful test of the theory, on this view, would be to see whether the exchange-oriented couples are actually doing better on objective grounds. Are their households managed more efficiently? Do they have better jobs or higher incomes? How are their children doing in school?

Murstein et al. did not pursue these questions, but there are a variety of other investigations that bear on them. Several studies suggest, for example, that reports of happiness are clearly related to objectively measurable concomitants of well-being. Low self-reports of happiness are strongly correlated with physical distress symptoms such as dizziness, rapid heartbeat, digestive disorders, and headaches,[21] and also with clinical symptoms of anxiety, depression, and irritability.[22] People who consider themselves happy are more likely to initiate social contacts with friends, to join groups, and to behave in other ways suggestive of well-being.[23] Of particular reassurance to economists should be the consistent finding that self-reports of happiness are very strongly linked to position in the distribution of income.[24] The higher people rank, the happier they say they are.

On the strength of such findings, it appears reasonable to conclude that there is, in fact, a negative link between marital satisfaction and exchange-orientation. Of course, precisely the opposite link is predicted by the exchange, or self-interest, model.

EVIDENCE FROM FANTASY STUDIES

The connection between self-reports and objective reality, though often strong, is by no means perfect. A substantial body of research suggests that people's fantasies often provide a much clearer indication of how they actually feel. People's answers to questions sometimes suggest conformance with the exchange model of relationships while, at the same time, their fantasies paint an entirely different picture.

The contrast is clearly illustrated when the two approaches are applied to the question of why people fall in love. When psychologist Zick Rubin, a member of the exchange school, asked subjects involved in romantic relationships why they were in love, their answers were often strongly consistent with the exchange view.[25] Using their responses, he constructed an index of "mutual advantage," a summary measure of the reasons that were clearly linked to concrete benefits from the relationship. This index was strongly positively correlated with the strength of reported romantic attachment.*

The alternative approach is to focus not on what people say about their motives but on what they reveal about them in imaginative storytelling. The social psychologist's main tool for studying fantasies is the Thematic Apperception Test (TAT).

---

*More specifically, Rubin found a correlation coefficient of .5, which, as a critic of the exchange view would be quick to point out, leaves 75 percent of the variation in romantic attachment unexplained.

In this test, the subject is given several drawings or photographs, usually ones that depict interactions between people, and is then asked to write a story about each one. Extensive evidence suggests that TATs are more effective than direct questioning for assessing a subject's motivational state. One study found, for example, that achievement concerns revealed in fantasy were good predictors of performance on a moderately difficult task.[26] Self-reports of achievement-orientation, by contrast, were correlated neither with objective performance nor with achievement concerns in fantasy. There are similar findings with respect to feelings and behavior related to hunger,[27] power,[28] and affiliation.[29] These findings suggest that exchange-orientation might be better plumbed not by asking about it directly, as Rubin and Murstein et al. did, but by examining people's fantasies.

This is precisely the approach taken by psychologist Donald McAdams.[30] He administered TATs to samples of people in various states of romantic involvement. The relevant comparisons were between a group of "in-love" subjects (as defined by their having exceeded a threshold score on a questionnaire about feelings toward their partners) and a control group whose members were not thus involved. McAdams found that the fantasies of the in-love subjects displayed almost none of the exchange-orientation characteristic of the responses to Rubin's direct questions. Instead, they were rife with such feelings as the traditionalists describe. Characters in the stories typically expressed a sense of commitment or concern toward others. They emphasized a sense of surrender to fate, of wanting to escape to situations of shared intimacy. Harmony was also a recurrent theme, and characters often mentioned feeling "on the same wave length" with one another. With respect to all of these themes, the fantasies of control subjects were markedly different.

McAdams constructed a 10-item "intimacy-motivation index" that summarizes the strength of feelings of intimacy revealed by the TATs. This index is roughly the opposite of the mutual-advantage and exchange-orientation indexes used by exchange theorists. Contrary to the predictions of the exchange model, McAdams discovered that members of a large, nationwide sample who scored high on his index reported higher levels of happiness and security.

McAdams and his coauthor George Vaillant have also examined longitudinal evidence on the relationship between intimacy-motivation and well-being.[31] They began with TATs administered to a group of 57 Harvard graduates in 1943 (when the graduates were about 30 years old). Using these stories, they next constructed scores for intimacy, power, achievement, and affiliation-motivation. Finally, they related these early motives to a "life-adjustment index" calculated when the men averaged 47 years of age. This index was an aggregation of nine categories, many of which would win immediate approval from the hardheaded rational choice theorist: income, occupational advancement, recreational activities, vacations, enjoyment of job, psychiatric visits, drug or alcohol misuse, days of sick leave, and marital satisfaction. Of the four motives they measured from the TATs, only intimacy showed a strong positive relationship with successful adjustment later in life.

Working in the same tradition, psychologist James McKay found that people whose fantasies expressed an attitude of selfless love are more likely than others to enjoy good health, as measured by the incidence of infectious diseases.[32] One reason, apparently, is that such persons have elevated concentrations of T cells, virus-fighting lymphocytes in the blood. Several earlier studies report similar relationships between concerns about friendship and concentrations of salivary immunoglobulin A, which helps defend against upper respiratory infections.[33]

Again, none of these investigations proves that people in love behave irrationally. It seems fair to say, however, that the TAT studies, taken as a whole, are in much greater harmony with the commitment model than with the self-interest model of close personal relationships.

THE MODULAR BRAIN INTERPRETATION

Why the curious disparity between people's conscious descriptions of their motives and their motives as revealed by fantasies? Psychologist David McClelland suggests that the difference has something to do with the modular organization of the brain. In his 1985 book, *The Social Brain,* psychologist Michael Gazzaniga describes more than two decades of research he and his colleagues have carried out on the localization of brain function. On their interpretation of the evidence, the brain is organized into a host of separate modules, each with its own capacity to process information and motivate behavior. Most of these modules lack language capability, which in most people is centralized in a specific region of the left hemisphere. Not all of the nonlanguage modules are equally well connected with this central language module, and in this observation lies the basis for McClelland's explanation of the disparity between the different methods of assessing motivation. The argument is provocative, and well worth careful examination.

To begin, we must go back to some of the details of Gazzaniga's experiments, which involve patients who have undergone a rare form of brain surgery. In normal persons, the two lateral hemispheres of the neocortex of the brain are connected by a dense network of nerve fibers called the corpus callosum. In a small number of patients who suffer from severe epilepsy, however, the treatment of last resort is to sever this network surgically. For reasons that are not completely understood, this almost always prevents the recurrence of severe seizures. It is from a series of experiments involving these "split-brain" patients that psychobiologist Roger W. Sperry and, later, Gazzaniga (who was Sperry's student) and his colleagues have learned much of what is now known about the modularity of brain function. In particular, these experiments have taught us that specific areas of the brain can process information, generate an emotional response to it, and motivate behavior, all without any conscious knowledge whatsoever on the part of the central language module.

The most astounding thing about the split-brain patients is that their behavior appears almost completely normal. Millions of nerve fibers in their brains have been severed, and yet an untrained observer would never know it! The effects of their surgery show up clearly only under carefully controlled laboratory conditions in which sensory information can be transmitted to only one hemisphere of the brain. For example, when the eyes focus on a single point, an image flashed to the left of that point will be transmitted to only the right hemisphere. In normal persons, the right hemisphere would then transmit the image to the left hemisphere via the corpus callosum. But in the split-brain patient, this transmission pathway no longer exists, which means that the image cannot cross over.

A typical experiment flashes a visual stimulus—a picture of a knife, say—in the left side of the split-brain patient's visual field, which the optic nerves then transmit directly to his right hemisphere. Because the image never reaches the language module of the left hemisphere, the patient is unable to report what he has just seen. Nonetheless, if he is asked to choose from among a group of objects—a knife, fork, and a spoon, say—invariably he reaches for the correct one. Unable to express why he reached for it, he is genuinely puzzled by his own behavior.

If an image that would normally evoke an emotional response is flashed to the mute right hemisphere, the expected feeling is manifested in the usual ways. The split-brain patient is aware of the feeling, but is unable to explain what triggered it. For our purposes, a key finding is that when subjects experience a feeling whose cause has been concealed from the language module, they generally try to invent an explanation. Thus, for example, when the image of an office fire was shown to a subject's right hemisphere, she became frightened, and said to the investigator: "I don't really know why but I'm kind of scared. I feel jumpy. I think maybe I don't like this room, or maybe it's you. You're getting me nervous."[34]

Given that her corpus callosum has been severed, how does this patient's language center—located in the left hemisphere—even *know* she is afraid? Gazzaniga never explains, but presumably it is because the surgery does not eliminate all pathways between the two sides of the brain. The severed nerves all lie in the neocortex, or uppermost part of the brain, the most recent addition in evolutionary terms. Thus the right hemisphere of the patient's neocortex can still transmit information to the limbic system (a more primitive structure that surrounds the brain stem, well beneath the neocortex), where it can trigger an emotional response. The limbic system, in turn, is linked to various other parts of the brain, including the language module of the left neocortex, which means that the surgery leaves at least some indirect passages between the two hemispheres intact.

Whatever the technical details of the transmission process may be, we know the language module somehow has access to what the rest of the brain feels, even when it has no information about what caused the feeling. It is also able to observe the specific behaviors that are motivated by these feelings. Confronted with these feelings and behaviors, the language center seems to feel a compelling need to explain them. Gazzaniga views the language module as our center of rational consciousness, obsessed with rationalizing all that we feel and do. He stresses, however, that the explanations it invents are not always the right ones.

Information obviously flows much more freely in brains that have not been surgically altered. And yet, even in normal persons, there is a great deal of information that enters the central nervous system that cannot be accessed by the language module. We have long known, for example, that stimuli of very short duration can affect behavior, even when the subject is unaware of them. In one experiment, psychologist Anthony

Marcel demonstrates the existence of subliminal "priming."[35] Priming refers to the phenomenon that people can perceive a stimulus more rapidly if their attention has recently focused on something closely related to it. For example, numerous experimenters have first shown people a word, then asked them to say whether a subsequent group of letters constitutes a word or a nonword. The general finding is that they can perform this classification much more quickly if the group of letters is related to the word they have just seen. Thus, a subject who has just seen the word "cat" is able to respond more quickly that "dag" is not a word. Marcel shows that priming also happens even when the first word is flashed so quickly that subjects are not consciously aware of it.

Daniel Goleman,[36] building on the work of psychologist Donald Norman,[37] argues persuasively that the brain employs an "intelligent filter" that screens out most sensory input from conscious awareness. That the filter is intelligent is clearly evidenced in what he calls the "cocktail party effect":

> At a cocktail party or in a crowded restaurant there is typically a din of competing conversations, all carried at high volume within earshot of the others . . . you don't simply hear the loudest voice. For example, if you are stuck listening to a bore recount the gruesome details of his last vacation, rocky relationship, or nearly consummated deal, it is easy to tune him out and tune in on a more interesting conversation nearby—particularly if you hear your own name mentioned.[38]

Without the protection of this intelligent filter, environmental stimuli would simply overwhelm us. But the fact that the filter is intelligent means that, at some level, our brains have access to much more information than we realize. That much of it is screened from conscious awareness does not mean it has no effect on emotions and behavior.

Many of the emotions that affect behavior in close personal relationships appear to lie outside conscious awareness. Psychologists tell us, for example, that subtle nuances of body language often communicate a great deal more than even the most detailed and explicit verbal messages. That we often are not consciously aware of body language apparently matters not the slightest.

Indeed, who would pretend to understand how behavioral idiosyncrasies affect our feelings and behavior toward our partners? There is a particular look that appears on my wife's face when she experiences intense, pleasant surprise. I first noticed it when we would unexpectedly pass one another on the sidewalk, shortly after we met. Years have gone by since then and she now shows only a vestige of this expression when we meet by chance. But it still appears as strongly as ever in other contexts, as when our son, now a toddler, first fluttered in her womb. It is an expression I have never seen on anyone else and, so far as I know, it is of no direct usefulness whatsoever. And yet, for reasons I cannot explain, I find it deeply endearing. By all accounts, such effects are common in close personal relationships. We simply take it for granted that no rational explanation exists for them.

McClelland suggests that if forces beyond awareness do in fact play a major role in binding partners together, we should not be surprised that the reasons people give for pairing bear little relation to their true motives. What we are getting, in effect, is the language module's attempt to account for feelings and behaviors motivated by parts of the brain that cannot speak for themselves. In a culture that places a premium on rationality and the pursuit of self-interest, it seems hardly surprising that the explanations we hear are often of the rationalist mold.*

But how does the TAT get around this difficulty? One advantage is that when people describe their fantasies, they are merely *revealing* their feelings, not trying to account for them. Another advantage stems from the fact that emotions are much more closely linked to visual images than to verbal statements. Thus, McClelland reasons, the drawings that summon the imagina-

---

*In other contexts, these same observations say that the rationalist position may often be *stronger* than it appears. For example, because people know that society encourages altruistic behavior, their language modules may contrive altruistic explanations for behaviors that were in fact prompted by self-interest.

tive stories reported in TATs are much more likely than a verbal questionnaire to capture the subject's true feelings.

The modular view of the brain has clear intuitive appeal. It helps us, for example, to make sense of the curious practice whereby some people deliberately set their watches five minutes ahead. People who do this often explain that it helps them get to appointments on time. They *know,* of course, that their watches are fast. Still, they cannot prevent their eyes from seeing what the watch says. The language module may very well discount this visual image, just as the rationalists say it ought to. But it cannot control how other parts of the brain react to it. The language module may even be amused at how easily the rest of the brain is "fooled" by this image into "thinking" it is later than it really is. Rational or not, however, the practice often seems to serve its purpose.

The modular brain view may also help us understand why so many cultures attempt to play down the importance of physical beauty and at the same time to reinforce appreciation for inner traits of character. The difficulty is that, while inner beauty is what counts most for the long haul, the extreme conspicuousness of physical appearance often causes it to play a disproportionate role in the feelings that motivate behavior. With effort, one can look past a pretty face and focus on what lies inside, just as one can, with effort, look past the image on a clock.

The modular brain view sheds similar light on the Krebs and Dawkins account of the stickleback's reaction to the red mail van, and of the man's reaction to the erotic drawing. In the same vein, it helps explain why it is sometimes hard to fall asleep after watching a film like *Aliens,* even though we "know" such creatures do not really exist. The modular view even helps us make better sense of the growing literature on self-control. (See Chapter 4.) When we say that we are "of two minds" about something, we may be speaking literally as well as figuratively.

As Gazzaniga emphasizes, the modular view challenges "two thousand years of Western thought" in support of the belief "that our actions are the product of a unitary conscious system."[39] The new interpretation suggests that when economists talk about people maximizing utility, they are really talking about the language module of the left hemisphere. This is the part of the brain that reasons in the manner contemplated by the rational choice model. Clever as it is, however, the language module does not account for all of our behavior. The explanations it offers, moreover, will be accurate only some of the time.

The superior performance of the TATs is a demonstrated fact. McClelland accounts for it by saying that the language module does not have very good access to much of the relevant motivational information. If this explanation is even approximately correct, it provides yet another reason to believe that intimate relationships are based much less on rational calculation than on emotion. The rational, utility-maximizing language module of the brain may simply be ill-equipped to deal with many of the most important problems we face.

I want to stress again that my main point is not that the exchange model is wrong, but that it fails to capture an essential element of the process. As the rationalists emphasize, we live in a material world and, in the long run, behaviors most conducive to material success should dominate. Again and again, however, we have seen that the most adaptive behaviors will not spring directly from the quest for material advantage. Because of important commitment and implementation problems, that quest will often prove self-defeating. In order to do well, we must sometimes stop caring about doing the best we can.

The commitment model thus embraces the essential elements of both the traditionalist and exchange views of love. It openly concedes the material imperatives implicit in the exchange view. At the same time, it suggests why "an eyelash, a perfume, a haunting walk," or "the smell of almonds on the breath" might play an important role in the process. And it suggests, with Yates, why people who are sensible about love might indeed be incapable of it.

ELEVEN

HUMAN DECENCY

On the night of October 10, 1975, 18-year-old Bradley T. VanDamme of Fulton, Illinois, was involved in a serious one-car accident. As he lay unconscious in the front seat, the rear of his vehicle burst into flames. By the time bystander Billie Joe McCullough reached the car, the fire had spread into the front of the passenger compartment. McCullough crawled into the car and, with great difficulty and at obvious risk to his own life, pulled VanDamme free. Moments later the entire car exploded into flames. Although VanDamme suffered extensive injuries and was badly burned, he eventually recovered.

McCullough, a 22-year-old laborer, was later awarded the Carnegie Medal, an honor given for "outstanding acts of self-less heroism performed in the United States and Canada."[1] To be considered for a Carnegie Medal, an act must meet these four criteria: (1) it must be voluntary; (2) the actor must risk his or her own life to an extraordinary degree; (3) the actor must not be directly related to the victim; and (4) the actor must not be in an occupational role (such as police or life-guards) in which duty would have required the act.

There were 56 medals awarded in 1977, eight of them post-humously. The emergencies included "twenty instances of drowning, sixteen of burning in automobiles or buildings, six suffocations from smoke or fumes, four rock falls, three cases of electric shock, two oncoming trains, two attacking animals, one shooting, one falling sheet of metal, and one possible fall from a tree."[2] Because opportunities to perform such acts are extremely rare, 56 awards in one year seems a very large number.

The 48 persons who survived to receive their medals in 1977 will undoubtedly enjoy lifelong respect and admiration from their communities. Even so, the criteria for the awards appear to rule out self-interested motives. Kin selection cannot be at work here since the victim cannot have been a relative. Moreover, when the chances of dying during a rescue attempt are 1 in 7, it appears unlikely that reciprocal altruism of tit-for-tat could be significant motives. (See Chapter 2.) Acts of heroism often come at such cost that not even society's highest accolades could possibly compensate. The Congressional Medal of Honor, our highest military honor, has often been awarded posthumously to soldiers who threw themselves atop live grenades to save their comrades. Surely not even the most dedicated rationalist would pretend that these soldiers somehow figured to come out ahead.

Acts of heroism occur very frequently. They leave skeptics to wonder whether people in ordinary circumstances often show similar disregard for material self-interest. In Chapters 9 and 10, we saw that, in at least many circumstances, we do. We often bear costs in the name of fairness; and we often act selflessly in the context of love relationships. In this chapter, I will survey evidence that selfless behavior is common in a variety of other contexts as well. Once again, the picture that will emerge is flatly inconsistent with the classical portrait of economic man.

FIELD EXPERIMENTS ON HONESTY

New York City transit workers are not noted for their solicitous manner with the riding public. By one account, a Manhattan bus driver once slammed his doors in the face of a frail, elderly woman who was taking too long to board. His parting words were, "Lady you don't need a bus, you need an ambulance." The city's baseball fans are also an unruly bunch. On July 4, 1985, a stray bullet pierced the right hand of Joanne Barret as she and her husband and two sons sat in the stands watching a Yankee game. In August of 1986, also at Yankee

Stadium, first baseman Wally Joyner of the California Angels was hit in the arm by a 12-inch knife thrown from the upper deck. That same season, Mets manager Davey Johnson said he hoped his team would clinch the division title on the road, so that celebrating Mets fans would not destroy Shea Stadium. It was not to be, however. The Mets clinched at Shea and their fans, many of them clutching fistfuls of souvenir sod, made a moonscape of the playing field. Not to belabor the point, New York is a tough town.

But it has also been the site of a host of field experiments that reveal considerably more noble strands of human character. It was in New York, for example, that psychologist Harvey Hornstein and several of his colleagues were pleasantly surprised to discover what happens when people are given an opportunity to do a good deed.[3] In their basic experiment, they placed hundreds of wallets, each with a small amount of cash (roughly $5 in today's purchasing power), in different locations on the crowded city sidewalks. Each contained a variety of membership cards and personal papers, and an identification card bearing the name, address, and telephone number of its ostensible owner, one Michael Erwin (whose name was chosen "to avoid any unequivocal ethnic or religious group identification").[4]

For several months during the spring of 1968, Hornstein and his colleagues "lost" these wallets at the rate of roughly 40 per day. Of the many hundreds they lost, an astonishingly high 45 percent were returned completely intact! Needless to say, some inconvenience is involved in wrapping up a wallet and getting it to the post office. With such a small amount of cash involved, it would not have been reasonable for the finders to have expected a reward. (Indeed, many of them returned the wallets anonymously.) It is thus difficult to imagine a self-interested motive that might have driven so many people to return them.

Hornstein et al. were able to manipulate the return rate by manipulating subjects' attitudes about the benevolence of other people. In one version of their experiment, they placed each

wallet on the sidewalk inside an unsealed envelope addressed
to the owner. People who picked up the envelope found not
just the wallet inside, but also a letter, one ostensibly written
to the owner by someone who had earlier found his wallet.
More precisely, each subject found one of three versions of the
letter—"positive," "neutral," or "negative." The neutral version
said merely:

> Dear Mr. Erwin:
>   I found your wallet which I am returning. Everything is here
> just as I found it.

The positive and negative letters, however, went on to describe
the sender's feelings about finding and returning the wallet.
The positive letter continued:

> I must say that it has been a pleasure to be able to help somebody
> in the small things that make life nicer. Its really been no prob-
> lem at all and I'm glad to be able to help.

The negative version, by contrast, finished with this statement:

> I must say that taking responsibility for the wallet and having to
> return it has been a great inconvenience. I was quite annoyed at
> having to bother with the whole problem of returning it. I hope
> you appreciate the efforts that I have gone through.[5]

Of the 105 wallets involved in this phase of the experiment,
40 percent were returned intact. Only 18 percent of the ones
accompanied by negative letters were returned, while the rates
for the positive and neutral letters were 60 percent and 51 percent, respectively. In short, people who found negative letters
were markedly less likely to return the wallets. Hornstein et
al. argue that the writer of the letter serves as a role model for
the experimental subject. When the role model expresses negative feelings about his action, the subject is significantly less

likely to return the wallet, even though the letter provides no reason for him to have negative feelings about the *owner* of the wallet.

The letter writer is a *role model*? Somehow, that conveys a purposefulness that seems altogether lacking in these actions. It is hard to accept that people really take the writer's attitude as a model for what their own attitudes ought to be. The pattern in the return rates can be given a simpler interpretation, one based on the modular view of brain function discussed in Chapter 10. People are obviously aware of opposing currents in human nature: From experience, we know that some people are benevolent, others much less so. Our experiences with the former are linked with positive feelings, those with the latter with negative ones. Exposure to either type of person will naturally evoke the emotions associated with that type. These emotions, in turn, may affect behavior, even though the language module of the brain may have no idea why. Just as the spectacle of a science-fiction monster summons fright, even when there is no rational basis for fear, mere exposure to a nonbenevolent attitude will summon negative feelings from past experience. These feelings will naturally be salient when the subject decides whether to return the wallet; and it is hardly surprising, therefore, that they affect behavior in the observed ways.

This interpretation emphasizes that it is feeling, not reason, that motivates the decision about the wallet, and is thus in clear harmony with the commitment model. The role of negative feelings is further underscored by the extraordinary observation that not one of the wallets set out on June 4, 1968, the day Robert F. Kennedy was murdered, was returned.[6] Whether the reason was that Sirhan Sirhan was a negative role model—Hornstein's interpretation—or merely that his action triggered negative feelings—the modular brain view—one thing remains clear: there are simply no *rational* grounds for a third party's behavior to have affected anyone's decision about returning a lost wallet.

VICTIM-IN-DISTRESS EXPERIMENTS

New York's image gets a further boost from a series of experiments designed to see how people respond to a victim in distress. In one study, psychologists Irving Piliavin, Judith Rodin, and Jane Piliavin staged a mock distress scene to discover whether riders on a New York subway would come to the aid of a fellow passenger who had suddenly collapsed.[7]

Because the experimenters wanted a captive audience, they selected the 8th Avenue express line between 59th and 125th streets, a journey that lasts almost eight minutes. While one research assistant inconspicuously took notes at the rear of one of the cars, another, a male student, stood at the front. About one minute out of the station, he staggered forward and collapsed. His instructions were to remain supine on the floor until someone came to his aid. If no one did so by the time the train reached its stop, another research assistant helped him to his feet. In either event, the researchers disembarked at the station, then repeated the procedure on the next train going the other direction.

The experiment was run in two versions. In the first, which was designed to make passengers think the victim had become ill, the student stood holding a cane before falling. In the second, the intent was for the victim to appear drunk. In these trials, he doused himself with a strong-smelling liquor and carried a bottle wrapped tightly in a brown paper bag.

Piliavin et al. found that the victim with the cane received help from at least one passenger in 62 of 65 cases. As expected, the drunk victim received help much less frequently, but even he was assisted in 19 of 38 cases.

Psychologists Bibb Latané and John Darley report the results of a series of similar experiments.[8] Unlike the Piliavin et al. experiments, however, many of theirs were designed so that only a single subject was in a position to aid the victim. In one, a research assistant interviewed a subject in one room, then retreated to an adjacent room while the subject filled out some forms. From the adjacent room, which was separated from the first by only a cloth curtain, the researcher then cried out in pain: "Oh, my God, my foot . . . I . . . I . . . can't move . . . it. Oh, my ankle. I . . . can't . . . can't . . . get . . . this thing off . . . me."[9] In this particular experiment, which was typical of many of the others, 70 percent of the subjects quickly tried to assist the victim in some way.

KITTY GENOVESE REVISITED

New York City, the site of these victim-in-distress experiments, is of course also the place where 38 of Kitty Genovese's neighbors ignored her screams for more than half an hour as she was brutally stabbed and raped. (See Chapter 3.) Why this stark difference in behavior? Pursuing this question, Latané and Darley found that if an unresponsive bystander was stationed in the room with the subject, the subject was markedly less likely to aid the victim. In the experiment involving the woman with the injured foot, for example, only 7 percent of the subjects accompanied by a passive stooge intervened. Latané and Darley suggest that when more than one subject is at the scene, there is a diffusion of responsibility:

> When only one bystander is present at an emergency, if help is to come it must come from him. Although he may choose to ignore them (out of concern for his personal safety or desire "not to get involved"), any pressures to intervene focus uniquely on him. When there are several observers present, however, the pressures to intervene do not focus on anyone; instead, the responsibility is shared among all the onlookers. As a result each may be less likely to help.[10]

Latané and Darley point out that, although Genovese's neighbors were alone in their apartments, each was surely aware that many others could also hear her screams. Thus feeling part of a larger group, no single neighbor felt the full focus of responsibility.

This explanation sounds reasonable enough. But it appears completely inconsistent with the findings of the Piliavin et al. subway experiments. In those experiments there were, on the average, more than eight other passengers present in the end of the car where the victim fell. And yet in almost all of the cases involving the victim with the cane, at least one person quickly helped. Piliavin et al. also found that the likelihood of assistance did not go down as the number of bystanders increased. The diffusion-of-responsibility explanation just doesn't seem to fit here.

There is at least one important difference between the situations confronting subjects in the Piliavin et al. and Latané and Darley experiments. In the former, subjects had every reason to believe that the other people in the subway car were, like themselves, strangers to the victim. In the Latané and Darley experiment, however, the subjects may have thought the unresponsive bystander was a fixture in the office, someone who knew the victim. Subjects might well have supposed such a person had a reason for not acting.

But how can the Piliavin findings be reconciled with the behavior of Kitty Genovese's neighbors? Most of them, as noted, had to have been aware that many others could also hear her screams. What differentiated them from the subway bystanders is that none could possibly have known that no one else had come to the victim's aid. It is understandable that each person might want very much for *someone* to help the victim, and yet at the same time not want to be the one to do it.* If none of the subway bystanders acted, each would know immediately that the victim was still in jeopardy. Kitty Genovese's neighbors, by contrast, had no way of knowing that none of the others had

---

*Situations like this are often described as the "volunteer's dilemma," a discussion of which appears in Kliemt, 1986.

taken the simple, obvious step of calling the police. We may hope that, had they known that, someone almost surely would have acted.

RESPONSES TO REQUESTS FOR ASSISTANCE

In addition to conducting victim-in-distress experiments, Latané and Darley also sent their students into the streets of New York to ask complete strangers for a variety of different types of assistance. The students, who were "clean-cut undergraduates" for the most part, were told to be as unselective as possible about whom to approach. They asked for three different types of minor assistance (time, directions, or change), for money, or for the subject's name. The results for one version of the experiment are summarized in Table 11.1.

Anyone who has ever walked or driven in New York cannot help thinking how busy and in a hurry most New Yorkers seem. Still, all but a few were willing to stop and give a stranger directions or the time of day. Not as many would give money or their names, but more than one-third responded favorably even to these requests. The proportion of positive responses was still higher if the experimenter took the trouble to phrase his or her request in a more polite way. For example, when the name request was put as, "Excuse me, my name is ———. Could

TABLE 11.1. Responses to Requests for Assistance in New York City

"Excuse me, I wonder if you could . . .	Number asked	Percent helping
a. tell me what time it is?"	92	85
b. tell me how to get to Times Square?"	90	84
c. give me change of a quarter?"	90	73
d. tell me what your name is?"	277	39
e. give me a dime?"	284	34

Source: Latané and Darley, 1970, p. 10.

you tell me what your name is?", 64 percent of the people gave their names. When the students asked, "Excuse me, I wonder if you could give me a dime? My wallet has been stolen.", 72 percent gave the dime.

Studies like these have been conducted in virtually every city or town that has a major university. All of the ones I have seen produced results very similar to the ones discussed here. I have focused on the experiments that took place in New York because it is difficult to conceive of an environment more highly conducive to self-interested behavior. The conditions favoring tit-for-tat and other forms of reciprocal altruism are almost completely lacking in interactions among strangers there. The obvious difficulty for the self-interest model is that, in virtually every study, New Yorkers do not behave in the predicted manner.

THE FREE-RIDER PROBLEM

Economists and others have long been concerned about the so-called free-rider problem, a difficulty encountered when groups try to produce public or collective goods voluntarily. The problem springs from the two simple properties that characterize a public good: (1) once it is produced, it is difficult to prevent people from consuming it; and (2) one person's consumption does not diminish the value of consumption by others. Programs for public television are a clear example. Once an episode of "Masterpiece Theater" is broadcast, it is difficult to prevent people from tuning in; and when people do tune in, they do not diminish the strength of the signal available to others. The free-rider problem is that, while most people may want the public good very much, each has an incentive to rely on others to pay for it. It is thus very similar to the prisoner's dilemma: the behavior that best serves the group does not best serve each individual.

One way to solve the free-rider problem is to use the coercive power of the state. Because taxes are compulsory, we effectively deny ourselves the option of not contributing to public goods like street-cleaning services. In this fashion, we escape the difficulty often encountered in apartment houses, where each tenant has an incentive to wait for someone else to vacuum the vestibule.

The self-interest model predicts that people will not contribute voluntarily to the production of public goods. More precisely, it predicts that, as the number of potential contributors grows, the amount each person will voluntarily contribute shrinks quickly to zero. This prediction is often called the "strong free-rider hypothesis." When psychologists Gerald Marwell and Ruth Ames asked a sample of distinguished economists if they believed that economic theory did indeed generate this prediction, all but one affirmed that it did.[11] (The lone exception said that economic theory makes no relevant predictions about *anything*). For those who accept the strong free-rider hypothesis, the notion of a "voluntary public good" is an oxymoron.

The empirical evidence against the free-rider hypothesis is just as strong and consistent as the economic logic that supports it. As economist James Andreoni points out, for example, charitable activities are essentially voluntary public goods, and yet each year they receive far more than token levels of support.[12] More than 85 percent of all American households make private donations to charities, with an average gift of more than $200 in 1971 dollars. Religious organizations raised approximately $10 billion in 1981, health organizations and hospitals over $7 billion, and civic orchestras more than $150 million.[13] And notwithstanding their quarterly protests to the contrary, public TV and radio stations usually do manage to generate sufficient contributions to remain afloat.

Experienced lawyers usually have a contingency strategy available in the event their case does not proceed as hoped. ("My client did not shoot Mr. Higgins, your honor; but if she did, it was in a moment of temporary insanity.") Economists employ a similar strategy when people do, for some reason, contribute voluntarily to public goods. In these uncomfortable cases, economic theory predicts that increased government contributions toward the public goods should completely "crowd out" the private contributions. That is to say, for every extra dollar of government support for a public good, private contributions should go down by a dollar. Economists Burtran Abrams and Mark Schmitz have estimated, however, that an extra dollar of government support for charitable activities results in only 28 cents less in private support.[14]

There have also been a host of experimental studies whose findings sharply contradict the free-rider hypothesis.[15] Psychologist Robyn Dawes, who has been personally involved in many of these studies, estimated that, by the late 1970s, there had already been more than one thousand of them.[16]

An experiment conducted by Dawes, Jeanne McTavish, and Harriet Shaklee[17] epitomizes much of the work in this vast literature. Each trial of this experiment involved a group of eight people who did not know one another. Subjects were asked to give one of two responses, "cooperate" or "defect," which resulted in payoffs in the form of a multiperson prisoner's dilemma: defecting always had a higher payoff than cooperating, but if all defected, each did worse than if all cooperated. In such experiments, "defect" has the same meaning as "free-ride" in the public goods case. By defecting, one gets a benefit at the expense of the other parties.

Dawes et al. ran four versions of this basic experiment. In the first, players were not permitted to talk to one another before choosing. In the second, they were permitted to talk about any subject, provided it was not related to the experiment itself. The third version permitted them to discuss the experiment, but not to make explicit declarations about their choices. In the fourth version, all restrictions were lifted. Players were permitted to make promises about their choices and, in most groups, players declared themselves in a roll call.

In all four versions of the experiment, players were required to mark their choices in private. They were also promised that none of the other players would be told what others had chosen. The intention was that there be no reason for a defector to fear retaliation, and hence no practical way to enforce promises to cooperate.

Under these conditions, the free-rider hypothesis predicts that everyone will defect. Because confidentiality meant promises were not binding, communication should have made no difference. Contrary to this prediction, however, unanimous defection did not occur in any of the four versions. In addition, the results differed systematically with the amount of communication permitted: The more people were allowed to communicate, the less often they defected. The specific findings are summarized in Table 11.2.

Numerous other studies have also found that cooperation tends to increase with communication.[18] This tendency cannot be accounted for by the self-interest model. The unsentimental rationalist understands, after all, that to have made a promise does not mean it is rational to keep it. On the contrary, the payoff structure in these experiments dictates clearly that it be broken.

The commitment model, by contrast, holds that decisions about cooperation are based not on reason but on emotion. As noted in Chapter 7, it thus suggests a basis for the association between communication and cooperation. To cheat a stranger and to cheat someone you have met personally amount to precisely the same thing in rational terms. Yet in emotional terms, they are clearly very different. Face-to-face discussion, even if not directly relevant to the game itself, transforms the other players from mere strangers into real people. Discussion about what is the "right" thing to do in prisoner's dilemmas

TABLE 11.2. Percentage of Subjects Defecting

VERSION I (no communication)	VERSION 2 (irrelevant communication)	VERSION 3 (open communication)	VERSION 4 (open communication + promises)
73%	65%	26%	16%

Source: Dawes et al., 1977, p. 5.

further arouses the relevant emotions. And still higher levels of emotional involvement are evoked by explicit promises to cooperate.

There is, in any event, little doubt that emotions were strongly involved in the players' choices. As Dawes et al. write:

> One of the most significant aspects of this study, however, did not show up in the data analysis. It is the extreme seriousness with which the subjects take the problem. Comments such as, "If you defect on the rest of us you're going to have to live with it the rest of your life," were not at all uncommon. Nor was it unusual for people to wish to leave by the back door, to claim that they did not wish to see the "sons of bitches" who double-crossed them, to become extremely angry at other subjects, or to become tearful . . .
>
> The affect level was so high that we are unwilling to [experiment with pre-existing groups] because of the effect the game might have on the members' feelings about each other.[19]

Thus, feelings about defection ran high even though confidentiality prevented anyone from knowing who the actual defectors were. The mere knowledge that *someone* defected often poisoned the atmosphere for the entire group.

In a preliminary version of their experiment, Dawes et al. told one group their choices would later be revealed. Nonetheless, three persons defected, to the expected outrage of others. In this instance, people's reactions were naturally much more focused:

> The three defectors were the target of a great deal of hostility ("You have no idea how much you alienate me," one cooperator shouted before storming out of the room); they remained after the experiment until all the cooperators were presumably long gone.[20]

The free-rider experiments are not confined to artificial games played in the laboratory. In one important early study, economist Peter Bohm paid subjects to participate in what he described as an audience research study for the research department of the Swedish TV Broadcasting Company (the Swedish equivalent of the BBC).[21] Subjects came to the television studio to view a tape of a pilot program produced by two of Sweden's best-known humorists. They were told that the broadcasting company needed to find out how people felt about the show in order to determine whether closed-circuit television revenues would cover production costs. After watching the tape, subjects were asked to report the maximum amount they would be willing to pay to receive the program.

For present purposes, the two variations of interest are (1) a group that was told that they would actually be charged the amount they reported if the program was adopted; and (2) a second group that was told the program would be subsidized and that the fee would be completely independent of the value they reported. Given these instructions, the prediction of the free-rider hypothesis is clear: the first group should report much less, and the second group much more, than the amounts they were truly willing to pay.

Yet Bohm found virtually no difference between the two. He noted that subjects in both groups appeared to take their task seriously, and seemed to believe that "a valuation of TV programs in terms of money would be an important piece of information to the decision makers."[22] Contrary to the predictions of the self-interest model, they apparently made an honest attempt to provide that information.

The emotions that lead people to cooperate clearly reduce their material gain in these free-rider experiments. The commitment model suggests, however, that people with these emotions might nonetheless carve out a niche for themselves, even in a bitterly competitive material world.

ECONOMISTS AS FREE-RIDERS

It is interesting that the only group for which the strong free-rider hypothesis receives even minimal support in this vast experimental literature turns out to be a group of economics graduate students. In experiments essentially like the ones run by Dawes et al., Marwell and Ames discovered that economics students were significantly more likely to defect than any of the other groups they studied.[23] This finding agrees with the finding by Kahnemen et al.[24] that commerce students are more likely than psychology students to make one-sided offers in ultimatum bargaining games. (See Chapter 9.)

These authors are by no means the only ones to have observed that economists behave differently. Consider this brief report from a recent issue of *The Chronicle of Higher Education:*

> Over the last 200 years, economists have made great strides in describing how an economy functions, but people mistrust them as much as they did a century ago, said Robert M. Solow, professor of economics at the Massachusetts Institute of Technology, in a speech marking the centennial of the American Economic Association.
>
> In 1879, Mr. Solow said, Francis Amasa Walker, an economist who would later be elected the group's first president, wrote an essay on "why economists seemed to be in bad odor amongst real people."
>
> Economists, Walker argued, disregard important international differences in laws, customs, and institutions that affect economic issues. They also ignore, he said, the customs and beliefs that tie individuals to their occupations and locations and lead them to act in ways contrary to the predictions of economic theory.
>
> Walker, Mr. Solow observed, could have been talking about the economists of the 1980's.[25]

But *why* are economists so different? Two possible explanations suggest themselves. One is that economics students are just like others, but have been influenced by economic theory to think that they *should* always try for maximum material gain. Materialist theories have a compelling logic, after all, and sustained exposure to them can be seductive. On the most charitable interpretation of this view, the free-rider experiments are little more than an intellectual exercise—an IQ test of sorts—in which the economics student tries to figure out the "right" answer. Whatever feelings he or she might normally bring to these situations become temporarily disengaged. Alternatively, and less charitably, it may be that sustained exposure to materialist theories tends to extinguish the impulse to cooperate, not just in laboratory experiments, but in other situations as well.

Another possibility is that economists are a distinct personality type to begin with. If some people in the population are, by nature, much more materialistic, much less given to emotion, than others, it is easy to imagine many of them being attracted by the teachings of economics. (Someone once said of an economist friend, "He wanted to become an accountant but didn't have enough soul.") My own impression is that both factors play a role. Many of the students who respond most enthusiastically to introductory economics courses *do* appear to be a little different. There is also ample evidence that most people, economists or not, feel dissonance when their beliefs and behavior are inconsistent. It seems hardly surprising, therefore, that this dissonance might sometimes lead economists to modify their predispositions. Economics, like any other discipline, acquires all the trappings of a separate culture; and like other cultures, it has the power to instill values and beliefs. The difficulty, for economists, is that the ones it instills are often sharply at variance with those embraced by most other people.

The commitment model offers economists an alternative path to dissonance reduction, one that requires them to change only surface elements of their belief structure. It makes clear that actions based on emotion need not be materially disadvantageous, despite their obvious costs in each given instance. As we saw in Chapter 3, a person known to eschew self-interest faces opportunities that a pure rationalist does not, even though he gains less than a pure rationalist would in each exchange.

Drawing by Ed Arno: © 1974 The New Yorker Magazine, Inc.

"I'd like you to meet Marty Thorndecker. He's an economist, but he's really very nice."

The rationalist's problem, which the self-interest model repeatedly overlooks, is that he tends to be excluded from many profitable exchanges.

SELF-INTEREST AND VOTING

The self-interest model has made inroads not only into psychology and sociology but into political science as well. Several authors suggest that voters calculate how each party or candidate would affect their material interests, then vote for the one that scores best.[26] Others envision a less complex process whereby voters look back on how the incumbents' performance has affected them, and then re-elect them or not in accordance with that assessment.[27] Both views suggest that voting will be most strongly affected when important material issues are at stake.

There is support for some of these predictions. Conventional political wisdom, buttressed by empirical study,[28] tells us that incumbents often do suffer in the wake of severe economic recessions. But many other predictions do not fare very nearly as well. Measures of self-interest, for example, have been found to have very little impact on attitudes and voting with respect to such issues as civil rights, the Vietnam War, and the energy crisis.[29] In the conclusion to their careful quantitative study of voting motives, political scientists David Sears, Richard Lau, Tom Tyler, and Harris Allen write:

> What we can say with certainty is that both symbolic attitudes and policy preferences are remarkably indifferent to the individual's current personal situation, even when it involves such very striking phenomena as personal unemployment, the threat of catastrophic medical expenses, or having one's own child bused to distant ghetto schools.[30]

Perhaps the most obvious difficulty for the self-interest model in the political sphere is the simple act of voting itself. It is virtually certain that a single person's vote will never influence the outcome of any national election. Self-interest clearly dictates a "free-ride" by staying home. The standard rejoinder, "But what if *everyone* who favors your candidate did that?" is unmindful of the fundamental incentive problem: If all the supporters of my candidate stayed home, my vote would make no difference anyway. My trip to the polls simply does not affect the number of others who turn out. And yet people trudge to courthouses, fire stations, and elementary schools by the tens of millions each election, often at considerable expense of time and inconvenience, and often in nasty November weather.

Rationalists have suggested that people should be much more likely to vote when an election is expected to be close.[31] Political philosopher Brian Barry reports, however, that an index of "citizen duty" explains most of the variation in voting behavior, closeness of the election only very little.[32] Even those people who *are* more likely to vote in close elections can hardly be said to do so on rational grounds, for even the closest national elections are almost certain not to be decided by a single vote.

Political scientist Anthony Downs, in his influential *An Economic Theory of Democracy,* recognizes this difficulty, and responds that each citizen "is willing to bear certain short-run costs he could avoid in order to do his share in providing long-run benefits."[33] To do his *share?* As Brian Barry points out,[34] this is no *rational* explanation of why people vote. By the very terms of the rational model, long-run benefits will accrue (or fail to accrue) irrespective of the actions of any individual. Downs is merely *asserting* that the voter is not a free-rider. The challenge, for the self-interest model, is to explain *why.*

Most democratic cultures teach that voting is a duty. The commitment model suggests there may be genuine material advantages in being known as the type of person who takes duty seriously. It suggests further that the surest path to being known as such a person is to *be* one.

HIGH-STAKES HELPING

A determined rationalist might grudgingly concede that people do not always pursue self-interest when very small costs are involved. Voting, giving directions, returning wallets with small amounts of cash, cooperating in free-rider games—all of these run counter to self-interest, to be sure, but the costs involved in each case are minimal.* To the observation that people sometimes risk their lives to save perfect strangers, the rationalist may respond that such behavior is not representative: heroism obviously exists, but that does not mean most

---

*The German philosopher Hartmut Kliemt (1987) has indeed developed a theory that predicts systematic departures from self-interested behavior whenever ethical norms can be satisfied at minimal cost.

people would act heroically in similar situations. The rationalist may claim that when the stakes are genuinely high, people will behave in the predicted selfish ways. On this view, the instances of non-self-interested behavior are a minor annoyance for the self-interest model, nothing more.

Because the occasions that might summon heroic behavior are by nature very rare, this version of the rationalist position is inherently difficult to examine. There is one study, however, that is at least indirectly relevant: an experiment in which sociologist Shalom Schwartz attempted to recruit volunteers to be bone marrow donors.[35]

Subjects were first approached by an interviewer as they relaxed in a Red Cross lounge after having donated a pint of blood. The interviewer introduced herself as a medical sociologist from the University of Wisconsin who was trying to talk to everyone who gave blood that day. More than 80 percent agreed to her initial request, which was to spend 15 to 20 minutes talking with her.

Once the subject was seated, the interviewer recorded background information and explained that she wanted to ask permission to do special tests on some of the blood the subject had just donated. But before allowing a response to that question, she went on to give this explanation:

> I'm working with a team at the UW hospital that is doing bone marrow transplanting. Bone marrow is the soft substance that produces new blood. In blood diseases like leukemia, a person's bone marrow produces an excessive number of white cells. Even with the best drug treatment we eventually get to the point where the patient is unlikely to survive for more than a few months. In these cases we are now trying to replace diseased bone marrow with healthy transplanted marrow. This is a somewhat experimental procedure, but it is worth while since otherwise the patients really have no hope. The transplant is like a blood transfusion. Marrow is drawn from the donor's hip bones and later it is injected into the recipient. This leaves the donor with some soreness in the hips for a couple of days, but there are no permanent after-

effects, since the body quickly replenishes its supply of bone marrow. By now we have perfected the process so that there is almost no danger to the donor. The donor enters the hospital in the evening; early the following morning marrow is drawn under general anesthesia; and he may leave the hospital that afternoon. The major problem is getting a good match between donor and recipient so that the transplant isn't rejected. Members of the immediate family usually serve as donors, because their blood and other characteristics are the closest match with the recipient's.[36]

The interviewer then gave subjects one of three randomly chosen descriptions of a specific patient's case. The first said only that the hospital had "a 30-year-old female who might be helped by a transplant, and there is no possible matching donor from her family." The second said the same except that in place of "30-year-old female who might be helped" it said "a young mother who is in need of a transplant." The third description began exactly as the second, but had this vivid addition: "Without a match, survival for this woman is very unlikely. And of course losing their mother will be a tragedy for her kids, what with the emotional shock and the hardship of growing up without her."

The 144 subjects in Schwartz's experiment were mostly males (76 percent) and mostly married (78 percent). Having been given the relevant background information, they were asked whether they would be willing to have their blood tested. The interviewer told them that allowing the test did not imply any commitment to go further. Only 5 percent refused at this stage. To the 95 percent who agreed, the interviewer went on to say that testing was complicated and very expensive, and the hospital did not want to proceed unless the subject felt there was at least a 50–50 chance he or she would be willing to donate if found compatible. Only 12 percent of the subjects declined to accept this commitment. At each stage, those who did refuse tended to be those who had been given the less detailed descriptions of the victim's plight.

It is tempting to try to explain the high volunteer rates on the grounds that blood donors are very different from other people. The difficulty is that a great many of us, at one time or another, *are* blood donors. Schwartz reports that there was no relationship between how frequently a subject had given blood in the past and the likelihood he or she would commit to be tested. There is, moreover, every indication that the subjects took their pledges seriously. Often they "debated with themselves for 10–15 minutes while the interviewer waited for their decisions; they mentioned numerous costs to the interviewer; and in the weeks following the encounter they sought social validation for the assessment of costs they had made in deciding."[37]

By any reasonable standard, to undergo general anesthesia and to have someone cut through your flesh and penetrate your bones to dig out some of your bone marrow is to make a nontrivial sacrifice. The prospective beneficiary was not related to the subjects, or even known to them. Nonetheless, a substantial majority of ordinary people were prepared to volunteer.

It seems fair to say that Schwartz's study provides no support whatever for the rationalist's fallback position: even among ordinary, nonheroic people, altruistic behavior is apparently not limited to cases in which its costs are insignificant. To Schwartz, the high volunteer rates were "quite unexpected." To a truly determined rationalist, however, they must be nothing short of astonishing.

AN ALTRUISTIC PERSONALITY?

The question of whether stable personality traits exist was for many years a controversial one in psychology. Walter Mischel[38] argued that there are no such traits, that people's behavior is specific to every circumstance. No one any longer questions that circumstances matter. As we have repeatedly seen, even very simple experimental manipulations can strongly affect behavior. Yet there is an emerging consensus that general behavior patterns do exist—that, in a broad range of circumstances, some people are much more likely than others to respond in particular ways.

Are some people more altruistic than others? Almost certainly so, argues sociologist J. Philippe Rushton in his 1980 book, *Altruism, Socialization, and Society.* He notes first that independent observers substantially agree about how altruistic a given person is. These personal evaluations are also strongly consistent with the results of psychological tests designed to measure altruistic tendencies. Most important, all of these measures have strong predictive power: they can identify children who are more likely to share their candy with others, adults who are more likely to donate to charity, aid a victim in distress, and so on.

Rushton notes that a person who scores high on indexes of altruism also tends to differ in other specific ways:

> . . . he or she is more empathic to the feelings and sufferings of others and able to see the world from their emotional and motivational perspective . . . Altruists also behave consistently more honestly, persistently, and with greater self-control . . . Furthermore, the consistently altruistic person is likely to have an integrated personality, strong feelings of personal efficacy and well-being, and what generally might be called "integrity."[39]

Rushton also reports that while numerous studies have looked for a link between altruism and intelligence, no consistent relationship has emerged. Altruists, however, do appear to do better economically: the experimental studies consistently find that altruistic behavior is positively correlated with socioeconomic status.[40] Of course, this does not mean that altruistic behavior necessarily *causes* economic success. But it does suggest that an altruistic posture cannot be too seriously burdensome in material terms.

All of these findings are broadly consistent with the commitment model's interpretation of altruism. Recall from Chapter 3 that in a world in which all people were equally altruistic, it would not pay to scrutinize one another for symptoms of trustworthiness. Nonaltruistic persons would quickly gain ground in such a world. The model predicts that the only stable outcome is one involving an uneasy mix of more altruistic and less altruistic persons. Rushton's evidence confirms the common impression that it is just such a world we have.

The commitment model also predicts that the locus of control for altruistic behavior will be emotional rather than cognitive. This was the crucial step, recall, in solving the commitment problem. All of the evidence we have seen supports this prediction. Altruists are neither more nor less rational than nonaltruists. They are simply pursuing different goals.

TWELVE

REFLECTIONS

Views about human nature have important practical consequences. They affect the conduct of foreign affairs, the
design and scope of regulation, and the structure of taxation.
They dictate corporate strategies for preventing workers from
shirking, for bargaining with unions, and for setting prices. In
our personal lives, they affect how we choose mates and jobs,
even how we spend our incomes.

More important, our beliefs about human nature help shape
human nature itself. As critics of materialist theories emphasize, we are the most malleable of the earth's inhabitants. But
we are not infinitely so. Our ideas about the limits of human
potential mold what we aspire to become. They also shape what
we teach our children, both at home and in the schools.

The commitment and self-interest models paint strikingly
different pictures not only of human nature, but also of its consequences for material welfare. We have seen that people who
love, who feel guilty when they cheat, vengeful when they are
wronged, or envious when they get less than their fair share
will often behave in ways that reduce their material payoffs.
But precisely because of this, they will also enjoy opportunities
that would not be available to a purely opportunistic person.
In many cases, a person or society armed with this knowledge
will make better choices than one exposed only to the self-
interest tradition.

SHIRKING ON THE JOB

In the workplace, as in other areas of life, there are frequent
opportunities to cheat and shirk. In recent decades, econo-

mists have written at length about this issue under the rubric of the so-called "principle-agent" problem.[1] In the standard treatment, the firm, or principal, has some task it wants the worker—its agent—to perform. The problem is that it is costly to monitor the worker's performance.

Economists have focused on the design of contracts that provide material incentives not to shirk. One ingenious proposal makes use of the observation that firms can often rank the performance of different workers even when they cannot measure exactly how much each produces.[2] Under these circumstances, firms can elicit better performance by making part of each worker's pay depend on his or her rank in the productivity ordering.

But even the most sophisticated of these contracts is limited by the fact that behavior is often virtually impossible to monitor. In the language of Chapter 4, workers confront golden opportunities to shirk, ones that are altogether beyond the reach of material incentive contracts. In the modern industrial firm, people tend to work in teams rather than as individuals. The classical monitoring problem is that while the firm can easily discover how much a team produces, it has little way of knowing how much each individual contributes to this total. The self-interest model emphasizes that each worker thus has an incentive to free-ride on the efforts of his coworkers.

The commitment model suggests two approaches for solving this problem—one rather obvious, the other somewhat less so. The first is to hire workers who feel bad when they shirk. How can firms do this? In Chapter 4, we saw that although it is not possible to observe what a worker does when confronted with a golden opportunity, his reputation may nonetheless provide useful clues. Sometimes even learning the groups to which people belong will provide relevant information. (Recall from Chapter 5 the New York City couples who advertise for governesses in Salt Lake City newspapers.) Firms that encounter serious monitoring problems are well advised to gather information about the reputations of job candidates, and most of them of course already do so.

Where the commitment model may offer more novel insight is in suggesting ways to increase a given worker's propensity to cooperate. Most people have at least some capacity to experience the emotions that support cooperation. The extent to which they actually experience them depends strongly on environmental factors. The practical problem confronting the firm is to design a working environment that will encourage these emotions. A useful starting point is the observation, discussed in Chapter 10, that feelings of moral responsibility are much more focused on people with whom we have close personal ties. This suggests that shirking might be attacked by creating a work environment that fosters closer personal ties between coworkers.

Exactly this strategy has been followed by many successful firms in Japan. In the typical Japanese corporation, the worker "is a member of the company in a way resembling that in which persons are members of families, fraternal organizations, and other intimate and personal organizations in the United States."[3] Many Japanese companies provide housing, athletic, and medical facilities for their workers, and educate their children in company schools. Coworkers vacation together in mountain or shore retreats maintained by the company. In contrast to the typical American worker, who works for many different firms during his lifetime, the Japanese ideal is lifetime tenure with a single employer.

This pattern enables the Japanese firm to solve monitoring problems in a way that the typical American firm cannot. Because of the close ties that exist between Japanese coworkers, their employers can link pay to the *group's* performance and rely on feelings of coworker solidarity to overcome the inherent free-rider problem.* By contrast, the pay schemes suggested by the self-interest model, which focus on *individual*

---

*For a detailed and illuminating discussion of how Japanese firms deal with free-rider problems, see Harvey Leibenstein's 1987 book, *Inside the Firm: The Inefficiencies of Hierarchy.*

performance, not only do not encourage cooperation, they actively militate against it.

This is not to say that the particular solutions adopted by Japanese firms will always be appropriate in the United States, where we place such a high premium on individuality and mobility. On the contrary, firms that blindly imitate the behavior of Japanese firms, as many American companies have begun to do, are not likely to prosper. If the commitment model is useful here, it is because it suggests the specific purpose the Japanese practices serve, namely, to encourage the emotions that support cooperation. The successful firms will be those that find ways of solving this problem in the American context. The self-interest model, with its exclusive focus on material incentives, steers management's attention in entirely different directions.

WAGE AND PRICE SETTING

Views on human nature affect not only a firm's policies for dealing with shirking, but also those toward wage and price setting. In highly profitable firms, for example, it is not uncommon for union members to threaten to abandon their jobs permanently in the event management does not accede to their demands. In these situations, management must decide whether to take the threat seriously.

Now, to abandon one's livelihood is an extraordinarily costly step—much more costly, most of the time, than the loss employees would suffer by moderating their demands. Threats of this sort would be utterly without credibility if union members behaved as predicted by the self-interest model. But if their concerns about fairness play a prominent role, it is easy to see why such threats are so often effective. A labor relations policy based on traditional rational bargaining models would serve a firm very poorly indeed.

Workers are not the only ones who care about how the economic pie is divided. In Chapter 9 we saw that consumers too make frequent sacrifices in the name of fairness. In particular, they will often accept losses in order to avoid patronizing firms whose prices they perceive to be unfair. We also saw in the case of ski resorts that perceptions of fairness and the underlying reality are often very different. In such cases, a firm can enhance its position if it can discover ways to make its prices seem more in line with its costs.

Richard Thaler cites the example of hotel room packages during Super Bowl weekend.[4] The Super Bowl is played each year on a Sunday late in January. In the host city, it is all but impossible to find a hotel room for the Saturday night before the game. And yet hotel chains are reluctant to charge a market-clearing price for essentially the same reason that ski operators do not charge market-clearing rates during holiday weekends: they fear that customers would perceive $300 per night as unfair, and refuse to patronize their hotels in other cities or at other times.

The solution some hotels have adopted is to sell a Super Bowl package: a room for Thursday through Sunday for $400 total. Since they have vacant rooms on the other nights anyway, including them in the package does not cost much. Making them part of the deal causes the buyer to see a price of $100 per night, which seems "fair." He is happy to pay it, even though he really didn't need a room for the other three nights.

FOREIGN RELATIONS

Military and strategic planning has become increasingly dominated by game theory of the sort first employed for these purposes by the Rand Corporation in the 1950s. But the behaviors predicted by traditional game theory often bear little resemblance to the actual behavior of countries in conflict. Many analysts, for example, have remarked on the apparent stupidity of the British war with the Argentines over the desolate Falkland Islands. As noted in Chapter 1, they point out that for much less than the amount spent in that conflict, each Falkland

Islander could have been given a Scottish castle and a generous pension for life.

At one point in history, the Falklands war might have been viewed as a rational investment in deterring aggression against other, more economically valuable, territories of the British Empire. With so little of that empire left to defend, however, it could hardly be justified on those grounds any longer. (How seriously, for example, would British interests be compromised if the Spanish were to take Gibraltar?) It is thus easy to see how an Argentine military planner equipped only with traditional game theory models might have concluded it would be safe to invade the Falklands.

Of course, the British did not respond as predicted by traditional models, and both they and the Argentines incurred heavy losses. Yet despite having spent so much to accomplish so little, the British show few signs of remorse. Notwithstanding their generally understated manner, perhaps they are like others in having a capacity for outrage and desire for revenge. If so, their lack of remorse is not surprising. Nor may anyone insist that these feelings, which in the end proved so costly, were not worth having *before the fact*. For despite the message of traditional game theory models, the Argentines ought well to have anticipated the British response, which ought have kept them from attacking in the first place. But of course, they too were driven by a sense of outrage, arising from their own prior territorial claims to the islands.

Similar issues arise in connection with the question of whether a military adversary can be "bombed into submission." Both the German bombardment of England during World War II and the American bombardment of North Vietnam twenty-five years later were undertaken in the belief that the answer is "yes." In both cases, however, the policy served only to increase the opposition's determination to resist. From the perspective of the rational choice model, this outcome is puzzling. But the commitment model's portrayal of human nature makes it seem much more intelligible.

The self-interest and commitment models make conflicting observations about a variety of other strategic issues as well. One is the defense doctrine of Mutually Assured Destruction (MAD). The idea behind MAD is simple. It is to maintain sufficient armaments to be able to deliver a devastating counterstrike to any nation that might consider launching a nuclear first strike against us.

Rationalists have argued that this form of deterrence makes no sense. Once we know we are the victim of a first strike, they reason, it is obviously too late to deter anything. At that point, our interests clearly dictate that we *not* retaliate, for to do so would only increase the likelihood of total world destruction. The problem with the MAD strategy, they conclude, is that the potential launcher of a first strike knows perfectly well what our incentives will be once its attack is launched. And this knowledge completely undercuts the capacity of MAD to deter.

Taken at face value, the critics' case is correct. If a nation makes policy decisions by strict reliance on the self-interest model, MAD *is* an irrational strategy. In order for MAD to be rational, our adversaries must know we have either (1) a doomsday machine (a tamper-proof device that *automatically* retaliates); or (2) policy makers who do not react rationally. The commitment model makes clear that because human beings are in charge of such decisions, they may indeed react irrationally. With the stakes so high, no prudent nation would be willing to gamble on a perfectly rational response to its first strike.*

While the commitment model thus identifies cases where our interests are better served by a policy maker subject to human

*David Gauthier (1985) has argued that it would be rational for policy makers to "predispose" themselves to retaliate against a first strike. The utility of such a predisposition, if known by the other side, is clear: it will deter a first strike. Gauthier then argues that if it is rational to become thus predisposed, it must also be rational to retaliate if a first strike is in fact launched. I prefer to say that it is *not* rational to retaliate at that point. This is only a semantic difference, however, for Gauthier and I would want to hire precisely the same policy maker, namely, someone the other side could predict would retaliate. And we would both stress that the surest route to their making such a prediction is to hire someone who really would push the button.

emotion, it also points to others where they are less well served. A difficulty often arises, for example, when the legitimate interests of one group seem to dictate the imposition of devastating costs on another. Consider this vivid illustration: At a critical juncture in World War II, just after the Allies had broken the Axis code, England deciphered a communication that the Germans were about to bomb Coventry. This confronted Winston Churchill with a terrible dilemma. If he ordered Coventry evacuated, he would save the lives of its citizens, but in the process reveal the code had been broken. By remaining silent, the secret would be preserved, and the war likely foreshortened.

Churchill reckoned the gains from a faster and more certain victory justified the sacrifice of Coventry. It was surely with this decision at least partly in mind that he later wrote:

> The Sermon on the Mount is the last word in Christian ethics. Everyone respects the Quakers. Still, it is not on these terms that Ministers assume their responsibilities of guiding states.[5]

But even if we grant that Churchill's was the right decision, it is easy to imagine that many leaders would not have been able to implement it. Their sympathies for the immediate, known victims in Coventry would have overwhelmed their concerns for the unknown persons who might later be spared.

A case in point is Ronald Reagan's decision to ship armaments to Iran in exchange for American hostages. This was clearly a bad decision. It promised to spare the lives of a small number of known persons in the short run, at the almost certain expense of substantially greater hostage-taking in the future. Just as clearly, however, it was a decision motivated by an honest human concern for the specific people held captive.

In these examples, we see that the emotions can function not only as the *solution* to commitment problems, but also as the *cause* of them. In such cases, they can sometimes be overridden by commitment devices of a more formal sort. For example, one proposal in the wake of the Iran arms-for-hostages deal called for the president to ask for a law forbidding him to negotiate with terrorists.[6] Like Odysseus who tied himself to the mast, he could thus prevent his sentiments from getting the better of him.

TAXES AND REGULATIONS

As we saw in Chapter 9, the commitment model makes clear that people who care only about absolute wealth will be less effective bargainers than those who care also about how gains are divided. The emotion of envy acts as a commitment device that prevents people from accepting profitable, but one-sided, transactions. Envious persons often behave irrationally, but there is genuine material advantage in being an effective bargainer.

But here too, an emotion solves one commitment problem only to create others. To experience the emotion of envy is to feel concern about relative position in some hierarchy. Such concerns distort our decisions about a variety of important decisions, including the one of how much to save.[7] At any point, a family can save more of its income for retirement, or spend more now for a house in a better school district. For most parents, the lure of providing relative educational advantages for their children is powerful. Yet the laws of simple arithmetic tell us that no matter how much each family spends on housing, only 10 percent of the children can occupy seats in the top decile of the educational quality distribution. As in the familiar stadium metaphor, people leap to their feet to get a better view, only to discover the view no better than when all were seated. In the aggregate, saving less and spending more for houses in better school districts serves only to bid up the prices of those houses. It does nothing to alter the overall distribution of educational opportunities.

Positional concerns thus often cause the individual payoff from spending to appear spuriously large, the payoff from saving spuriously small. Indeed, most families would have grossly inadequate incomes for retirement were it not for the Social Security system and private forced-savings programs. Concerns about relative position help solve the bargaining problem, but in the process create a prisoner's dilemma with respect to savings. Forced-savings programs may be interpreted as an attempt to solve it. Viewed in this light, both the positional concerns themselves and the programs that restrain them are commitment devices.

Hoping to move forward in relative terms, people not only save less, they often work longer hours and skimp on the amounts they devote to safety and insurance. Here too, however, the payoffs are much smaller in the aggregate than they appear to individuals. For when everyone works longer hours, or in riskier jobs, no one moves forward in relative terms. And again the problem is one of simple arithmetic: no matter how many hours we all work, no matter what risks we take on the job, only 10 percent of us can be in the top 10 percent of the income distribution.*

The commitment model suggests that workplace safety standards and various other labor laws may be interpreted as commitment devices that help solve these prisoner's dilemmas. If they are helpful, it is not because firms have too much power or because workers are incompetent—the reasons traditionally offered—but because concerns about relative position are such an important component of human nature. Knowing this is important. It can help confine regulation to the areas in which it has at least a chance of doing some good. It also suggests specific alternative policies that can achieve the same ends much less intrusively.**

---

*Of course, there can be very real advantages to having more income, in absolute terms, even if relative position remains the same. This will especially be so for people who have little to begin with. But the fundamental point remains that, when relative income matters, income-enhancing actions will appear misleadingly attractive to individuals.

**For a much more detailed discussion of these claims, see my 1985 book.

THE IMPORTANCE OF STABLE ENVIRONMENTS

For different reasons, both the commitment model and the tit-for-tat model suggest why environments that encourage repeated interactions might be advantageous. In the tit-for-tat model, repetition is useful because it gives teeth to the threat of retaliation: someone who defects can be punished on a future occasion. The commitment model suggests that stable environments are also useful for the opportunities they provide to discern traits of character and to foster personal ties and loyalty. These, in turn, can sustain cooperation even in situations where defection is impossible to detect (and hence impossible to retaliate against.) Both models thus suggest a reason for the attractiveness of living in small towns, or of forming cohesive neighborhood groups in large cities.

The idea that geographic mobility is a good thing is firmly enshrined in American conventional wisdom. In defense of it, economists have stressed that incomes will be highest when resources are free to move to their most highly valued uses. Stated in this way, their claim seems true by definition. But it does not consider the possible effects that increased mobility may have on our ability to solve commitment problems. A stable population will naturally be much better able than a transient one to form effective bonds of trust. Being firmly rooted has economic costs, just as the self-interest model says. But it also has important economic benefits. People who turn down high-paying jobs in impersonal environments are not necessarily unmindful of their material welfare.

BEHAVIOR TOWARD INSTITUTIONS

The commitment model says that emotional predispositions are the driving force behind moral behavior, an assertion for which we have seen extensive independent support. The role of emotion makes it easy to see why there are many people who would never dream of cheating a friend but think nothing of stealing company property or paying too little income tax. The sympathy that motivates proper conduct toward individuals tends to be much less strongly summoned by large institutions.

At an earlier point in human history, it did not much matter whether people were predisposed not to cheat large organizations, for there were none. But today, of course, they are a large and growing fixture of life, and it is clearly disadvantageous to live in a society where people feel free to cheat them.

The modern strategy for dealing with this problem has been to rely on detection and punishment—industrial stool pigeons, lie detectors, and drug tests for catching miscreants, and fines, lost jobs, or imprisonment for punishing them. The commitment model suggests that an effective alternative, or complement, to this strategy might be to *personalize* people's attitudes toward institutions. Institutions do, after all, act on behalf of real people. We establish governments to take actions for us that we find it impractical to undertake individually. Large corporations, similarly, exist because they enable us to produce more than we could on our own. When we cheat the government, we cheat our neighbors. When we steal from our employers or take drugs on the job, we steal from our coworkers. The difficulty is that we do not experience these connections directly. Because moral behavior is driven largely by emotion, and because emotion is more naturally summoned by persons than by institutions, it would surely help to stress these linkages when we teach our children moral values.

TEACHING VALUES

People of earlier times had a keen appreciation of the importance of character development. Moral lessons learned early in life are not easily forgotten, and churches and families spared little effort in seeing to it that children received them.

Moral behavior almost always calls for self-sacrifice, for the interests of others to be put ahead of our own. Slowly but steadily, the willingness to heed this call has eroded under the forces of materialism. Contrary to Adam Smith's clear intention, his invisible hand planted the idea that moral behavior might not be necessary, that the best of all possible worlds might result if people were simply to pursue their own interests. Darwin's survival of the fittest went a step farther, creating the impression that failure to pursue self-interest might even be hazardous to our health. Smith's carrot and Darwin's stick have by now rendered character development an all but completely forgotten theme in many industrialized countries.

In materialist theories, to be moral is to be a chump. To the extent the "chump model" is believed, it has surely encouraged the adoption of opportunistic values.[8] The late British economist Fred Hirsch argued that the capitalist system cannot function without widespread adherence to the values inherent in the Protestant work ethic. He noted that these values, which took centuries to foster, are deteriorating rapidly. The contradiction of capitalism, he concluded, is that its emphasis on individual self-interest tends to erode the very character traits without which it cannot function.

The commitment model casts this contradiction in a new light. Like the chump model, it acknowledges that doing the right or just thing entails costs on each specific occasion; but it stresses that being thus predisposed need not be a losing strategy. Commitment problems abound and, if cooperators can find one another, material advantages are there for the taking. From the perspective offered by the commitment model, the self-denying traits of character required for efficient markets no longer appear in tension with the materialist premises of the marketplace.

The practical importance of this realization is that it might make a difference to someone faced with the choice of what kind of person to become. Attitudes and values are not etched with great specificity at birth. On the contrary, their development is, as noted, largely the task of culture. Most people have the capacity to develop emotional commitments to behave unopportunistically. Unlike the chump model, the commitment model suggests a simple answer to the nagging question of why even an opportunistic person might want to do so.

Teaching moral values was once the nearly exclusive province of organized religion. The church was uniquely well equipped to perform this task because it had a ready answer to the question, "Why shouldn't I cheat when no one is looking?" Indeed, for the religious person, this question does not even arise, for God is *always* looking. But the threat of damnation appears to have lost much of its punch in recent years. And no alternative institutions have emerged to take over this role of the church.

The decline of religion is not the only important change. Families, even those that want to teach moral values to their children, find themselves increasingly less able to devote the necessary time and energy. Half of all American children now spend some portion of their childhood in single-parent homes. Of those with two parents, it is increasingly the norm for both to work full-time. When the choice is between, on the one hand, having one parent stay home to teach the children moral values (or both stay home part-time) and, on the other, having both work full-time to be able to afford a house in a better school district, most parents feel irresistibly drawn to the latter.

If moral values are important, and are not being taught in the home, why not teach them in the public schools? Few subjects excite greater passions than proposals to teach moral values in the public schools. Liberal watchdogs spring into action the moment any item in the curriculum seems to embody a value judgment. For them, the idea of teaching values means that "someone is going to try to stuff *his* moral values down *my* kid's throat." Conservative fundamentalists, for their part, insist that religious doctrine be presented to students with the same status as scientific facts. As they see it, the failure to teach *their* particular slate of values amounts to a public repudiation of them.

On many specific issues, such as abortion, there is little room for the two groups to compromise. Unfortunately, the salience of these issues obscures our very substantial consensus on questions of value. Most people living today in the United States would agree, for example, that people should

- not lie,
- not steal,
- not cheat,
- keep their promises,
- follow the golden rule, and
- have tolerance and respect for diversity.

This is not to say there is agreement over hard cases. White lies are often considered acceptable, but sometimes hard to define. Even so, there remains striking consensus on most of the concrete examples covered by these simple rules. Why then have *they* not been made part of the curriculum in public schools?

Ironically, part of the difficulty stems from the last item on the list, our respect for diversity. Many judgments about values are of course deeply personal. Even if all but a few of us strongly endorse each item on the list, at least some of those few feel strongly to the contrary. And because of that, many of us feel reluctant to force "our" values on them in a forum like the public schools.

But tolerance, like any of the other virtues, is not absolute. To accommodate the tiny minority who would not be happy to see even this limited slate of values promoted vigorously in the public schools, the rest of us must sacrifice a great deal. If values were merely personal opinions, there might still be ample reason to make this sacrifice. But they are not. When people are taught not to lie and cheat, the world becomes a more attractive place for almost everyone. More important, the gains are not merely general: they will accrue more than proportionately to persons who effectively internalize these values.* Thus

*Because the commitment model says that cooperators and defectors will receive the same average payoff in equilibrium, it may seem to say that there is no particular advantage to becoming more cooperative. But it does not say this at all. As noted in Chapter 4, it describes an equilibrium in which the two competing strategies are defined in *relative* terms. The facts seem to indicate that even defectors must acquire at least *some* moral sentiments if they are to make their way in the world.

the people who insist that values not be taught in the public schools are insisting that other people's children—our children—settle for smaller portions of the character traits that will help them make their way in the material world. It is not clear why the community should be willing to accept this cost on behalf of so few.

Teaching values in the public schools has also encountered political opposition because many people believe it blurs the important boundary between church and state. The commitment model stresses, however, that values spring not only from religious teachings, but also from material considerations quite independent of them. In this respect, of course, it is no different from numerous other materialist accounts of moral values. It *is* different from other accounts, though, in stressing that values benefit *individuals,* not just society as a whole. It thus makes clear what other accounts cannot—namely, that the case for teaching moral values in the public schools is, in this sense, much the same as the traditional case for teaching science and math.

Although the forces described by the commitment model suggest that there can be individual advantage in moral behavior, it is important to bear in mind that these forces, by themselves, do not assure high levels of social cooperation. On the contrary, we know that cooperation rates differ widely across societies; and that even within a society, they tend to differ sharply over time.[9] Such differences are surely not explained by inherited differences in the propensity to cooperate. Much more likely, they reflect differences in the extent to which societies invest in the maintenance of social norms.

The importance of such norms is further underscored by the effect each person's behavior has on the behavior of others. As we saw in the prisoner's dilemma experiments in Chapter 7, people have a strong tendency to cooperate when they expect others to do likewise. By the same token, they are much more likely to defect when they expect defection. Behavioral systems that have this kind of feedback property tend to be highly unstable. If defection rates rise for some reason one year, there will be a tendency for even more people to defect the next year, and still more the year after. Likewise, a rise in cooperation rates will tend to be self-reinforcing.

Societies that fail to intervene in this process miss a valuable opportunity. As sociologist James Coleman has emphasized, a society's norms are an important part of its capital, no less so than its roads or factories.[10] Failure to maintain them will lead to a backward society just as surely as will failure to maintain the more concrete and visible elements of the economic infrastructure.[11]

IS MATERIAL GAIN A PROPER MOTIVE FOR MORALITY?

Some may object that the prospect of material gain is not a proper motive for adopting moral values. This objection, however, misinterprets the principal message of the commitment model. For the model to work, satisfaction from doing the right thing must *not* be premised on the fact that material gains may later follow; rather, it must be *intrinsic* to the act itself. Otherwise a person will lack the necessary motivation to make self-sacrificing choices; and once others sense that, material gains will not, in fact, follow. Under the commitment model, moral sentiments do not lead to material advantage unless they are heartfelt.

Moreover, if it is true that adopting moral values is beneficial, it is surely useful for people to know this. The role of material rewards in the commitment model is logically equivalent to religion's threat of damnation, and there is no more reason to conceal knowledge of one than of the other.

On the contrary, it is not clear that anything short of the prospect of material gain would be sufficient to counteract the opposing tendencies encouraged by the chump model. I recently saw a distressing documentary on PBS in which an interviewer probed the attitudes of high-school students about moral behavior in the world of business. One question he asked was, "If the chemical company you own were about to go bankrupt, and you could save it by dumping toxic wastes, which would cause serious harm to other people, would you do it?" All but one of the students responded without hesitation that they would! I find it difficult to believe that the chump model of morality has not been a major force behind these attitudes. If so, the alternative perspective suggested by the commitment model ought to have given some of these students pause. Or at least, such is my fondest hope.

I believe that the evidence we have seen firmly justifies these four conclusions:

1. *People often do not behave as predicted by the self-interest model.* We vote, we return lost wallets, we do not disconnect the catalytic converters on our cars, we donate bone marrow, we give money to charity, we bear costs in the name of fairness, we act selflessly in love relationships; some of us even risk our lives to save perfect strangers. Traditional attempts to rationalize such behaviors have fallen short. Kin selection is clearly important, and yet many beneficiaries are completely unrelated to their benefactors. Reciprocal altruism and tit-for-tat are also important, but cannot explain cooperation in prisoner's dilemmas that happen only once or in which defection simply cannot be detected. Many of the exchanges we have seen are of precisely this sort and each party knows it.

2. *The reason for irrational behavior is not always that people miscalculate.* To be sure, we often do make mistakes. I hear that First National is lending at 9 percent but forget and pay 10 percent at Citizens' Federal. Or perhaps I am unable to calculate that the tax laws favor buying over renting. If someone pointed out these mistakes to me, I would almost surely change my behavior. Yet many of the most salient examples of irrational behavior do not involve mistakes at

all. The husband who devotedly remains with his wife despite her lingering illness could instead leave her for someone healthy. In many cases, it would be strongly in his material interest to do so. But he stays, and not because he is unable to make the relevant calculation. It is the same with people who reject one-sided offers. Most know perfectly well that to accept would increase their wealth, yet they reject with not the slightest trace of regret.

3. *Emotion is often an important motive for irrational behavior.* Abundant evidence suggests that emotional forces lie behind our failure to maximize. Developmental psychologists tell us that moral behavior emerges hand-in-hand with the maturation of specific emotional competencies. The psychopath fails not because of an inability to calculate self-interest, but because of an inability to empathize, a fundamental lack of emotional conditionability. Thematic Apperception Tests reveal that affection, not concern for material self-interest, is the motivating force behind successful intimate relationships. We know that the way people feel has a strong effect on the likelihood of their performing good deeds, such as helping a stranger or returning a lost wallet. And experiments consistently reveal that cooperators react with outrage when one of their "partners" defects in a prisoner's dilemma.

4. *Being motivated by emotion is often an advantage.* There are many problems that purely self-interested persons simply cannot solve. They cannot make themselves attractive for ventures that require trust. They cannot threaten credibly to walk away from unfair transactions that will increase their wealth. Nor can they deter aggressors when retaliation would be prohibitively costly. Nor can they make credible commitments in intimate personal relationships.

All of these problems are important. We have seen that people who are known to have specific emotional predispositions are often able to solve them. The problems require that we tie our hands, and the emotions have just the desired effect. We have also seen a variety of plausible means whereby others might discern our predispositions. It is not necessary that we be able to judge everyone's character with complete accuracy. The commitment model requires only that we be able to make reasonably accurate judgments concerning people we know very well.

Most of us believe we have this capacity. If we are right, it follows that noble human motives, and the costly behaviors they often summon, will not only survive the ruthless pressures of the material world, but even be nourished by them.

On the strength of the evidence, we must say that the self-interest model provides a woefully inadequate description of the way people actually behave. Yet the model continues to flourish. Its proponents have driven out traditionalists from field after field in the behavioral sciences. One reason is that, where traditionalism is often vague, the self-interest model is painstakingly precise. Many of its predictions may be wrong, but at least it *makes* predictions. And in fairness, a great many of them turn out to be right.

But the most important reason for the self-interest model's success is that its logic is so compelling. It reveals an elegant coherence behind countless seemingly unrelated patterns of experience. The most familiar examples come from the animal kingdom. Darwin's theory tells us that hawks see so well because the ones with keener eyesight always caught more prey, and thus left more descendants.

The model has proved equally useful for understanding the evolution of organizations.[12] It tells us, for example, that because firms that pollute the environment have lower costs, they will inexorably drive out their more socially conscious rivals. Most people may want lower pollution, but will find it irresistibly tempting to free-ride, to rely on others to buy the more expensive products of the nonpolluting firms.

Similar material pressures, the model argues, have molded the behavior of human beings. Its hardnosed, if unhappy, conclusion is that, over the millennia, selfish people have gradually driven out all others.

And yet despite the compelling logic in favor of this conclusion, the fact remains that it is wrong. In attempting to explain why, most critics want to deny that material payoffs played such a pre-eminent role. They often point out that people with high incomes tend to have fewer children, and conclude that ordinary selection pressures simply do not apply in the case of humans.

But this response fails on a closer look, for the negative relationship between fecundity and income is only very recent. During most of human history, environmental conditions were much more stressful than now, and there was always a very strong link between a family's material success and the number of its children who survived. Moreover, polygynous societies were the rule in early human history, and men who were not successful in material terms often did not even marry at all. Surely it is an unfruitful strategy to criticize the materialist model by merely asserting that humans are somehow exempt from its logic.

Critics are also quick to say that culture overwhelms the tendencies encouraged by material incentives. But this criticism, too, falls short. Even within the most strictly materialist theory, it is easy to see why societies would try to restrain the pursuit of self-interest: prisoner's dilemmas abound, and all stand to gain when each shows restraint. Materialists also have no difficulty understanding why opportunistic persons might find it attractive to live in such societies. What critics have not explained, however, is why opportunists would comply with efforts to instill moral values in their *own* children. Why don't they instead teach them to cooperate only when it is in their narrow interests, and to behave opportunistically otherwise?

There are many intelligent persons who appear able to resist cultural conditioning. By the logic of the materialist theories, these people should have long since driven others out. We need not deny the obvious importance of culture to say that, *by itself,* it cannot account for why this has not happened. Granted, evolution has put us on an extraordinarily long leash, and cultural indoctrination is surely necessary to explain the details of unopportunistic behavior. But just as surely, it is not sufficient.

A FRIENDLY AMENDMENT TO THE SELF-INTEREST MODEL

The difficulty confronting critics is that they have failed to come forward with an alternative theory. None of the evidence they cite against the self-interest model is really new. The experiments with prisoner's dilemmas date from the 1950s, those with honesty and victims-in-distress from the 1960s. Even Kagan's recent work on the role of emotional competencies merely provides modern scientific footing for beliefs that were all but universal during the nineteenth century. But as the philosopher Thomas Kuhn has stressed, a reigning theory is almost never displaced by mere contradictions in the data.[13] If it is to be challenged at all, it must be by an alternative theory that better fits the facts.

The commitment model is a tentative first step in the construction of a theory of unopportunistic behavior. It challenges the self-interest model's portrayal of human nature in its own terms by accepting the fundamental premise that material incentives ultimately govern behavior. Its point of departure is the observation that persons *directly* motivated to pursue self-interest are often for that very reason doomed to fail. They fail because they are unable to solve commitment problems.

These problems can often be solved by persons known to have abandoned the quest for maximum material advantage. The emotions that lead people to behave in seemingly irrational ways can thus indirectly lead to greater material well-being. Viewed in these terms, the commitment model is less a disavowal of the self-interest model than a friendly amendment to it. Without abandoning the basic materialist framework, it suggests how the nobler strands of human nature might have emerged and prospered.

It does not seem naive to hope that such an understanding might have beneficial effects on our behavior. After all, the self-interest model, by encouraging us to expect the worst in others, does seem to have brought out the worst in us. Someone who expects always to be cheated has little motive to behave honestly. The commitment model may not tell us to expect the best in others, but it does encourage a markedly more optimistic view.

APPENDIX

A FORMAL VERSION OF THE COMMITMENT MODEL

This appendix lays out some of the technical details of a more general version of the commitment model described in Chapter 3.

Consider a population, each of whose members bears one of two traits, H or D. Those bearing H are honest, but those bearing D are not.[1] To be honest here means to refrain from cheating one's partner in a cooperative venture, even when cheating cannot be punished. To be dishonest means always to cheat under the same circumstances.

Suppose people face one of two options:

1. They may pair with someone in a joint venture whose payoffs are as given in Table A.1. This venture will occur only once and dishonest behavior cannot be punished.

or

2. They may pair with someone in an alternative venture in which behavior can be perfectly monitored. Call this the "work-alone" option, because it does not involve activities that require trust. It too will occur only once, and its payoff is x_2 for each person, irrespective of the combinations of types who interact. Thus, the work-alone option offers the same payoff as when two dishonest persons interact in venture 1.

Many readers will find it more plausible to assume that persons who cheat one another in venture 1 do worse than those who participate in ventures that do not require trust (that is, to assume a payoff larger than x_2 for the work-alone option). But since the goal of this exercise is to see whether honest persons can prosper in

TABLE A.1: The Payoffs to A from Interaction with B

		B	
		H	D
A	H	x_3	x_1
	D	x_4	x_2

the material world, I retain the more conservative assumption that the work-alone option pays only x_2. If honest persons can survive with that payoff, they will certainly do so with an even higher one.

Since working alone pays only x_2, it will never appeal to a dishonest person, who can always do at least as well in venture 1. Its obvious attraction for an honest person is that there is no chance of being cheated; the downside, however, is that its payoff is less than x_3, the gain from successful cooperation in venture 1. (More below on how honest persons choose between the two options.)

In addition to their behavioral differences, let the Hs and Ds differ with respect to the genes that influence some observable characteristic S, which is also influenced by random environmental forces. More specifically, suppose that the observable characteristic for person i takes the value,

$$S_i = \mu_i + \epsilon_i$$

where

$$\mu_i = \begin{array}{l} \mu_H \text{ if } i \text{ is honest,} \\[6pt] \mu_D \text{ if } i \text{ is dishonest, } \mu_H > \mu_D, \end{array}$$

and ϵ_i is an independently, identically distributed random variable with zero mean. The μ_i component of S_i is heritable, the ϵ_i component is not.

A. CASE 1: A PERFECTLY RELIABLE SIGNAL

If the variance of ϵ_i were zero, everyone could tell with certainty whether any given person was an H or a D. In that case, Hs would pair only with other Hs in venture 1, and would receive a payoff of x_3. The Ds would be left to pair with one another, for which they would receive only x_2. Thus, if the signal that accompanied each trait were *perfectly* reliable, the Hs would soon drive the Ds to extinction.

B. CASE 2: IMPERFECT SIGNALS

By contrast, when ϵ_i has sufficiently large variance, S_i provides merely a measure of the probability that i is trustworthy. As an illustration of this more interesting case, suppose people draw their S-values independently from the probability densities f_D and f_H shown in Figure A.1.[2]

In terms of the discussion in Chapter 3, the relative position of the two densities reflects imperfect mimicry by the Ds of the trait used by the Hs to identify themselves as trustworthy. For the densities shown, whose ranges do not overlap completely, we are sure that individuals with $S > U_D$ are honest, and that those with $S < L_H$ are dishonest. Individuals whose S-values lie in the region where the two densities overlap may be either H or D. If h denotes the proportion of the population bearing H, the probability that an individual j with $S = S_j$ is honest is then given by

$$(1) \qquad Pr\{H_j | S_j\} = \frac{h f_H(S_j)}{h f_H(S_i) + (1 - h) f_D(S_j)}.$$

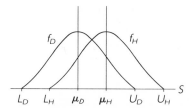

FIGURE A.1   Probability Densities for an Observable Signal of Trustworthiness

For the two densities shown in Figure A.1, $Pr\{H_j|S_j\}$ is plotted in Figure A.2 for two different values of h.

i. The Threshold Signal Value

Given the payoffs in Table A.1, both Hs and Ds will clearly do best by interacting (if they choose venture 1) with other individuals whom they believe to be Hs. Consider the problem confronting individual i, who is H and must decide whether to interact with individual j, who has $S = S_j$. Let $E(X_{ij}|S_j)$ denote the expected payoff to i from pairing with this individual. If the alternative is the work-alone option (which has payoff x_2), the condition that makes it worth i's while to work with j is given by

$$(2) \qquad E(X_{ij}|S_j) = x_3 Pr\{H_j|S_j\} + x_1[1 - Pr\{H_j|S_j\}] \geq x_2.$$

Call S^* the value of S_j that satisfies $E(X_{ij}|S_j) = x_2$. S^* is the smallest value of S_j for which it would be as attractive for i to work with j as to work alone. Using the densities from Figure A.1, this threshold signal value is shown in Figure A.3 for the particular case of $h = 1/2$ and $x_2 = (x_1 + x_3)/2$.

Using equations 1 and 2, we can easily show that S^* is a decreasing function of h: as the proportion of the population that is honest grows, it becomes ever more probable that an individual whose S lies between L_H and U_D is honest, and ever more likely, therefore, that the expected payoff from interacting with that individual will exceed x_2. It is also easy to show that S^* decreases with increases in $(x_3 - x_2)$ and increases with increases in $(x_2 - x_1)$. The greater the payoff to successful coop-

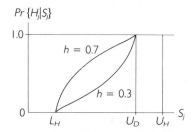

FIGURE A.2   The Probability of Being Honest Conditional on *S*

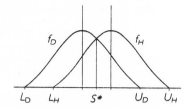

FIGURE A.3   The Threshold Signal Value When $h = \frac{1}{2}$ and
$$x_2 = (x_1 + x_3)/2$$

eration, and the smaller the penalty for being cheated, the lower will be the threshold signal for cooperation. For the particular case of $(x_4 - x_3) = (x_3 - x_2) = (x_2 - x_1) = x_1$, the schedule $S^*(h)$ that corresponds to the densities from Figure A.1 is plotted in Figure A.4.

ii. The Sorting Process Whereby Interacting Pairs Form

It is not strictly correct to say that an individual who is honest faces only the alternatives of working alone or working with someone with $S = S_j$. There are other members of the population besides j; and, of those with $S > S^*$, i will want to choose a partner with the highest possible S-value. The problem is that *everyone* prefers to interact with such a partner, and there are only so many of them to go around.

The bearer of a high S-value, whether he is honest or not, owns a valuable asset. The natural way to exploit it will be to use it to attract a partner whose own S-value is also high. Without going into technical details, we can see that the outcome will be for the two with the highest S-values to pair up, then the next two, and so on until all those with $S \geq S^*$ are paired. Needless to say, the expected total payoff to any pair increases with the S-values of its members. If the population is sufficiently dense, as I will assume here, the S-values within each pair will be virtually the same.[3]

iii. The Expected Payoff Functions

With the foregoing discussion in mind, let us now investigate what happens if a mutation provides a small toehold for the Hs in a population that initially consisted

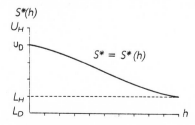

FIGURE A.4   The Threshold Signal Value as a Function of h

entirely of Ds. Will the Hs make headway or be driven to extinction? To answer this question, we must compare the average payoffs for Hs and Ds, denoted $E(X|H)$ and $E(X|D)$, respectively, when h is near zero. To calculate $E(X|H)$, note from equations 1 and 2 that $S^*(h)$ approaches U_D as h approaches zero (see Figure A.4). As the share of the population that is honest approaches zero, the rational strategy for an honest person, in the limit, is to interact only with people whose S-values lie to the right of U_D—that is, with people who are certain to be honest. As h approaches zero, the expected payoff to the Hs thus approaches the limiting value

$$(3) \qquad \lim_{h \to 0} E(X|H) = x_3 \int_{U_D}^{U_H} f_H(S)dS \; + \; x_2 \int_{L_H}^{U_D} f_H(S)dS.$$

The second term on the right-hand side of equation 3 reflects the fact that an H with $S < U_D$ does best by not interacting—that is, by choosing the work-alone option. (He would be delighted to interact with an H with $S > U_D$, but that person would not agree to interact with him).

The corresponding limiting expected payoff for the Ds is simply x_2. So when the proportion of the population that is honest is very small, we have $E(X|H) > E(X|D)$, which means h will grow.

What if we had started at the opposite extreme—in a population in which the proportion of Ds was near zero? In the limit, the decision rule for the Hs would be "interact with anyone whose S-value exceeds L_H." As h approaches one, the expected payoff for the Ds would thus approach

$$(4) \qquad \lim_{h \to 1} E(X|D) = x_2 \int_{L_D}^{L_H} f_D(S)dS \; + \; x_4 \int_{L_H}^{U_D} f_D(S)dS.$$

The corresponding expected payoff for H will approach x_3 as h approaches one. Comparing the right-hand side of equation 4 with x_3, we see that the former will be larger for sufficiently large values of x_2 or x_4, or for sufficiently extensive overlap of the ranges of f_H and f_D. Assuming that $E(X|D)$ does exceed x_3 for values of h close to one, h will then begin to fall.

To investigate the behavior of this population as it evolves away from either of the two pure states, we need general expressions for $E(X|H)$ and $E(X|D)$.

The first step in finding $E(X|H)$ is to use equations 1 and 2 to find S^* as a function of h (as was done to generate Figure A.4). Given $S^*(h)$, we then calculate P_H and P_D, the respective shares of the honest and dishonest populations with $S > S^*$:

$$(5) \qquad P_H = \int_{S^*}^{U_H} f_H(S)dS$$

and

$$(6) \qquad P_D = \int_{S^*}^{U_D} f_D(S)dS.$$

Given equations 5 and 6, we can compute $E(X|H)$ as a weighted sum of the payoffs from (1) working alone, (2) interacting with someone who is honest, and (3) interacting with someone who is dishonest. Noting that $(1-P_H)$ is the probability that an honest individual works alone, and using $\lambda = hP_H/(hP_H^+ \; (1-h)P_D)$ to denote the share of the population with $S>S^*$ that is honest, we have

$$(7) \qquad E(X|H) = (1-P_H)\,x_2 + P_H\lambda x_3 + (1-\lambda)x_1].$$

In like fashion, we may calculate $E(X|D)$ as weighted sum of the payoffs to working alone, interacting with someone who is honest, and interacting with someone who is dishonest:

$$(8) \qquad E(X|D) = (1-P_D)x_2 + P_D[\lambda x_4 + (1-\lambda)x_2].$$

For our illustrative densities from Figure A.1, $E(X|H)$ and $E(X|D)$ are plotted as functions of h in Figure A.5. Both $E(X|H)$ and $E(X|D)$ will in general be increasing functions of h. For the particular densities from Figure A.1, the two curves cross exactly once.

The equilibrium value of h is the one for which $E(X|D)$ and $E(X|H)$ intersect. For an equilibrium to be stable, $E(X|H)$ must cross $E(X|D)$ from above. Since $E(X|H)$ will always be greater than $E(X|D)$ at $h=0$, the intersection of the two curves (assuming they intersect at all) will thus correspond to a stable equilibrium value of h, like the one depicted in Figure A.5.

C. CASE 3: COSTS OF SCRUTINY

The model can be made more complete, and the existence of an equilibrium assured, if we now add the assumption that resources must be expended in order to inspect the S-values of others. Let us assume specifically that these values can be observed only by people who have borne the cost C of becoming sensitized.

First consider the limiting case of a population in which h approaches zero. A necessary condition for any interaction to occur at all is that $x_3 - C > x_2$. Assuming that condition is met, only those honest persons whose own S-values exceed U_D will find it worthwhile to spend C to become sensitized. Hs with $S < U_D$ will work alone (because there is no prospect of their finding an H with whom to interact). Thus the latter Hs will receive payoff x_2, the same as $E(X|D)$ when h is zero. No Ds will pay to become sensitized because they too have no chance of finding an unclaimed H,

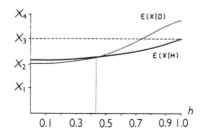

FIGURE A.5 **Expected Payoffs for H and D**

so the expected payoff for Ds here is x_2. For very small values of h, then, some Hs will fare the same as the Ds, others better. Thus, as before, h will grow when it starts near zero.

For values of h near one, no one will find it worthwhile to pay C to become sensitized. With everyone's S thus effectively out of sight, even Ds with $S < L_H$ will find honest partners with whom to interact. $E(X|D)$ will thus approach x_4 as h approaches one. So, unlike the case where S could be observed for free, it is no longer possible for the Hs to take over the entire population, regardless of how close x_3 may be to x_4.

A key step in understanding the nature of the equilibrium that results when h starts near zero is to recognize that it will always be most strongly in the interests of those with the highest S-values to bear the expense of becoming sensitized. To see this, recall from the earlier discussion that the bearer of a high S-value owns a valuable asset he can use to attract a partner whose own S-value is also high. It is in the interests of bearers of high S-values to interact with others who are H. And, having become sensitized, they are then able to identify others with high S-values (the people who are most likely to be H) and interact with them. Persons with relatively low S-values, who can only hope to claim a partner whose own S-value is also low, therefore face a lower expected payoff to the investment of becoming sensitized.

Knowing this enables us to conclude that the equilibrium h must be sufficiently low that it pays at least *some* of the population to become sensitized. We can show this by noting that, if we assume the contrary, we get a contradiction. That is, suppose we assume that, in equilibrium, the expected payoff to the person with the highest S-value is higher if he does *not* become sensitized. Recall that his expected payoff if he had become sensitized, call it $E(X,C)$, would be

$$(9) \qquad E(X,C) = x_3 - C,$$

which we have already assumed is greater than x_2. We know that if it does not pay the H with the highest S-value to become sensitized, it does not pay any other H to do so either. And when nobody pays C, the odds of Hs with low S-values pairing successfully are the same as for those with high S-values. *All* of the Hs must thus expect a payoff higher than x_2. This means it pays all of the Hs to interact, and all will expect the same payoff, call it $E(X|O)$:

$$(10) \qquad E(X|O) = hx_3 + (1-h)x_1.$$

But the expected payoff for each D when everyone interacts is $hx_4 + (1-h)x_2$, which is clearly larger than $E(X,O)$.

Thus, if we assume that the equilibrium h is so large that it does not pay even those with the highest S-values to become sensitized, we are forced to conclude that the expected payoff to D exceeds the expected payoff to H at that value of h. This means that it could not have been an equilibrium value after all. The equilibrium h must therefore be small enough that it is in the interests of at least those with the highest S-values to become sensitized.

To gain further insight into the nature of the equilibrium here, let us again consider a population in which h started near zero and has grown to some positive value, say, h_0. At h_0, who will interact with whom, and in whose interests will it be to become sensitized? We can show it will pay those persons with S greater than some threshold value, $S^*(h_0) < U_D$, to become sensitized and interact with others with like S-values. And we can also show that it may or may not pay Hs with $S < S^*(h_0)$—i.e., those who do not find it profitable to become sensitized—to interact at random with other members of the truncated population (people with $S < S^*(h_0)$).

The threshold value $S^*(h_0)$ is determined as follows. Again making use of the notation defined in equations 5 and 6, note that

(11)
$$1 - P_H = \int_{L_H}^{S^*(h_0)} f_H(S)dS$$

and

(12)
$$1 - P_D = \int_{L_D}^{S^*(h_0)} f_D(S)dS$$

are the respective shares of the honest and dishonest populations for which $S < S^*(h_0)$. Let $\delta = (1 - P_H)h_0/[1 - P_H)h_0 + (1 - P_D)(1 - h_0)]$ denote the share of this truncated population that is honest. $S^*(h_0)$ is the value of S that solves the following equation:

(13)
$$Pr\{H|S^*(h_0)\}x_3 + (1 - Pr\{H|S^*(h_0)\})x_1 - C$$
$$= \max\{x_2, \, \delta x_3 + (1 - \delta)x_1\}.$$

The left-hand side of equation 13 is the expected payoff to an H with $S = S^*(h_0)$ who pays C to become sensitized and then interacts with someone with the same S-value (see equation 1). The second expression within the brackets on the right-hand side of equation 13 is the expected payoff to that same H (or, for that matter, to any other H) if he does not become sensitized and interacts with a randomly chosen person from the truncated population (again, those Ds and Hs with $S < S^*(h_0)$). If x_2 is larger than that figure, as it is likely to be for small values of h_0, all Hs with $S < S^*(h_0)$ will work alone. Otherwise all Hs will interact—those with $S > S^*(h_0)$ interacting with others with $S > S^*(h_0)$, those with $S < S^*(h_0)$ interacting with randomly chosen members of the remaining population. Depending on the particular densities used for f_h and f_D, either outcome is possible.

Once $S^*(h_0)$ is determined, it is straightforward, albeit tedious, to calculate $E(X|H)$ and $E(X|D)$. Using the rule that h grows when $E(X|H) > E(X|D)$, the equilibrium value of h is the one for which the two expected payoff curves cross. If we again employ the densities from Figure A.1, and use $C = x_1/4$, the expected payoff curves and the equilibrium h are as depicted in Figure A.6.

Two features of Figure A.6 merit discussion. Note first the discontinuities in the two payoff curves. To see why these occur, recall that it would not be in the interests of any persons to become sensitized if the population initially consisted almost entirely of Hs. Even when the S-values of others cannot be seen without first bearing the costs of scrutiny, it will pay all of the Hs, even those with the highest S-values, to interact at random with people from the population at large. For values of h close to 1, the expected payoff to the Ds exceeds that to the Hs, which, as noted earlier, cause h to fall. Once h reaches the value for which

(14) $$E(X|O) = hx_3 + (1-h)x_1 = x_3 - C,$$

however, it abruptly becomes in the interests of those Hs with $S > U_D$ to become sensitized, thereby to interact selectively with one another, rather than with individuals chosen at random. At the value of h that solves equation 14, the Hs who incur the costs of becoming sensitized are exactly compensated for those costs by the

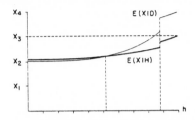

FIGURE A.6 Equilibrium When There Are Costs of Scrutiny

higher gains from selective interaction. But their sudden unavailability for interaction with the remainder of the population produces an abrupt decline in everyone else's expected payoff. This decline is reflected in the discontinuities in the expected payoff curves in Figure A.6.

Note also that the equilibrium value of h in Figure A.6 is larger than the corresponding value in Figure A.5. Although the costs of scrutiny reduce the expected payoffs to both groups in absolute terms, the reduction is more pronounced for the Ds. This happens because the costs of scrutiny cause the schedule $S^*(h)$ to shift to the right. And given that f_D lies to the left of f_H, any such shift in $S^*(h)$ will cause a proportionally greater reduction to the Ds' payoff than to the Hs'. It is perhaps fitting that, in their struggle with the Ds, the Hs are abetted by the fact that it requires some effort to observe the symptoms of trustworthiness.

NOTES

CHAPTER 1

1. Rice, 1982, pp. 62, 63.
2. See, for example, Hirschman, 1977.
3. 1960.
4. 1960, pp. 43, 44.
5. Ekman, 1985, pp. 15, 16.
6. 1984, p. xiv.
7. 1968.

CHAPTER 2

1. 1976 (1759), p. 47.
2. 1976, p. 139.
3. 1964.
4. 1975.
5. 1974.
6. 1978, p. 155.
7. 1985, p. 401.
8. Again, see Wilson, 1975.
9. 1971.
10. 1978, p. 162.
11. 1965.
12. 1984.
13. 1980.
14. 1980, p. 103.
15. Herbert Read, quoted by Ashworth, 1980, p. 104.
16. Mayer, quoted by Axelrod, 1984, pp. 59, 60.
17. Axelrod, 1984, p. 60.
18. 1971, pp. 50, 51.
19. Trivers, 1985, p. 388.
20. 1985.

21. Eldredge and Gould, 1972.
22. 1975, p. 113.
23. 1971, p. 83.

CHAPTER 3

1. 1976 (1759), p. 194.
2. 1965 (quoted by Banfield, 1985, p. 278).
3. See, e.g., Parfit, 1984.

CHAPTER 4

1. 1971, p. 50.
2. 1976 (1759), p. 194.
3. 1975.
4. Chung and Herrnstein, 1967; Baum and Rachlin, 1969; Herrnstein, 1970; Ainslee and Haendel, 1983; Solnick et al., 1980.
5. 1871 (1911), pp. 72–73.
6. 1956.
7. Becker and Stigler, 1977.
8. Ainslie, 1975; Elster, 1979; Schelling, 1980; Thaler and Shefrin, 1981; Herrnstein, 1981.
9. Ainslie, 1982; Winston, 1980; Mello, 1972; Cook, 1982.
10. Pattison, Sobell, and Sobell, 1977.
11. Cook and Tauchen, 1982.
12. 1981, p. 481.

CHAPTER 5

1. Davies and Halliday, 1977, quoted by Krebs and Dawkins, 1984.
2. Caryl, 1979; Krebs and Dawkins, 1984.
3. Krebs and Dawkins, 1984.
4. 1952.
5. 1977, p. 104.
6. Krebs and Dawkins, 1984.
7. 1970.

CHAPTER 6

1. 1873 (1872), p. 50.
2. 1873 (1872), p. 50.
3. 1873 (1872), p. 28.
4. 1873 (1872), p. 29.
5. 1873 (1872), p. 50.
6. 1873 (1872), p. 51.
7. 1873 (1872), p. 7.
8. 1873 (1872), p. 66.

9. Ekman, 1985, p. 124.
10. 1985, p. 132.
11. Ekman, 1985, p. 134.
12. Ekman, 1985, p. 134.
13. 1985, p. 136.
14. Darwin, 1873 (1872), pp. 262–63.
15. 1985, pp. 141–42.
16. 1873 (1872), pp. 262–63.
17. 1873 (1872), pp. 337–38.
18. 1985.
19. Ekman, 1985, p. 93.
20. Scherer, 1982.
21. DePaulo, Zuckerman, and Rosenthal, 1980; Zuckerman, DePaulo, and Rosenthal, 1981.
22. 1985, pp. 99–102.
23. 1985, pp. 415–16.
24. For an excellent interpretive summary, see Goleman, 1985.
25. Bruell, 1970.

CHAPTER 7

1. Lykken, 1981.
2. DePaulo, Zuckerman, and Rosenthal, 1980; and Zuckerman, DePaulo, and Rosenthal, 1981.
3. DePaulo, Zuckerman, and Rosenthal, 1980, p. 130.
4. Zuckerman, DePaulo, and Rosenthal, 1981, p. 139.
5. Zuckerman, DePaulo, and Rosenthal, 1981, p. 139.
6. DePaulo and Rosenthal, 1979.

CHAPTER 8

1. Lenneberg, 1967; Chomsky, 1957, 1965.
2. 1984.
3. Schwartz, 1986; Bowles and Gintis, 1986.
4. Konner, 1982.
5. Quoted in Konner, 1982, p. 28.
6. Seligman and Hager, 1972, p. 8.
7. Kagan, 1984, p. 45.
8. Harkness, Edwards, and Super, 1981, p. 600, quoted in Kagan, 1984, p. 119.
9. 1739, p. 520, quoted in Kagan, 1984, p. 119.
10. Kagan, 1984, p. 125.
11. Bruner, 1983.
12. Kagan, 1984, p. 127.
13. 1984, p. 127.
14. Restak, 1979.
15. Frank, 1985, p. 18

16. 1984, p. 122.

17. 1978, p. 256.

18. 1976.

19. 1971.

20. Hare, 1975, 1978, 1979; Ziskind, 1978; Ziskind, Syndulko, and Melzman, 1978.

21. Surveyed by Hare and Hare, 1967.

22. 1970, p. 14.

23. For a comprehensive survey, see Wilson and Herrnstein, 1985.

24. Barndt and Johnson, 1955; Black and Gregson, 1973; Mischel, 1961; Stein, Sarbin, and Kulik, 1968.

25. Kelley and Veldman, 1964.

26. 1984, p. xiv.

CHAPTER 9

1. Quoted by Barrett, 1986.

2. Kahneman, Knetsch, and Thaler, 1986b, p. 18.

3. Kahneman et al., 1986b, p. 19.

4. 1982.

5. 1986a.

6. Bazerman, 1985; Binmore et al., 1985; Guth and Tietz, 1985; Guth, 1986.

7. 1985.

8. 1985, p. 206.

9. Kahneman et al., 1986b.

10. Stigler, 1946; Seidman, 1979; Krueger and Summers, 1986.

11. Elsewhere (Frank, 1984a, b; 1985) I develop this claim at length.

12. Frank, 1985. Chapter 4.

CHAPTER 10

1. 1981, p. 39.

2. 1982.

3. 1961.

4. 1964.

5. Thibaut and Kelley, 1959.

6. 1983, p. 289.

7. 1983, p. 141.

8. Walster, et al., 1978, p. 7.

9. 1986.

10. McClelland, 1986.

11. 1960, p. 106, quoted by Berscheid and Walster, 1974.

12. Mincer, 1963; Willis, 1973; Ben-Porath, 1973.

13. Becker, Landes, and Michael, 1977.

14. Keeley, 1977.

15. 1984.

16. Krebs and Dawkins, 1984, p. 385.

17. Sonnet 116.
18. 1977, p. 543.
19. Clark and Mills, 1979.
20. Clark and Mills, 1979, p. 24.
21. Bradburn and Noll, 1969.
22. Bachman, Kahn, Davidson, and Johnston, 1967.
23. Bradburn and Caplovitz, 1965.
24. Easterlin, 1973.
25. 1973.
26. DeCharms, Morrison, Reitman, and McClelland, 1955.
27. Atkinson and McClelland, 1948; McClelland, 1951.
28. McClelland, Davidson and Saron, 1979 quoted by McClelland, 1986; McClelland, Ross, and Patel, 1985.
29. McClelland, Stier, Patel, and Brown, 1985, quoted by McClelland, 1986.
30. 1980, 1982.
31. 1980, quoted by McAdams, 1982.
32. 1986, quoted by McClelland, 1986.
33. McClelland and Jemmott, 1980; McClelland, Alexander, and Marks, 1982.
34. Gazzaniga, 1985, p. 77.
35. 1983.
36. 1985.
37. 1968.
38. 1985, pp. 63, 64.
39. 1985, p. 81.

CHAPTER 11

1. Rushton, 1980.
2. Rushton, 1980, p. 3.
3. Hornstein et al., 1968, 1971.
4. 1968, p. 223.
5. 1968, p. 223.
6. Hornstein, 1976, p. 118.
7. 1969.
8. 1970.
9. 1970, p. 58.
10. 1970, p. 90.
11. 1981.
12. 1986a.
13. Andreoni, 1986a, p. 1.
14. 1978, 1984.
15. Bohm, 1972; Sweeney, 1973; Smith, 1978; Marwell and Ames, 1981; Isaac, Walker, and Thomas, 1984; Isaac, McCue, and Plott, 1985; Isaac and Walker, 1985; Andreoni, 1986b; Dawes, Orbell, and van de Kragt, 1986.
16. 1980.
17. 1977.

18. Bonacich, 1972; Rapoport et al., 1962; Bixenstein et al., 1966; Brechner, 1977; Edney and Harper, 1978.
19. 1977, p. 7.
20. 1977, p. 7.
21. 1972.
22. 1972, p. 126.
23. 1981.
24. 1986a.
25. January 8, 1986.
26. Page, 1977; Riker and Ordeshook, 1973.
27. Fiorina, 1978; Kramer, 1971; Tufte, 1978.
28. Kramer, 1971.
29. Fiorina, 1978; Gatlin et al., 1987; Kinder and Kiewert, 1978; Lau et al., 1978; Sears et al., 1978.
30. 1980, p. 681.
31. Riker and Ordeshook, 1968.
32. 1970, pp. 16, 17.
33. 1957, p. 270.
34. 1970.
35. 1970.
36. 1970, pp. 286–87.
37. 1970, p. 291.
38. 1968.
39. p. 84.
40. Schwartz, 1970; Kohn, 1969.

CHAPTER 12

1. Grossman and Hart, 1983; Harris and Raviv, 1978; Holmstrom, 1979, 1982; Milgrom and Weber, 1982; Pratt and Zeckhauser, 1985; Radner, 1981; Riley, 1975; Rothschild and Stiglitz, 1976, Shavell, 1979.
2. Lazear and Rosen, 1981.
3. Abegglen, 1973, p. 62.
4. 1985.
5. Quoted by Banfield, 1985, p. 300.
6. Reich, 1987.
7. Duesenberry, 1949.
8. Hirsch, 1976; Schwartz, 1986.
9. Hirschman, 1982.
10. Coleman, 1986.
11. Banfield, 1958.
12. Nelson and Winter, 1978.
13. 1962.

APPENDIX

1. More precisely, imagine a population with two alleles, a_1 and a_2, at a given genetic locus. Individuals homozygous in a_1 are "honest," those homozygous in

a_2 are not. Regardless of what effect honest behavior may have on fitness, each allele in heterozygous individuals will be affected equally by the interactions of these individuals with others. We may thus disregard these individuals when analyzing the competition between a_1 and a_2. In the text, H refers to individuals homozygous in a_1, D to those homozygous in a_2.

2. Each density shown in Figure A.1 is derived from the standard normal density, $f(S)$, in the following manner: First the tails are truncated at two standard deviations from the mean by subtracting $f(2)$ from every point. Let I denote the area under the resulting functions. The functions are then normalized by dividing each by I. Letting 2 and 3 be the respective means, we thus have

$$f_H = (1/\sqrt{2\pi}) \, (1/I)[\exp(-(x-3)^2/2) - \exp(-2)],$$

and

$$f_D = (1/\sqrt{2\pi}) \, (1/I)[\exp(-(x-2)^2/2) - \exp(-2)].$$

3. In less dense populations, S-values could differ within pairs, suggesting that the member in any pair with the lower S-value might have to pay his partner in order to induce him to participate. Any such transfer payments will obviously not affect the average payoff to members of a cooperating pair. Even if the assumption of dense populations did not hold, therefore, complications of this sort would create no difficulties: we are concerned only with average payoffs to the two genotypes here.

REFERENCES

Abegglen, James. *Management and Worker*. Tokyo: Sophia University, 1973.

Abrams, Burtran, and Mark Schmitz. "The Crowding Out Effect of Government Transfers on Private Charitable Contributions," *Public Choice* 33 (1978): 29–39.

Abrams, Burtran, and Mark Schmitz. "The Crowding-Out Effect of Governmental Transfers on Private Charitable Contributions—Cross-Section Evidence," *National Tax Journal* 37 (1984): 563–68.

Ainslie, George. "Specious Reward: A Behavioral Theory of Impulsiveness and Impulse Control." *Psychological Bulletin* 21 (1975): 485–89.

———. "A Behavioral Economic Approach to the Defense Mechanisms: Freud's Energy Theory Revisited." *Social Science Information* 21 (1982): 735–79.

———. "Behavioral Economics II: Motivated, Involuntary Behavior." *Social Science Information* 23 (1984): 47–78.

Ainslie, George, and Richard Herrnstein. "Preference Reversal and Delayed Reinforcement," *Animal Learning and Behavior* 9 (1981): 476–82.

Ainslie, George, and V. Haendel. "The Motives of the Will." In *Etiologies of Alcoholism and Drug Addiction,* edited by E. Gottheil, A. McLennan and K. Druley. Springfield, N.J.: Thomas, 1982.

Akerlof, George. "The Market for 'Lemons.' " *Quarterly Journal of Economics* 84 (1970): 488–500.

———. "Loyalty Filters." *American Economic Review* 73 (March 1983): 54–63.

Andreoni, James. "Private Giving to Public Goods: The Limits of Altruism." University of Michigan Department of Economics Working Paper, 1986a.

———. "Why Free Ride." University of Wisconsin Working Paper, 1986b.

Aronson, E. *The Social Animal.* 4th ed. New York: Freeman, 1984.

Arrow, Kenneth. "Political and Economic Evaluation of Social Effects and Externalities." In *Frontiers of Quantitative Economics,* edited by M. Intrilligator. Amsterdam: North Holland, 1971: 3–25.

———. "Gifts and Exchanges." In *Altruism, Morality and Economic Theory,* edited by E. S. Phelps. New York: Russell Sage, 1975: 13–28.

Ashworth, Tony. *Trench Warfare, 1914–18: The Live and Let Live System.* New York: Holmes and Meier, 1980.

Atkinson, J. W., and David McClelland. "The Effect of Different Intensities of the

Hunger Drive on Thematic Apperception." *Journal of Experimental Psychology* 38 (1948): 643–58.

Aumann, Robert. "Survey of Repeated Games." In *Essays in Game Theory and Mathematical Economics in Honor of Oskar Morgenstern,* Mannheim: Bibliographisches Institut, 1981.

Axelrod, Robert. *The Evolution of Cooperation.* New York: Basic Books, 1984.

Bachman, J., R. Kahn, T. Davidson, and L. Johnston. *Youth in Transition.* Vol. 1. Ann Arbor: Institute for Social Research, 1967.

Baker, Russell. *Growing Up.* New York: Congdon and Weed, 1982.

Banfield, Edward. *Here the People Rule.* New York: Plenum, 1985.

Banfield, Edward. *The Moral Basis of a Backward Society.* Glencoe, Ill.: Free Press, 1958.

Barndt, R. J., and D. M. Johnson. "Time Orientation in Delinquents." *Journal of Abnormal and Social Psychology* 51 (1955): 343–45.

Barrett, Paul. "Influential Ideas: A Movement Called 'Law and Economics' Sways Legal Circles." *The Wall Street Journal,* August 4, 1986: 1, 16.

Barry, Brian. *Sociologists, Economists, and Democracy.* London: Collier-Macmillan, 1970.

Baum, W., and H. Rachlin. "Choice as Time Allocation." *Journal of the Experimental Analysis of Behavior* 27 (1969): 453–67.

Bazerman, Max. "Norms of Distributive Justice in Interest Arbitration." *Industrial and Labor Relations* 38 (July 1985): 558–70.

Becker, Gary. *A Treatise on the Family.* Cambridge, Mass.: Harvard University Press, 1981.

Becker, Gary, E. M. Landes, and R. Michael. "An Economic Analysis of Marital Instability." *Journal of Political Economy* 85 (1977): 1141–87.

Becker, Gary, and George Stigler. "De Gustibus Non Est Disputandum." *American Economic Review* 67 (1977): 76–90.

Ben-Porath, Yoram. "Economic Analysis of Fertility in Israel: Point and Counterpoint." *Journal of Political Economy* 81 (1973): S202–S233.

Bergstrom, Theodore, Lawrence Blume, and Hal Varian. "On the Private Provision of Public Goods." *Journal of Public Economics,* 1986.

Berscheid, Ellen. "Emotion." In *Close Relationships,* edited by H. H. Kelley et al. San Francisco: Freeman, 1983: 110–68.

Berscheid, Ellen, and Elaine Walster. "A Little Bit about Love." In *Foundations of Interpersonal Attraction,* edited by Ted L. Huston. New York: Academic Press, 1974.

Binmore, K. A., A. Shaked, and J. Sutton. "Testing Noncooperative Bargaining Theory: A Preliminary Study." *American Economic Review* 75 (December 1985): 1178–80.

Bixenstein, V., C. A. Levitt, and K. R. Wilson. "Collaboration Among Six Persons in a Prisoner's Dilemma Game." *Journal of Conflict Resolution* 10 (1966): 488–96.

Black, W. A., and R. A. Gregson. "Time Perspective, Purpose in Life, Extroversion and Neuroticism in New Zealand Prisoners." *British Journal of Social and Clinical Psychology* 12 (1973): 50–60.

Blau, Peter. *Exchange and Power in Social Life.* New York: Wiley, 1964.

Bohm, Peter. "Estimating Demand for Public Goods: An Experiment." *European Economic Review* 3 (1972): 111–30.

Bonacich, P. "Norms and Cohesion as Adaptive Responses to Political Conflict: An Experimental Study." *Sociometry* 35 (1972): 357–75.

Bowles, Samuel, and Herbert Gintis. *Capitalism and Democracy.* New York: Basic Books, 1986.

Bradburn, N., and D. Caplovitz. *Reports on Happiness.* Chicago: Aldine, 1965.

Bradburn, N., and C. E. Noll. *The Structure of Psychological Well Being.* Chicago: Aldine, 1969.

Brechner, K. "An Experimental Analysis of Social Traps." *Journal of Experimental Social Psychology* 13 (1977): 552–64.

Brennan, G., and L. Lomasky. "Inefficient Unanimity." *Journal of Applied Philosophy* 1 (1984): 151–63.

Bruell, Jan. "Heritability of Emotional Behavior." In *Physiological Correlates of Emotion,* edited by Perry Black. New York: Academic Press, 1970.

Bruner, J. *Child's Talk.* New York: Norton, 1983.

Caryl, P. G. "Communication by Agonistic Displays: What Can Games Theory Contribute to Ethology?" *Behavior* 68 (1979): 136–69.

Chomsky, Noam. *Syntactic Structures.* The Hague: Mouton, 1957.

——. *Aspects of the Theory of Syntax.* Cambridge, Mass.: MIT Press, 1965.

Chronicle of Higher Education, January 8, 1986: p. 5. (Solow article)

Chung, Shin-Ho, and Richard Herrnstein. "Choice and Delay of Reinforcement." *Journal of the Experimental Analysis of Behavior* 10 (1967): 67–74.

Clark, M. S., and J. Mills. "Interpersonal Attraction in Exchange and Communal Relationships." *Journal of Personality and Social Psychology* 37 (1979): 12–24.

Cleckley, Harvey. *The Mask of Sanity.* 4th ed. St. Louis: Moseby, 1964.

Coleman, James. "Norms as Social Capital." In *Economic Imperialism,* edited by Gerard Radnitzky and Peter Bernholtz. New York: Paragon House, 1986.

Collard, David. *Altruism and Economy,* Oxford, Eng.: Martin Robertson, 1978.

Cook, Philip. "Alcohol Addition." Unpublished paper, Duke University, 1982.

Cook, Philip, and George Tauchen. "The Effect of Liquor Taxes on Heavy Drinking." *Bell Journal of Economics* 13 (1982): 379–90.

Crawford, V. "A Theory of Disagreement in Bargaining." *Econometrica,* 50 1982: 606–37.

Darwin, Charles. *The Origin of Species.* Cambridge, Mass.: Harvard University Press, 1966 (1859).

——. *The Expression of the Emotions in Man and Animals.* New York: D. Appleton, 1873 (1872).

———. *The Descent of Man and Selection in Relation to Sex.* New York: Modern Library, n.d. (1871).

———. *Autobiography.* New York: Oxford University Press, 1983 (1876).

Davies, N. B., and T. Halliday. "Optimal Mate Selection in the Toad *Bufo Bufo.*" *Nature* 269 (1977): 56–58.

Dawkins, Richard. *The Selfish Gene.* New York: Oxford University Press, 1976.

———. *The Blind Watchmaker,* New York: Norton, 1986.

Dawes, Robyn. "Social Dilemmas." *Annual Review of Psychology* 31 (1980): 169–93.

Dawes, Robyn, Jeanne McTavish, and Harriet Shaklee. "Behavior, Communication, and Assumptions About Other People's Behavior in A Commons Dilemma Situation." *Journal of Personality and Social Psychology* 35 (1977): 1–11.

Dawes, Robyn, John Orbell, and Alphons van de Kragt. "Cooperation in the Absence of Incentive Compatibility." Carnegie Mellon University Working Paper, 1986.

deCharms, R., H. W. Morrison, W. R. Reitman, and D. C. McClelland. "Behavioral Correlates of Directly and Indirectly Measured Achievement Orientation." In *Studies in Motivation,* edited by D. C. McClelland. New York: Appleton-Century-Crofts, 1955.

DePaulo, Bella, Miron Zuckerman, and Robert Rosenthal. "Humans as Lie Detectors." *Journal of Communications,* Spring, 1980.

DePaulo, Bella and Robert Rosenthal. "Ambivalence, Discrepancy, and Deception in Nonverbal Communication." In *Skill in Nonverbal Communication,* edited by R. Rosenthal. Cambridge, Mass.: Oelgeschlager, Gunn, and Hain, 1979.

Derlega, V., and J. Grzelak, eds. *Cooperation and Helping Behavior.* New York: Academic Press, 1982.

Deutsch, M. *Distributive Justice.* New Haven, Conn.: Yale University Press, 1985.

Diekmann, A. "Volunteer's Dilemma." *Journal of Conflict Resolution* 29 (1985): 605–10.

Dixit, Avinash. "The Role of Investment in Entry Deterrence." *Economic Journal* 90 (March 1980): 95–106.

Downs, Anthony. *An Economic Theory of Democracy.* New York: Harper and Row, 1957.

Duesenberry, James. *Income, Saving, and the Theory of Consumer Behavior.* Cambridge, Mass.: Harvard University Press, 1949.

Durrell, Lawrence. *Clea.* New York: Dutton, 1960.

Easterlin, Richard. "Does Economic Growth Improve the Human Lot? Some Empirical Evidence." In *Nations and Households in Economic Growth: Essays in Honor of Moses Abramovitz,* edited by P. David and M. Reder. Stanford, Calif.: Stanford University Press, 1973.

Eaton, B. C., and R. G. Lipsey. "Capital, Commitment, and Entry Equilibrium." *Bell Journal of Economics* 12 (1981): 593–604.

Edgerton, R. *Rules, Exceptions, and the Social Order.* Berkeley: University of California Press, 1985.

Edney, J., and C. Harper. "The Effects of Information in a Resource Management Problem: A Social Trap Analog." *Human Ecology* 6 (1978): 387–95.

Ekman, Paul. *Darwin and Facial Expression: A Century of Research in Review.* New York: Academic Press, 1973.

———. *Telling Lies.* New York: Norton, 1985.

Ekman, Paul, Wallace Friesen, and Phoebe Ellsworth. *Emotion in the Human Face,* New York: Pergamon, 1972.

Ekman, Paul, Wallace Friesen, and Klaus Scherer. "Body Movements and Voice Pitch in Deceptive Interaction." *Semiotica* 16 (1976): 23–27.

Ekman, Paul, Joseph Hager, and Wallace Friesen. "The Symmetry of Emotional and Deliberate Facial Actions." *Psychophysiology* 18 / 12 (1981): 101–6.

Elster, Jon. *Ulysses and the Sirens.* Cambridge, Eng.: Cambridge University Press, 1979.

———. "Weakness of Will and the Free-Rider Problem." *Economics and Philosophy* 1 (1985): 231–65.

———. "Sadder but Wiser? Rationality and the Emotions." *Social Science Information* 24, 2 (1985): 375–406.

———. *Sour Grapes.* Cambridge, Eng.: Cambridge University Press. 1983.

Fiorina, Morris. "Short and Long-term Effects of Economic Conditions on Individual Voting Decisions." Social Science Working Paper 244, California Institute of Technology, 1978.

Frank, Robert. "Are Workers Paid Their Marginal Products?" *American Economic Review* 74 (September 1984a): 549–71.

———. "Interdependent Preferences and the Competitive Wage Structure." *Rand Journal of Economics* 15 (Winter, 1984b): 510–20.

———. *Choosing the Right Pond.* New York: Oxford University Press, 1985.

———. "If *Homo Economicus* Could Choose His Own Utility Function, Would He Want One With a Conscience? *American Economic Review* 77 (September 1987): 593–604.

Friedman, J. W. *Oligopoly and the Theory of Games.* Amsterdam: North Holland, 1977.

Gansbury, Martin. "37 Who Saw Murder Didn't Call Police." *New York Times,* March 27, 1964: 1, 38.

Garcia, John, and Robert Koelling. "Relation of Cue to Consequence in Avoidance Learning." *Psychonomic Science* 4 (1966): 123–24. Reprinted in Seligman and Hager (1972, pp. 10–14).

Gatlin, D., M. Miles, and E. Cataldo. "Policy Support Within a Target Group: The Case of School Desegregation." *American Political Science Review* 72 (1978): 985–95.

Gauthier, David. *Morals by Agreement.* Oxford, Eng.: Clarendon, 1985.

Gazzaniga, Michael. *The Social Brain.* New York: Basic Books, 1985.

Goleman, Daniel, *Vital Lies, Simple Truths.* New York: Simon and Schuster, 1985.

———. "Psychologists Pursue the Irrational Aspects of Love." *New York Times,* July 22, 1986: C1, C8.

Gould, Stephen Jay. *Ever Since Darwin.* New York: Norton, 1977.

Grossman, S., and O. Hart. "An Analysis of the Principal Agent Problem." *Econometrica* 51 (1983): 7–46.

Guth, Werner. "Payoff Distributions in Games and the Behavioral Theory of Distributive Justice." Paper presented to the International Conference on Economics and Psychology, Kibbutz Shefayim, Israel, July 1986.

Guth, Werner, and Reinhard Tietz. "Strategic Power Versus Distributive Justice: An Experimental Analysis of Ultimatum Bargaining." In *Economic Psychology,* edited by H. Brandstatter and E. Kirchler. R. Trauner, 1985.

Guth, Werner, Rolf Sdhmittberger, and Bernd Schwarze. "An Experimental Analysis of Ultimatum Bargaining," *Journal of Economic Behavior and Organization* 3 (1982): 367–88.

Haggard, E. A., and K. S. Isaacs. "Micromomentary Facial Expressions." In *Methods of Research in Psychotherapy,* edited by L. A. Gottschalk and A. H. Auerbach. New York: Appleton-Century-Crofts, 1966.

Hamilton, W. D. "The Genetical Theory of Social Behavior." *Journal of Theoretical Biology* 7 (1964): 1–32.

———. "Selection of Selfish and Altruistic Behavior." In *Man and Beast: Comparative Social Behavior,* edited by J. Eisenberg and W. Dutton. Washington, D.C.: Smithsonian Institution Press, 1971.

Handel, Michael. "Intelligence and Deception." *Journal of Strategic Studies* 5 (1982): 136.

Hannan, Michael. "Families, Markets, and Social Structures: An Essay on Becker's *A Treatise on the Family, Journal of Economic Literature* 20 (1982): 65–72.

Hardin, Russell. *Collective Action.* Baltimore: Johns Hopkins Press, 1982.

Hare, Robert. *Psychopathy: Theory and Research.* New York: Wiley, 1970.

———. "Psychophysiological Studies of Psychopathy." In *Clinical Application of Psychophysiology,* edited by D. C. Fowles. Columbia University Press, 1975.

———. "Electrodermal and Cardiovascular Correlates of Psychopathy." In R. D. Hare and D. Schalling, 1978.

———. "Psychopathy and Laterality of Cerebral Function." *Journal of Abnormal Psychology* 88 (1979): 605–10.

Hare, Robert, and Averil S. Hare. "Psychopathic Behavior: A Bibliography." *Excerpta Criminilogica* 7 (1967): 365–86.

Hare, Robert, and M. J. Quinn. "Psychopathy and Autonomic Conditioning." *Journal of Abnormal Psychology* 77 (1971): 223–35.

Hare, Robert, and D. Shalling. *Psychopathic Behavior.* New York: Wiley, 1978.

Harkness, S., C. P. Edwards, and C. M. Super. "Social Roles and Moral Reasoning," *Developmental Psychology* 17 (1981): 595–603.

Harris, M., and A. Raviv. "Some Results on Incentive Contracts." *American Economic Review* 68 (1978): 20–30.

Harris, R. J., and M. Joyce. "What's Fair? It Depends on How You Phrase the Question." *Journal of Personality and Social Psychology* 38 (1980): 165–79.

J. Harsanyi. *Rational Behavior and Bargaining Equilibrium in Games and Social Situations.* Cambridge, Eng.: Cambridge University Press, 1977.

———. "Rule Utilitarianism, Rights, Obligations, and the Theory of Rational Behavior." *Theory and Decision* 12: 115–33.

Herrnstein, Richard. "On the Law of Effect." *Journal of the Experimental Analysis of Behavior* 13 (1970): 242–66.

———. "Nature as Nurture: Behaviorism and the Instinct Doctrine." *Behaviorism* 1 (1972): 23–52.

———. "Self-Control as Response Strength." In *Quantification of Steady-State Operant Behaviour,* edited by C. M. Bradshaw, E. Szabadi, and C. F. Lowe. Amsterdam: Elsevier / North Holland Biomedical Press, 1981.

Hirsch, Fred. *Social Limits to Growth.* Cambridge, Mass.: Harvard University Press, 1976.

Hirschman, Albert O. *The Passions and the Interests.* Princeton, N.J.: Princeton University Press, 1977.

———. *Shifting Involvements.* Princeton, N.J.: Princeton University Press, 1982.

Hirshleifer, Jack. "Economics from a Biological Viewpoint." *Journal of Law and Economics* 20 (April 1977): 1–52.

———. "Natural Economy Versus Political Economy." *Journal of Social Biology* 1 (1978): 319–37.

———. "The Emotions as Guarantors of Threats and Promises." UCLA Department of Economics Working Paper, August 1984.

Hobbes, Thomas. *The Citizen,* New York: Appleton-Century-Crofts, 1949.

Holmstrom, Bengt. "Moral Hazard and Observability." *Bell Journal of Economics* 10 (1979): 74–91.

———. "Moral Hazard in Teams." *Bell Journal of Economics* 13 (1982): 24–40.

Homans, George. *Social Behavior.* New York: Harcourt, Brace and World, 1961.

Hornstein, Harvey. *Cruelty and Kindness.* Englewood Cliffs, N.J.: Prentice Hall, 1976.

Hornstein, Harvey, Elisha Fisch, and Michael Holmes. "Influence of a Model's Feelings About His Behavior and His Relevance as a Comparison Other on Observers' Helping Behavior." *Journal of Personality and Social Psychology* 10 (1968): 220–26.

Hornstein, Harvey, Hugo Masor, Kenneth Sole, and Madeline Heilman. "Effects of Sentiment and Completion of a Helping Act on Observer Helping." *Journal of Personality and Social Psychology* 17 (1971): 107–12.

Hume, David. *A Treatise on Human Nature,* Oxford: Clarendon, 1888.

Isaac, R. Mark, Kenneth McCue, and Charles Plott. "Public Goods Provision in an Experimental Environment." *Journal of Public Economics* 26 (1985): 51–74.

Isaac, R. Mark, and James M. Walker. "Group Size Hypotheses of Public Goods Provision: An Experimental Examination." University of Arizona Working Paper, 1985.

Isaac, R. Mark, James M. Walker, and Susan H. Thomas. "Divergent Evidence on Free Riding: An Experimental Examination of Possible Explanations." *Public Choice* 43 (1984): 113–49.

Jevons, Stanley. *The Theory of Political Economy.* London: Macmillan, 1941.

Kagan, Jerome. *The Nature of the Child.* New York: Basic Books, 1984.

———. *Change and Continuity in Infancy.* New York: Wiley, 1971.

———. *The Second Year.* Cambridge, Mass.: Harvard University Press, 1981.

Kahneman, Daniel, Jack Knetsch, and Richard Thaler. "Fairness and the Assumptions of Economics." *Journal of Business* 59 (1986a): S285–S300.

———. Perceptions of Unfairness: Constraints on Wealth Seeking." *American Economic Review* 76 (1986b): 728–41.

Keeley, Michael. "The Economics of Family Formation." *Economic Inquiry* 15 (1977): 238–50.

Kelley, H. H. "Love and Commitment." In *Close Relationships,* edited by H. H. Kelley, et al., San Francisco: Freeman, 1983: 265–300.

Kelley, H. H., and J. W. Thibaut. *Interpersonal Relations.* New York: Wiley Interscience, 1978.

Kelly, F. J., and D. J. Veldman. "Delinquency and School Dropout Behavior as a Function of Impulsivity and Nondominant Values." *Journal of Abnormal and Social Psychology* 69 (1964): 190–94.

Kim, Oliver, and Mark Walker. "The Free Rider Problem: Experimental Evidence." *Public Choice* 43 (1984): 3–24.

Kinder, Donald, and D. R. Kiewert. "Economic Grievances and Political Behavior: The Role of Personal Discontents and Collective Judgments in Congressional Voting." *American Journal of Political Sciences* 23 (1979): 495–527.

Kirman, William, and Robert Masson. "Capacity Signals and Entry Deterrence." *International Journal of Industrial Organization* 4 (1986): 25–42.

Kitcher, Philip. *Vaulting Ambition,* Cambridge, Mass.: MIT Press, 1985.

Kliemt, Hartmut. "The Veil of Insignificance." *European Journal of Political Economy* 213 (1986): 333–44.

———. "The Reason of Rules and the Rule of Reason." Unpublished paper, 1987.

Konner, Melvin. *The Tangled Wing.* New York: Holt, Rinehart and Winston, 1982.

Kohn, M. L. *Class and Conformity.* Homewood, Ill.: Dorsey, 1969.

Kramer, Gerald. "Short-term Fluctuations in U. S. Voting Behavior, 1896–1964." *American Political Science Review* 65 (1971): 131–43.

Krebs, J., and R. Dawkins. "Animal Signals: Mind-Reading and Manipulation." In *Behavioral Ecology: An Evolutionary Approach,* edited by J. R. Krebs and N. B.

Davies, 2nd ed. Sunderland, MA: Sinauer Associates, 1984.

Kreps, David M., Paul Milgrom, John Roberts, and Robert Wilson. "Rational Cooperation in Finitely Repeated Prisoner's Dilemma." *Journal of Economic Theory* 27 (1982): 245–52.

Krueger, Alan B., and Lawrence Summers. "Reflections on the Interindustry Wage Structure." NBER Working Paper No. 1968, June 1986. (*Econometrica,* forthcoming).

Kuhn, Thomas. *The Structure of Scientific Revolutions.* Chicago: University of Chicago Press, 1962.

Latané, Bibb, and John Darley. *The Unresponsive Bystander: Why Doesn't He Help?* New York: Meredith, 1970.

Lau, Richard, Thad Brown, and David Sears. "Self-Interest and Civilians' Attitudes Toward the War in Vietnam." *Public Opinion Quarterly* 42 (1978): 464–83.

Lazear, E., and S. Rosen. "Rank Order Tournaments as Optimal Labor Contracts." *Journal of Political Economy* 89 (1981): 1261–84.

Leibenstein, Harvey. *Beyond Economic Man,* Cambridge, Mass.: Harvard University Press, 1976.

———. *Inside the Firm.* Cambridge, Mass.: Harvard University Press, 1987.

Lenneberg, Eric. *Biological Foundations of Language.* New York: Wiley, 1967.

Leonard, Elmore. *Glitz.* New York: Arbor House, 1985.

Levy, R. *The Tahitians.* Chicago: University of Chicago Press, 1973.

Locke, John. "Some Thoughts Concerning Education." In *John Locke on Education,* edited by Peter Gay. New York: Bureau of Publications, Teachers College, Columbia University, 1964.

Loewenstein, George. "Anticipation and the Valuation of Delayed Consumption." *Economic Journal,* 1987.

Lumsden, Charles, and Edward O. Wilson. *Genes, Mind, and Culture.* Cambridge, Mass.: Harvard University Press, 1981.

Lykken, David. *A Tremor in the Blood.* New York: McGraw-Hill, 1981.

MacDonald, John. *The Lonely Silver Rain,* New York: Knopf, 1985.

McAdams, D. P. "A Thematic Coding System for the Intimacy Motive." *Journal of Research in Personality* 14 (1980): 413–32.

———. "Intimacy Motivation." In *Motivation and Society,* edited by A. Stewart. San Francisco: Jossey Bass: 1982: 133–71.

McAdams, D. P., and G. Vaillant. "Intimacy Motivation and Psychosocial Adaptation: A Longitudinal Study." Unpublished paper, Loyola University of Chicago, 1980.

McClelland, D. C. "Some Reflections on the Two Psychologies of Love." *Journal of Personality* 54 (1986): 324–53.

———. *Personality.* New York: Sloane, 1951.

McClelland, D. C., R. J. Davidson, and C. Saron. "Evoked Potential Indicators of the Impact of the Need for Power on Perception and Learning." Unpublished paper,

Department of Psychology and Social Relations, Harvard University, 1979.

McClelland, D. C., G. Ross, and V. T. Patel. "The Effect of an Examination on Salivary Norepinephrine and Immunoglobulin Levels." *Journal of Human Stress* 11 (1985): 52–59.

McClelland, D. C., D. Stier, V. T. Patel, and D. Brown. "The Effect of Affiliative Arousal on Dopamine Release." Unpublished paper, Department of Psychology and Social Relations, Harvard University, 1985.

McClelland, D. C., and J. B. Jemmott III. "Power Motivation, Stress, and Physical Illness." *Journal of Human Stress* 6 (1980): 6–15.

McClelland, D. C., C. Alexander, and E. Marks. "The Need for Power, Stress, Immune Function, and Illness Among Male Prisoners." *Journal of Abnormal Psychology* 91 (1982): 61–70.

McGinness, Joe. *Fatal Vision.* New York: Signet, 1984.

McKay, James. Unpublished paper, Department of Psychology and Social Relations, Harvard University, 1986.

Marcel, Anthony. "Conscious and Unconscious Perception: An Approach to the Relations Between Phenomenal Experience and Perceptual Processes." *Cognitive Psychology* 15 (1983): 238–300.

Margolis, H. *Selfishness, Altruism, and Rationality.* Cambridge, Eng.: Cambridge University Press, 1982.

Marwell, Gerald, and Ruth Ames. "Economists Free Ride, Does Anyone Else?" *Journal of Public Economics* 15 (1981): 295–310.

Mello, Nancy. "Behavioral Studies of Alcoholism." In *The Biology of Alcoholism,* Vol. 2, edited by B. Kissin and K. Begleiter. New York: Plenum, 1972.

Messick, D., and K. Sentis, "Fairness Preference and Fairness Biases." In *Equity Theory,* edited by D. Messick and K. Cook. New York: Praeger, 1983.

Milgram, Stanley, and Paul Hollander. "The Murder They Heard." *The Nation,* June 15, 1964: 602–4.

Milgrom, P., and R. Weber. "A Theory of Auctions and Competitive Bidding." *Econometrica* 50 (1982): 1089–1122.

Mincer, Jacob. "Market Prices, Opportunity Costs, and Income Effects." In *Measurement in Economics,* edited by Carl Christ et al. Stanford, Calif.: Stanford University Press, 1963.

Mischel, W. "Preference for Delayed Reinforcement and Social Responsibility." *Journal of Abnormal and Social Psychology* 62 (1961): 1–7.

———. *Personality and Assessment.* New York: Wiley, 1968.

Murstein, B. I., M. Cerreto, and M. MacDonald. "A Theory and Investigation of the Effect of Exchange-Orientation on Marriage and Friendship." *Journal of Marriage and The Family* 39 (1977): 543–48.

Nash, J. "The Bargaining Problem." *Econometrica* 18 (1950): 155–62.

Nelson, Richard, and Winter, Sidney. *An Evolutionary Theory of Economic Change.* Cambridge, Mass.: The Belknap Press of Harvard University Press, 1978.

New York Times, Apr. 13, 1982: Al, D27. (CBS murders)

New York Times, Apr. 14, 1982: Al, B2. (CBS murders)

Norman, Donald. "Toward a Theory of Memory and Attention." *Psychological Review* 75 (1968): 522–36.

Oliver, P. "Rewards and Punishments as Selective Incentives for Collective Action." *American Journal of Sociology* 85 (1980): 1356–75.

Olson, Mancur. *The Logic of Collective Action.* Cambridge, Mass.: Harvard University Press, 1965.

———. *The Rise and Decline of Nations.* New Haven, Conn.: Yale University Press, 1982.

Parfit, Derek. *Reasons and Persons.* Oxford, Eng.: Clarendon, 1984.

Page, Benjamin. "Elections and Social Choice: The State of the Evidence." *American Journal of Political Science* 21 (1977): 639–68.

Pattison, E., M. Sobell, and L. Sobell. *Emerging Concepts of Alcohol Dependence.* New York: Springer, 1977.

Phelps, E. S. (ed.) *Altruism, Morality, and Economic Theory.* New York: Russell Sage, 1975.

Piliavin, Irving, Judith Rodin, and Jane Piliavin. "Good Samaritanism: An Underground Phenomenon? *Journal of Personality and Social Psychology* 13 (1969).

Posner, Richard. *Economics Analysis of Law.* Chicago: University of Chicago Press, 1972.

Pratt, John, and Richard Zeckhauser. *Principals and Agents: The Structure of Business.* Boston: Harvard Business School Press, 1985.

Quattrone, G., and A. Tversky. "Self-deception and the Voter's Illusion." In *The Multiple Self,* edited by J. Elster. Cambridge, Eng.: Cambridge University Press, 1986: 35–58.

Radner, Roy. "Monitoring Cooperative Agreements in a Repeated Principal-Agent Relationship." *Econometrica* 49 (1981): 1127–48.

Rapoport, Anatol, A. Chammah, J. Dwyer, and J. Gyr. "Three-Person Non-Zero-Sum Nonnegotiable Games." *Behavioral Science* 7 (1962): 30–58.

Rapoport, Anatol, and A. Chammah. *Prisoner's Dilemma.* Ann Arbor: University of Michigan Press, 1965.

Rawls, John. *A Theory of Justice.* Cambridge, Mass.: The Belknap Press of Harvard University Press, 1971.

Regan, Donald. *Utilitarianism and Cooperation.* Oxford, Eng.: Clarendon Press, 1980.

Reich, Walter. "How the President Can Thwart Terror." *New York Times,* Feb. 19, 1987: A31.

Restak, Richard. *The Brain: The Last Frontier.* New York: Warner, 1979.

Rice, Otis. *The Hatfields and McCoys.* Lexington: University of Kentucky Press, 1982.

Riker, William, and Peter Ordeshook. *An Introduction to Positive Political Theory.*

Englewood Cliffs, N.J.: Prentice Hall, 1973.

———. "A Theory of the Calculus of Voting." *American Political Science Review* 62 (1968): 25–42.

Riley, John. "Competitive Signalling." *Journal of Economic Theory* 10 (1975): 174–86.

Robins, Lee. "Aetiological Implications in Studies of Childhood Histories Relating to Antisocial Personality." In *Psychopathic Behavior: Approaches to Research,* edited by R. Hare and D. Schalling. Chichester, Eng.: Wiley, 1978.

Roth, Alvin, ed. *Game Theoretic Models of Bargaining.* Cambridge, Eng.: Cambridge University Press, 1985.

Roth, A., M. Malouf, and J. Murnighan. "Sociological versus Strategic Factors in Bargaining." *Journal of Economic Behavior and Organization* 2 (1981): 153–77.

Rothschild, M., and J. Stiglitz. "Equilibrium in Competitive Insurance Markets." *Quarterly Journal of Economics* 80 (1976): 629–49.

Rubin, Paul, and Chris Paul. "An Evolutionary Model of Taste for Risk," *Economic Inquiry* 17 (1979): 585–96.

Rubin, Zick. *Liking and Loving.* New York: Holt, Rinehart and Winston, 1973.

Rubinstein, Ariel. "Perfect Equilibrium in a Bargaining Model." *Econometrica* 50 (1982): 97–110.

Rushton, J. Philippe. *Altruism, Socialization, and Society.* Englewood Cliffs, N.J.: Prentice Hall, 1980.

Schelling, Thomas. *The Strategy of Conflict.* Cambridge, Mass.: Harvard University Press, 1960.

———. "Altruism, Meanness, and Other Potentially Strategic Behaviors." *American Economic Review* 68 (1978): 229–30.

———. "The Intimate Contest for Self-Command," *The Public Interest* 60 (1980): 94–118.

Scherer, Klaus. "Methods of Research on Vocal Communications: Paradigms and Parameters." In *Handbook of Methods in Nonverbal Behavior Research,* edited by Klaus Scherer and Paul Ekman. New York: Cambridge University Press, 1982.

Schmalensee, Richard. "Entry Deterrence in the Ready to Eat Cereal Industry." *Bell Journal of Economics* 9 (1978): 305–27.

Schwartz, Barry. *The Battle for Human Nature.* New York: Norton, 1986.

Schwartz, Shalom. "Elicitation of Moral Obligation and Self-Sacrificing Behavior: An Experimental Study of Volunteering to Be a Bone Marrow Donor." *Journal of Personality and Social Psychology* 15 (1970): 283–93.

Scitovsky, Tibor. *The Joyless Economy.* New York: Oxford University Press, 1976.

Sears, David, Richard Lau, Tom Tyler, and Harris Allen. "Self-Interest vs. Symbolic Politics in Policy Attitudes and Presidential Voting." *American Political Science Review* 74 (1980): 670–84.

Sears, David, Carl Hensler, and Leslie Speer. "Whites' Opposition to Busing: Self-Interest or Symbolic Politics." *American Political Science Review* 73 (1979): 369–84.

Sears, David, Tom Tyler, Jack Critin, and Donald Kinder. "Political System Support and Public Responses to the Energy Crisis." *American Journal of Political Science* 22 (1978): 56–82.

Seidman, Laurence. "The Return of the Profit Rate to the Wage Equation." *Review of Economics and Statistics* 61 (1979): 139–42.

Seligman, Martin, and Joanne Hager. *Biological Boundaries of Learning.* New York: Meredith, 1972.

Selten, R. "The Equity Principle in Economic Behavior." *Decision Theory and Social Ethics,* edited by H. Gottinger and W. Leinfeller. Dordrecht: Reidel, 1978: 289–301.

Sen, Amartya. "Goals, Commitment and Identity." *Journal of Law, Economics, and Organization* 1 (1985): 341–55.

———. "Rational Fools." *Philosophy and Public Affairs* 6 (1977): 317–44.

Shavell, S. "Risk Sharing and Incentives in the Principal and Agent Relationship." *Bell Journal of Economics* 10 (1979): 55–73.

Shubik, Martin. *Game Theory in the Social Sciences.* Cambridge, Mass.: MIT Press, 1982.

Skinner, B. F. *The Behavior of Organisms.* New York: Appleton-Century-Crofts, 1938.

Smith, Adam. *The Theory of Moral Sentiments.* New York: Kelley, 1966 (1759).

———. *The Wealth of Nations.* New York: Everyman's Library. 1910 (1776).

Smith, Vernon. "Incentive Compatible Experimental Processes for the Provision of Public Goods." In *Research in Experimental Economics,* Greenwich, Conn.: JAI Press. 1978.

Solnick, J., C. Kannenberg, D. Eckerman, and M. Waller. "An Experimental Analysis of Impulsivity and Impulse Control in Humans." *Learning and Motivation* 11 (1980): 61–77.

Sperry, R. "Consciousness, Personal Identity, and the Divided Brain." *Neuropsychologia* 22 (1984): 661–73.

Spinoza, Benedictus de. *Tractatus Theologico Politicus,* London: Trubner, 1868.

Stein, K. B., T. R. Sarbin, and J. A. Kulik. "Future Time Perspective: Its Relation to the Socialization Process and the Delinquent Role." *Journal of Consulting and Clinical Psychology* 32 (1968): 257–64.

Stigler, George. "The Economics of Minimum Wage Legislation." *American Economic Review* 36 (1946): 358–65.

Robert Strotz. "Myopia and Inconsistency in Dynamic Utility Maximization." *Review of Economic Studies* 23 (1955–56): 165–80.

Sugden, Robert. "Consistent Conjectures and Voluntary Contributions to Public Goods: Why the Conventional Theory Doesn't Work." *Journal of Public Economics* 27 (1985): 117–24.

Sweeney, J. "An Experimental Investigation of the Free Rider Problem." *Social Science Research* 2 (1973): 277–92.

Taylor, M. *Anarchy and Cooperation.* Chichester, Eng.: Wiley, 1976.

Telser, Lester. "A Theory of Self-enforcing Agreements." *Journal of Business* 53 (1980): 27–44.

Thaler, Richard. "Mental Accounting and Consumer Choices." *Marketing Sciences* 4 (Summer, 1985).

Thaler, Richard, and H. Shefrin. "An Economic Theory of Self-Control." *Journal of Political Economy* 89 (1981): 392–405.

Thibaut, J. W., and H. H. Kelley. *The Social Psychology of Groups.* New York: Wiley, 1959.

Tinbergen, Niko. "Derived Activities: Their Causation, Biological Significance, and Emancipation During Evolution." *Quarterly Review of Biology* 27 (1952): 1–32.

———. "The Evolution of Signaling Devices." In *Social Behavior and Organization among Vertebrates,* edited by W. Etkin. Chicago: University of Chicago Press, 1964.

Trivers, Robert. "The Evolution of Reciprocal Altruism." *Quarterly Review of Biology* 46 (1971): 35–57.

———. "Parent-Offspring Conflict." *Americal Zoologist* 14 (1974): 249–64.

———. *Social Evolution.* Menlo Park, Calif.: Benjamin / Cummings, 1985.

Tufte, Edward. *Political Control of the Economy.* Princeton, N.J.: Princeton University Press, 1978.

Walster, E., G. W. Walster, and E. Berscheid. *Equity: Theory and Research.* Rockleigh, N.J.: Allyn and Bacon, 1978.

Weller, Jack E. *Yesterday's People: Life in Contemporary Appalachia.* Lexington: University of Kentucky Press, 1965.

Williamson Oliver. "Predatory Pricing: A Strategic and Welfare Analysis." *Yale Law Journal* 87 (1977): 284–340.

———. *The Economic Institutions of Capitalism.* New York: Free Press: 1985.

Willis, R. J. "A New Approach to the Economic Theory of Fertility Behavior." *Journal of Political Economy* 81 (1973): S14–S64.

Wilson, Edward O. *Sociobiology: The New Synthesis.* Cambridge, Mass.: Belknap Press of Harvard University Press, 1975.

———. *On Human Nature,* Cambridge, Mass.: Harvard University Press, 1978.

Wilson, James Q., and Richard Herrnstein. *Crime and Human Nature.* New York: Simon and Schuster, 1985.

Winston, Gordon. "Addiction and Backsliding: A Theory of Compulsive Consumption." *Journal of Economic Behavior and Organization* 1 (1980): 295–394.

Yaari, M., and M. Bar-Hillel. "On Dividing Justly." *Social Choice and Welfare.* 1 (1984): 1–14.

Ziskind, E. "The Diagnosis of Sociopathy." In R. D. Hare and D. Schalling, eds., 1978.

Ziskind, E., K. Syndulko, and I. McItzman. "Aversive Conditioning in the Sociopath." *Pavlovian Journal of Biological Science* 13 (1978): 199–205.

Zuckerman, Miron, Bella De Paulo, and Robert Rosenthal. "Verbal and Nonverbal Communication of Deception." In *Advances in Experimental and Social Psychology*, Vol. 14. New York: Academic Press, 1981.

INDEX